THE
WILLIAM GOODHUGH DAWSON
FAMILY HISTORY

by
William Goodhugh (Hugh) Dawson
Capt. RAMC, Sqn.Ldr. RAF (rtd), MA (Cantab), FRCOG, DA,
MB B Chir, MRCS, LRCP

Front cover: North Foreland Lighthouse, water colour attributed to P Wareham. From the painting owned by William Goodhugh Dawson (WGD4) later gifted to Margate Museum.

THE WILLIAM GOODHUGH DAWSON FAMILY HISTORY

Published by William Goodhugh Dawson, who has asserted his rights under the Copyright, Designs and Patents Act 1988 to be identified as the author of this work.

First Edition published 15 July 1996
Second Edition published 1 September 2022

ISBN: 978-1-3999-2199-2

Printed in the United Kingdom by Chroma Group Ltd., Unit 8, Ely Road, Theale, Reading, West Berkshire RG7 4BQ
https://chromagroup.co.uk/

To my Father
for his example of duty and affection.

They shall still bring forth fruit in old age.
(Psalm 92 *v* 14)

Acknowledgements

With the passage of time since I published the first edition of this Family History, many of the people who stimulated my interest and supplied information are no longer with us. These include amongst my relatives my father and mother, my aunts Mrs. Bessie Hiller Thomas née Dawson, Miss Alice Mary (Sass) Dawson, and Miss Frances Harris, my cousins Mrs Isabel Ramsay née Dawson, Bryan Walton Cooper, who helped with the Harris history, and also my late second cousin Miss Marion Dunn. Mr Eric Smith FSA, husband of my cousin Muriel née Dawson, who informed me of his research into the Dawson history. I am also grateful for the assistance given by two other descendants of Rev. John Wesley Dawson, Mr Richard Leonard Goodhugh Dawson, plastic surgeon, and Mr Leonard Walker, schoolmaster. Dr A. Percival MBE, Director of The Faversham Society, also gave me much help and encouragement.

Among the living, I am very grateful for the assistance of my daughter Mrs Sarah M. Griffin, to Dr Gordon Sheffield Harris, whose mother wrote a history of her family which was an inspiration (i), and to Mr Colin James Harris, both cousins on my mother's side, who have also helped with the Harris history.

The first edition also benefited greatly from the assistance of the late Miss Penny Ward, Archivist of Margate Library, and also the Librarians of Faversham Public Reference Library.

I must mention particularly Mrs Thelma Dawson for typing the manuscript of the first edition, which forms the basis for much of this edition, and her husband Simon for his research and enormous effort in creating and maintaining genealogical tables. David Cooper, a son of my cousin Bryan, provided further details concerning the Harris and Cooper branches, and also helped produce this book.

Finally, my warm thanks to my wife, Margaret, who encouraged me with the first edition of this book.

Contents

Preface to the Second Edition of Family History

Twenty-five years have passed since the printing of the first edition. All copies were distributed long ago and I should particularly like to be able to offer copies to younger relatives.

Further research has been done, particularly by my kinsmen David Cooper and Simon Goodhugh Dawson. Looking back at my earlier literary efforts I realise how much I owe to Simon's hard work and advice, and to his most patiently guiding me in the first steps of computer literacy. David is giving much of his time for this second edition, including a stay at my home in July 2021, to forward the project. This edition incorporates further research by David on the Shuffill side of my mother's ancestry and Cooper involvement in the Crimean War, inter alia. Simon has added more information on the ministers, and his branch of the history. I have also added a short memorandum on the lives of my mother and her four Harris sisters.

The first edition of the Family History was dedicated to my father, and my autobiography, "A Long Life", to my mother. It is only fitting that special acknowledgement be given to Simon and David without whose help this Family History would never have seen the light of day.

Simon compiled detailed genealogical tables which were included in the first edition. We have had to make considerable cuts to them for this edition to remove reference to the living to protect their privacy, as it would be impractical to obtain individual permissions.

The most significant Family event during the past 25 years was undoubtedly the Family Reunion to celebrate the return from Chicago of the Regency Shopfront of the baker's shop of John Dawson, my great-great-grandfather, to Faversham. It is fully related in my autobiography.

WGD4 17 May 2022

The Family History: Introduction

The Dawson ancestry can be accurately traced to the mid eighteenth century (1). However, unconfirmed evidence shows a line of descent from the seventeenth century (2). Descent on my father's side from the Goodhugh family has been established to the early eighteenth century.

Early records show the name Dawson occurring in the north of England, mostly in Cumberland, Westmoreland, Durham, the West Riding of Yorkshire (from the fifteenth century), Lincolnshire, and Cheshire, and extending into central Scotland (from the sixteenth century). The name possibly may have come over in the Norman Conquest as d'Oson, from Osonvilla (locally known as Oson) near Dieppe, Normandy. It also may have links to the Scottish Davison and Davidson.

Lines of descent on my father's side involve the Hiller, Fagg, Day and Eggleston families. There is also kinship with the Berry, Dunn, Luke, Fitchew and Clay families.

My mother was from the Harris family, which we can also trace back to the late eighteenth century, although with less detail. There is interesting kinship with many other families, including the Shuffill/Sheffield, Shoobridge, Care and Dow families.

I will first record the direct Dawson genealogy with notes on the people mentioned from my records and also from traditions received from my father. I will then investigate the families that married into my father's line, before turning to my mother's antecedents.

The next page contains a diagrammatic summary of the family tree which locates the various branches. There are more detailed family tree diagrams in Appendix 4, and Appendix 5 contains a list of all individuals identified to date. These can be found after the lists of abbreviations, sources and references.

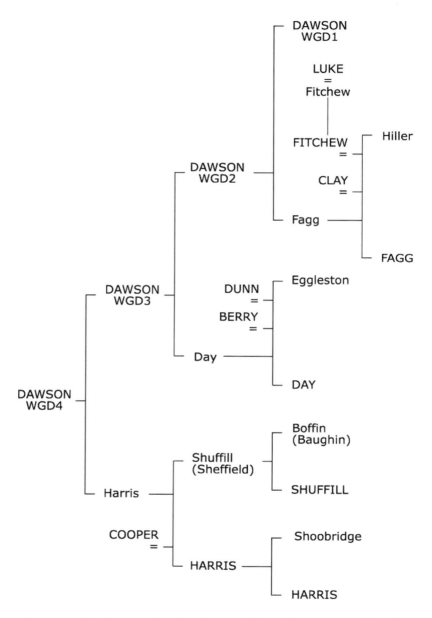

Summary family tree showing the main branches mentioned in the text. Males are shown in upper case.

Chapter 1

The Dawson Family

In this section I relate the direct genealogy of the Dawson family, from the earliest ancestor which we can trace with any degree of confidence. The family's roots lie in northeast Kent.

William Dawson

William Dawson, my great-great-great-grandfather, was a shipwright of Margate, Kent. The Archives of Margate Library for the year 1796 show that his address was Lower Parade, Bankside, which no longer exists and the rateable value of his house was £8.0.0. The site of the property is now an open space close to the old harbour and the presumed site of his boat yard.

There is an unconfirmed family tradition that William Dawson came from Norway (3). It may be relevant that a William Dawson did father a child (Karoline Williamsen born 28 January 1866, baptised 15 April 1866 in Sokndal, Rogaland, Norway) to a Norwegian woman, Karen Svensdrogden (SGD-IGI). Curiously, I received a genealogical inquiry from Norway concerning a Thanet Dawson and descendants near the Arctic Circle. I am told that in the eighteenth century there was a regular shipping trade between Margate and The Baltic (PW).

William was buried on 2 January 1818 when aged 70 so his date of birth would be about 1747. This agrees with a baptismal entry of 8 Febuary for 1746 or 1747 at St. Lawrence, Thanet (4). He was married to Susanna Presley (5). After her husband's death it appears that Susanna lived with her son, my great-great-grandfather, John Dawson in Faversham, as his tombstone in Faversham Churchyard records his mother and three of his children who died in infancy as well as his own and his wife's death (6). I have since seen the entry of Susanna Dawson aged 72 on 21 April 1822 in the burial register of St. Mary of Charity, Faversham (7).

The burial register of St John's, Margate records the deaths of three children in the first year of life and one aged 12, namely Susannah 1, Susannah 2, Ann and William respectively. Other children dying in

4

infancy or childhood, including two sets of twins, have been identified by SGD (3). Four children survived to adult life, Elizabeth, Sarah, Robert Staines, and John (1). Such losses were not unusual. For example, in Rev'd John Wesley's father's eighteenth-century family just five children out of nineteen survived childhood.

According to the International Genealogical Index of 1992 (SGD), Susanna Presley's mother may have been Hannah Staines. In addition to Robert, one of John Dawson's daughters, Ann, had the second name Staines. Incidentally, her daughter in turn married the painter Joseph Clark RA, (1834-1926) of the well-known painting *'The Sailor's Return'* (8). I have his portrait of my uncle Arthur Eggleston Dawson. An admiral named Staines is buried near the entrance to St John's Churchyard and he may have been a kinsman, although Staines appears to have been a common name in this part of Kent.

I have William Dawson's will of 1802 and also a letter written by him to his son John, then removed to Faversham, dated 28 March 1814 (9) (10). The writing shows the old form for S which had already been superseded in the newspapers. The text of the letter reads as follows:

M.r Dawson Confectioner
Market Place
Feversham

Margate March 28 th

My dear Child / I fear my long silence has in some measure
caus'd you some uneasinefs - yet I trust you have through one
channell or other often heard of us. My delay has not been owing
to my tender affection towards you but owing to our Indisposition
of Body - the day you left us I was obliged to come home after tea
& go to bed was very ill for a mont so that I could not attend ye
Chapell your poor Mother has been so bad with ye Rheumatism
that she has not been out but once to Chapell since Xmafs & still
continues very bad for some time she could scarcely move hand or
foot so that she could not drefs or undrefs Herself so that I have
been oblig'd to do for her as a child her trouble has kept moveing
her from ye sole of her foot to ye Crown of her Head there it seems

5

now to fix itself we have try'd & used various means but to little
purpose her head now is so bad as very much affects her sight
makes her very deaf besides such swiming in yᵉ head that a few
morning back she fell 2 or 3 stairs down & had the stairs foot door
being open would have come head foremast into yᵉ pafsage so that if
she does not get better in a day or two we must apply to yᵉ Faculty.
Robert told us he had wrote but he never knew yᵉ one half of your
Mother's Illnefs. Now under all these tryals I delay'd writing as I
could not bear to give you yᵉ least uneasinefs which I must have
done If I'd told you yᵉ truth & no use to tell you untruth or to
deceive you - We have experienced a very severe & long winter
many Familys at Margate haveing suffer'd much through yᵉ
Inclemency of yᵉ Weather & scarcely of Work - our Businefs also is
very Bad so that I'd scarcely done any thing all yᵉ Winter. In fact
had there been much to do I have been very unable to do it but I
must Rest Satisfy'd with yᵉ Dispensations of providence for we
must not presume to Dictate or say unto God why doest thou deal
with us thus - but I fully conceive & find that this is not Resting
place but its an Howling Wildernefs a way that strewed with
Briers & thorns but a little more toil & labour we shall soon get to
our Journeys End - I pray god to Enable us by faith & prayer to be
prefsing forward till we lay hold of Eternal life ever looking unto
Jesus as our King & Conquerer our Lord & Saviour - you Hinted
George would tell us some droll stories I think he has he tells us
one of a fine pincushion thick Courious by w.ʰ pins of makeing
pillowcases & such like but says he I told them they were Napkins
& that I was Up to their goshops - I suppose you have heard that
Geo Watson was forced to give up Businefs that he is now in a
Manner starving only as his Brothers supply him with a few
necefsarys of Life - Hen.ʸ Adams has taken yᵉ shop & Married Mifs
Freebody & turn'd Baker - your Moth.ʳ has wish'd much to come
up but I fear now that we shall not be able to come this Spring
without a great Alteration - and Abatement in your moth.ʳˢ
trouble. but I blefs god that under all our tryals - we still one
consolation of being Blefs'd with yᵉ best of Child.ⁿ it gives me great
comfort to hear from Rob.ᵗ you are doing well. that you can spare

6

money to redeem yᵉ Morgage - which I shall leave to your option I
have hinted it to Boncey & M.ʳ Cobb but you Mention'd 120 but it
is 125 which sum I pay yᵉ Int.ˢᵗ for so that with yᵉ half years Int.ˢᵗ
due this Lady will be 128-2-6 - altogether, now use your pleasure
but let me know in a day or two as the money lying dead will be of
no use to any body. If you think to redeem it better do it this
quart.ʳ think of yᵉ best plan to remit yᵉ money let me know - & if
done I shall give you security with Int.ˢᵗ For ye sum - I hope Moth.ʳ
will be better in a few days she seems better while writing this
letter. Rob.ᵗ Family & Dixon are all well Rob.ᵗ was here yest.ʸ all
join with us in love to you all hopeing you are all well.
  Yours Affectionately - W.ᵐ Dawson
  Busy at Work for yᵉ present

     William and Susanna Dawson were both religious, first attending the Parish Church and later an Independent Chapel of which William became clerk. I have an account of John Dawson's conversion in my great-grandfather's hand-writing (11). It appears that his sister Sarah 2, born 2 November 1781 and who worked for a Wesleyan haberdasher, persuaded her employer and his wife to invite her brother to a meal at which the Wesleyan Minister, Rev. Joseph Cusworth (Commissioned 1807, died 1857) was present (ii). The Rev. Cusworth was appointed to Margate in 1808 and he was later Governor of Kingswood School. Sarah was in Sister Sinnock's Class of 1808 (iii). Sarah was concerned for John's spiritual well-being despite the fact that even as a young adult he would frequently attend worship (his mother would often take the boy John to the Independent Chapel to hear the preaching). It is interesting to note that at least five of John's descendants became Methodist Ministers, which I will look at in more detail later.

     My daughter, Mrs Sarah Griffin has a sampler worked by Sarah Dawson when she was aged 9 (12 – see Chapter 8). Sarah Dawson was later one of the two witnesses to John Dawson's wedding on 14 August 1813 and wrote clearly in the Register. She was then aged 31 and unmarried. However, in his Will dated 1849 John Dawson left her ten pounds a year for the rest of her life in her married name of Gouger (10). At the age of fifty-seven, while living at 22 High Street, Margate, she married a widowed farmer, John Gouger, aged seventy-eight.

John, whose father Captain John Gouger had given him a farm, had been born in Ramsgate, and farmed the 135 acres employing 7 labourers and a boy at the time of the 1851 Census, by which time he was 91 years old. He died the next year aged 92. In those days the word retirement had not been coined. The American Evangelist Dr Graham reminds us that there is no Biblical reference to retirement!

John and Sarah Gouger lived at 42 Brickclamp, in the parish of St. Nicholas at Wade, a small village about 7 miles west of Margate. John had a son, Francis, by previous marriage, who was a grazier. He died when thrown from a trap, a two-wheeled carriage (iii).

John Gouger, Sarah's husband, was an important figure in the Margate Wesleyan Church. He would recall John Wesley's last visit to Margate in 1790 - his first visit had been in 1766. John wrote an account of the eighteenth-century church. He was Circuit Steward for 50 years, spanning 1792 and 1842. One Circuit Minute from 1831 reads 'agreed that a supply of Sherry wine be kept at each preaching place in the circuit for the refreshment of the Preachers after preaching.' A son Daniel (b.1800) followed in his footsteps (iv).

Old Methodist documents in the family were the Arminian Magazine of 1797 presented to Dr Sangster at Central Hall on 8 September 1944. This was a predecessor of the Methodist magazine of which copies from 1799, 1804, 1806, 1807, 1809, 1810 (one with the name Randall 1821) were presented to Wesley Chapel, City Road in 1934 together with a Map of Methodism (1824) by AMD (v).

John Dawson

Born 20 April 1785, married Ann Goodhugh 14 August 1813, died 2 October 1850. There is a discrepancy concerning the date of John Dawson's death: his tombstone records 3 October 1850 whereas according to the Parish Register of Deaths it was 2 October (6) (13). John Dawson was my great-great-grandfather.

After his conversion to Wesleyanism, John Dawson moved to Faversham, I believe in 1810. He had a bakery and confectionery shop at 4 Market Square which was still open when I was a boy. The shop front was sold and went to Chicago and has since been returned. The front of the pharmacy shop next door but one which was owned by my late Uncle Thomas J. Thomas (who married Bessie Hiller Dawson) remains unaltered.

John Dawson (1785-1850), from a set of three pictures with Ann, his wife, and Elizabeth Fagg marking the wedding of the latter with William Goodhugh Dawson (WGD1).

When he was 28, John married Ann Goodhugh with her father's consent. She was 17. Ann had 13 children, 10 surviving to adult life. The children were baptised in the Wesleyan Chapel in Preston Street.

John Dawson was an active member of the Wesleyan Church. On the formation of the local branch of the Wesleyan Methodist Missionary Society in 1819 he became its first Treasurer. Information from Dr A. Percival MBE of the Faversham Society shows that he was also active in public life. He stood as a Liberal Candidate for the Town Council in 1835 and was concerned about Faversham Creek improvements (14). In my possession are his Hymn Book and a drawing of him said to have been done at his son's wedding in 1845. I believe my son, WGD5, has his punch bowl spoon.

I am indebted to Miss Ruth Clay who has written her family history *Some Clays and Other Ancestors* for some details of John Dawson (vi). The Clays were tradespeople in Faversham in the nineteenth century. It seems likely that her ancestor Charles Clay (1794-1853) became a Wesleyan in 1813 through the influence of John Dawson. Charles' son John Lawson Clay (1830- 1900) was a witness to John Dawson's Will in 1849 (vii). He was only twenty at the time. He may have been John Dawson's apprentice as he became a baker. A sister of John Dawson's son William Goodhugh's wife, Georgina, née Fagg, married another son of Charles Clay, George William (1832-1905). For both it was a second marriage. Her first husband was Sergeant Bell of Her Majesty's Army. For many years my father used his swagger stick as a walking stick.

John Dawson died suddenly on 2 October 1850 when entering a horse-bus in Canterbury (6) (15). I have his Will leaving his business to his wife who only survived him by eighteen months. A note of insurance premium for the property of the late John Dawson dated 1852 shows numerous dwellings in Ospringe and Canterbury and his father's house in Margate (16).

William Goodhugh Dawson 1

Born 24 May 1814, married Elizabeth Fagg 11 July 1845, died 5 April 1884.

William Goodhugh Dawson (1814-1884).

He was my great-grandfather and known to his grandchildren as 'Ya-Ya'. He was the eldest child of John Dawson and was 31 when he married the 34-year-old Elizabeth Fagg at the Wesleyan Bethel Chapel in Rochester. His first cousin William Sandwell Dawson (2) was one of the witnesses, another being Sarah, younger sister of the bride. After six years of marriage Elizabeth had an only child, my grandfather, WGD2.

My great-grandfather described himself as a builder and undertaker, although on his tombstone only the former trade is mentioned (17). Nothing is known of his education. I have his book 'The Ready Reckoner', which also has his wife's maiden name in the cover so it must presumably predate their marriage in 1845.

Little is also known of the building work carried out by my great-grandfather in Faversham. It included renovating a cottage adjoining the Drill Hall (formerly the Assembly Hall) in Preston Street which was his workshop (18). It was told to my father that he gave the impression of a relaxed attitude to business and was often seen in desultory conversation on street corners.

He would seem to have prospered and he owned several sailing vessels. One drawing shows him wearing a yachting cap. The vessels brought building materials up the Creek to Faversham. He also engaged in coastal trade and trade with the Low Countries and France.

My great-grandfather was a Wesleyan and, although his brother John Wesley became a Wesleyan Minister, I know nothing of his work in the Church. Carrying my father in his arms in the garden as a baby, he was said to have been overheard singing the Hymn 'Lord, I hear of Showers of Blessings' (WGD3).

Ya-Ya lived next door to his son in Ospringe Road and died according to a memorial card 'with great suffering' on 5 April 1884. He is buried with his wife and son in Faversham Church Yard (17). The Faversham and North East Kent Advertiser contains, in marked contrast to its later tributes to his son in 1909, a bare notice of his death. Its columns were much preoccupied with the premature death from haemophilia of the Queen's youngest son, the Duke of Albany.

I have a good portrait and numerous photographs and caricatures of Ya-Ya. His appearance was rather forbidding and severe. He had a bald head and some resemblance to my father's younger brother, Howard. Ya-Ya took some interest in family history adding notes to old records. I have a family tree in his writing. I believe the account of his father, John Dawson's early life already mentioned, was also in his hand-writing.

He kept in touch with his sisters who had emigrated to America. I have two letters written to him during the Civil War by Sarah, who married Rev. Stephen Smith. They are written, presumably for paper economy, both horizontally and vertically (19). One nephew, John Dawson Smith (1842-1920), son of Mary Anne Smith née Dawson, served with the Union Forces in the Wisconsin Heavy Artillery. Hence it can be said that the family made a small contribution to the cause of the liberation of the slaves (vii).

The letters have been transcribed by SGD; and the text of one is given below, words defying deciphering being denoted by '???'

Geneva,

Walworth Co.
Wisconsin
Feby. 17/ 64

My dear Brother

Stephen is just about to send a letter to his Brother. I enclose a few lines to you just to ??? up your memory and let you know that we have been hoping to hear from you for some months past. How do you all do? How much I wish we could hear often but since poor Grandpa Smith died we seldom have a Faversham letter. I am thankful to say we are all now in the enjoyment of good health. My own health was poor last summer, suffering much with pain in my side but is now better. We are having a very pleasant winter although we have had some fearfully cold weather. I presume it is likely you may hear something of it through the papers. About New Year was the coldest that we have known of it to be since we have been in the Country. On Thursday Decr 31 was an ever memorable day to us, Stephen had an engagement to marry a couple about 4 miles in the country, the young lady a daughter of one of our local preachers and as is generally expected I must go too and dine with the party. Thursday morning came cold and snowing fast, however, we bundled up with shawls and buffalo hides and off we went. We reached the house in safety as did all the rest of the wedding party. The ceremony was performed, the dinner over but still the storm ???. We started for home, but did not get more than 10 yards from the house, were obliged to stay there all of us until Saturday. The next day was terrific, the thermometer was about 35° below zero or 67 below freezing. This will give you some idea of the intensity of the cold but we had a good time and returned home in safety. *I think I have told you Helen Smith lives with us I am obliged to have help and I would rather have her than a stranger. We pay her a dollar or 4/2 per week. Polly and Willy came to visit us at Xtmas. We heard from Polly today they are all well.*

I heard from Eliza a short time since and I thought from her letter she seemed to intimate there a possibility of our not getting Uncle William's property. Can you tell me at all what she means. I do trust her fears are groundless, it would indeed be a sad disappointment. I have kept hoping and expecting to hear something respecting it. Will you let me know what you think about the matter? I was thinking a while ago I would write to J. B. Sharp and see if I could <u>sell</u> my claim do you think he would buy it at 5 or 10 per cent or is there anyone else you think would. I mean provided you think it is not likely to be settled for some time longer. It would be such an advantage to us, now, gold is fetching 50 per cent but when the war closes (as we now hope it soon will) it will assuredly be down again. If you will write me at once I should feel greatly obliged as I am very anxious to know about it.

How is your dear wife and boy, do give them a kiss from me with my best love. How I wish you would send me your photographs. You don't know how much they would be prized. I have a splendid interleaf Morocco album already for them and have so many friends who would like to see them. We are now in our second year. We enjoy living in Geneva very much. Its a very pleasant little town, a good society, and some of the warmest hearts Wisconsin can produce. I never get homesick for the longer I live in America the better I like it although I do sincerely hope I shall be permitted to visit you once more. It is now bed time and I must close. The 3 boys send love to cousin Willy.

Accept our united love

and believe me

Your affectionate Sister,

Sarah Smith

William Goodhugh Dawson 2

Born 12 December 1851, married Mary Day 8 June 1876, died 25 June 1909.

William Goodhugh Dawson (1851-1909).

William's mother was 40 when she had her only child and there is ample evidence that she doted upon him. His copy of 'Treasure Island' given by his mother on his tenth birthday has an affectionate dedication to her 'Dear Willie'. I also have joint photographs and examples of his early paintings kept by her.

He had some artistic talent with water-colours and beautiful hand-writing. Some school exercise-books and text-books are in my possession – viz. French dictionary 1864, Latin dictionary 1865. A diary of 1868 makes numerous references to days in his father's workshop (vii). Inside the cover is a list of his prizes at Commercial School between 1862 and 1871. As a young man he drew beautiful dedications to the Family Albums given to his mother and to Miss Mary Frances Day whom he was to marry.

His marriage in 1876, a little before the Married Women Property Act made a wife legally more than a chattel, was a love-match which lasted until his death in 1909. The honeymoon was spent at Torquay (20).

The 1881 Census records WGD1 as living with his wife Elizabeth at 44 Ospringe Road, Faversham and his son, WGD2, living at number

45 with his young family. This is also given as their address on WGD2's second child's (Arthur) birth certificate in 1879. The houses appear to have been later renumbered 42 and 40 and several photographs exist.

When his father had died in 1884, he had inherited a prosperous building, undertaking and ship-owning business. However, he was not successful in business and was continually worried by declining fortunes. Houses were built and then there were long delays before suitable tenants were found. Sometimes there was insufficient money to complete houses. A letter preserved by my father thanks him for a loan in this respect (21). He was also a managing ship-owner, inheriting the boats from his father and losing most, if not all of them to the waves (see Chapter 6).

Financial failure was made no easier by his wife's desire for respectability and gentility, perhaps due to her sisters having married more wealthy husbands with secure employment. Annie was married to Benjamin Berry JP, step-brother of Sir Walter Berry, a prosperous farmer. In 1907, Benjamin Berry became President of the Methodist Mutual Aid Association. Hannah married Robert Dunn, the Town Registrar. Jamie, a music teacher, married Tom Attwater, one of the Harbour-Master's sons. Any lapse from formality was frowned upon by my grandmother as, for instance, the occasion when my grandfather sat on a table in the family photo taken on the 21st birthday of his oldest child Bessie.

Robert Dunn described my grandfather to my mother as a 'miserable man'. However, in later years when questioning my aunt, Miss Alice Dawson about the description she angrily discounted it. Certainly, my grandfather was very harassed by financial problems. In later years he was happy to earn ten shillings a week keeping the books 'of a farmer as the income was regular and reliable'. I have the cash book for a Homestall Farm for 1901-3. At a later date Marion, the daughter of Robert Dunn, kept the books of Sir Walter Berry's farm.

We are apt to say that earlier generations did not understand children. An earlier present to my grandfather of Isaac Watts' 'Hymns for Children' is full of cautions about Hell and the Final Judgement. On one occasion my grandfather took my father in one of his vessels to Ramsgate, and on landing he pretended to run away from the small boy - not a practical joke that would be considered suitable today. Yet there is no doubt he was a kind and caring father.

It was a Victorian home. Servants attended at breakfast for Bible reading and prayers. There was a governess for the younger children. However, there was concealed poverty. My grandfather with an egg for his breakfast would give the top to one of the children who had porridge for their normal fare.

He was fond of the garden and had a vine in the green-house which provided bunches of grapes for the Harvest Festival. My father's earliest memory of his father was of his sadness at seeing him thinning the bunches so as to improve those selected for the festival. My grandfather was a hard and willing worker for the Wesleyan Chapel as was testified in his funeral oration (22). I have a photo showing him seated by his floral exhibit at a Chapel Festival in 1907. At heart he was not a fully committed Puritan. He would have a drink with a farmer when on business although he commended my father when he signed the Pledge. On a cycle ride he once surprised my father by lighting a cigarette. He boasted that he could not cycle up Detling Hill, part of the North Downs in Kent, until he was fifty; the reason was that he had changed his penny-farthing for a safety bicycle.

He was fond of family entertainment and would sing 'The Bay of Biscay'. Perhaps he was a frustrated seaman. My father recalled a bank holiday outing to Maidstone in a hired conveyance with two ponies. On the return journey the boys had to walk up Detling Hill as the ponies were tired.

He suffered much during the last few years of his life. There was temporary improvement following an operation at the Bolingbroke Hospital. My father recalled visiting him there and at his request bringing him a small bottle of whisky.

He had an original letter of John Wesley of which I had a copy. As I recall it returns thanks for hospitality. The writer includes greetings from his wife so it must predate her desertion of him. She left him on 23 February 1771 two weeks after his visit of 7 February to Faversham (23). He wrote in his journal *Non eam reliqui, non dimissi, non revocabo. I did not desert her, I did not send her away, I will not recall her* (ix).

I have been selective of memories passed on by my father. He was undoubtedly a grandfather of whom one could feel proud. I should like to have known him.

William Goodhugh Dawson 3

Born 17 May 1883, married Florence (Fluff) Harris 9 April 1923, died 25 September 1976.

William Goodhugh Dawson (1883-1976).

It is difficult to write a brief resume of my father's life, as I knew him for fifty years. However, the task is necessary for the benefit of later generations who did not know him.

He was born the fourth child of his parents when, as his mother recalled in later years, the corn was springing up in the field opposite their house at 40 Ospringe Road in Faversham. He was named William Goodhugh after his father and grandfather. His older brother, Arthur, would have liked these names but he was told that at his birth it was considered a mistake to have three WGD's around. In later life he came round to accepting the fortuity of this decision, as in contradistinction to my father, he had no sons. As oldest son Arthur did, my father told me, require him to show him proper respect.

My father's education was first by a governess and later at a Dame School run by a Miss Ottoway. Later on, he went to the Wreight School whose Headmaster was a very much respected Mr Telfer, and there he received a good education. My grandmother was distressed that funds were not available for her sons to attend the Grammar School. My father's school reports are preserved and show a diligent application to school work. He had an early interest in cricket. His diaries of 1895 and 1898 are full of interest (x) (xi).

17

On leaving school at 16, he worked locally in a junior clerical capacity for a Mr Dobbie for four and later five shillings a week. His petty-cash books are kept from 1900. He then moved to London to join the very old shipping firm of Thompson Hankey and Co. where Clarence Fitchew, the son of his father's cousin William Fitchew, was already working (xii).

Office work was very different from today. There were no women employees except cleaners, no typewriters or telephones, and there were coal fires in every office. Outside there was prevailing smog and dense horse-drawn traffic. Often it was necessary to bend under the horses' heads to cross the road. The firm's produce of rum and sugar took six weeks to travel in sailing brigs from the West Indies. As a teetotaller my father always felt rather unhappy about his involvement in what was known as the *Drink Trade.*

He lived with his brothers Arthur and Howard and his sister Alice in a rented house in Clapham. Alice was the house keeper. Close by, his oldest sister Bessie owned a private school in Nightingale Lane. My father did the school account books. In those pre-first-war years my father had an opportunity of joining a Fitchew cousin in the Midland Bank. It was a life-long regret that he turned it down as it would have entailed an initial small fall of salary. The advantage of bank employment was that in the early years of this century, almost alone, it offered pensions and also widows' pensions.

My father worked long hours and when a quarterly balance was due would remain late at the office to account for every penny. Away from work he was much occupied with Chapel, cricket, and to a lesser degree with football. On one occasion he played with his two brothers at Lords. They did not do well in that match, but I have a photo which records the event. His brother, Howard, once bowled to Dr W. G. Grace. Howard had considered becoming a professional player for Kent. My father was a member of the Astronomical Association: his telescope is now in the possession of Robert Harris, son of my cousin Martin Harris.

He also took every opportunity to travel. In May 1908 crossing The Channel with his mother in the steamer *Onward,* there was a collision with *The Queen.* The look-out was killed. The Captain of *Onward* was held to have proceeded without reducing speed in fog and his Certificate was suspended for six months. Upon landing after this unfortunate incident my father and his mother returned to Folkestone and took a train to take another boat from Dover!

18

As a boy in South Croydon, he once pointed out to me a lady in the street whom I understood his mother had intended him to marry. She had subsequently married a Baptist Minister who had left her and I gathered that my father felt that he had been fortunate to escape an arranged match.

World War 1 broke out when my father was 31. He was peace loving and had heard Lloyd George voice his opposition to the Boer War at a public meeting. He said 'two wrongs don't make a right' and a heckler in the audience called 'Yes, but two Wrights made an aeroplane!' My father had a horror of blood and hand-to-hand fighting. Although convinced of the justness and inevitability of the war, he felt he could only serve in a non-combatant unit and so was very glad to enlist in a proud Territorial Unit, the 2/3 London Field Ambulance early in 1915. He trained assiduously as a nursing orderly and in due course served several years in France attached with the Field Ambulance to 169th Infantry Brigade of 56 London Division (xiii) (xiv). At times he was stretcher-bearer, ambulance orderly and hospital nursing orderly.

I should explain to those not familiar with military operations that a Field Ambulance gives medical support to an infantry brigade of three battalions. The 169th Infantry Brigade was one of the three brigades of the 56th London Division. The 56th London Division in their finest hour withstood the great German attack in March 1918. This was the last desperate attempt of the Germans to win the war as the Russians had been defeated and the Americans had not yet arrived in force on the Western Front. U-boat attacks were severely affecting British supplies. The London soldiers were very skilfully led by General Sir Amyatt Hull who organised defence in depth, and the attack was held with 1,500 casualties to the Division. The German Commander General Ludendorff later conceded in his memoirs that 28 March was the turning point in 1918.

My father would have liked to have achieved some promotion, but failed utterly to drill a squad of defaulters when given the opportunity. Morale was high in the 2/3 London FA with defaulters in short supply. One CO was censured after a full inspection as there were no names in the Punishment Book (WGD3). There is only one punishment in the CO's diary: 28 days detention for a transport driver for giving false grounds for compassionate leave. Relevant sections of the Army Act were read to the Unit on parade on two occasions (xv). One corporal was even checked for throwing back an unexploded grenade in contravention of the Geneva Convention!

My father was awarded the Military Medal in December 1917 (24) (25) (26) (27). I understand that he dressed a wounded Canadian soldier at a crossroads under heavy shell fire. The Citation has been lost and the CO's diary is uninformative. I noticed with interest that the CO himself was evacuated with shellshock in April and again finally in May 1917 (xv). In due course, my father was discharged with an excellent CO's commendation. *He has shown energy and grit in his work* is an extract from his 'special remarks' (28). Whilst waiting for discharge, he had taken some professional examinations and he returned to his office.

Life there was different: there were now lady typists. He resumed his Chapel activities, this time in Faversham where he lived at the family home, commuting daily to London. Before the War he had been an officer in the Boys' Brigade. However, after the War, he felt more affinity with the Scout movement. It was as Scoutmaster at the Church that he first met my mother who was an officer 15 years younger than him, in Lady Berry's own Company of Guides, also attached to the Chapel.

My mother was not anxious to be married and moved away to a school teacher post in the London area. However, my father was persistent. An offer to take my mother's class of boys around the Tower was declined. A later visit with my mother to Hyde Park was agreed and it was at a café near the Serpentine that my father proposed and was accepted. The Faversham News recorded a presentation to Scoutmaster W.G. Dawson, MM, by Sir Walter Berry - the only mention I recall of my father's gallantry award - on the occasion of his forthcoming wedding and resignation from the Scout Movement (29).

Wedding of William Dawson (WGD3) and Florence Harris on 9 April 1923. Individuals are identified on the next page.

Key to individuals at the wedding of William Dawson (WGD3) to Florence Harris: 5 Arthur Meux, later married 45. 16 Hubert Harris, younger brother of bride. 20 Albert Harris, older brother of bride. 23 Arthur Dawson, older brother of groom. 24 probably Elsie Dawson née Jarman wife of 23. 25 Thomas Thomas, husband of 43. 30 Best man, unknown. 35 Fred Cooper, later to marry 50. 40 Hannah Dunn née Day. 41 Robert Dunn, husband of 40. 42 Alice Mary Dawson. 43 Bessie Thomas née Dawson. 44 Mary Dawson née Day (my grandmother). 45 Annie Stewart, college friend of bride. 46 Jen Maltby, college friend of bride. 47 Frances Harris, eldest sister of the bride. 48 WGD3 (my father). 49 Florence Harris (my mother). 50 Ivy Harris. 51 Katie Harris. 52 Lilian Dawson, youngest sister of the groom. 53 William Harris, bride's father. 54 Hannah Harris née Sheffield, bride's mother. 56 Kathleen Fright, later married 20. 57 Marion Dunn, daughter of 41. 58 perhaps David, son of 25. 68 probably Irene Dawson, daughter of 23, 69 probably Muriel Dawson, sister to 68.

The Dawson Family History resumé will be left at this point as further descent would involve a description and discussion of relations and kinsfolk still living. Memoranda are, however, required for families which had an important input into successive Dawson generations.

These are the *Goodhughs,* since Ann Goodhugh married my great-great-grandfather; the *Hillers,* since a grand-daughter Elizabeth Fagg married my great-grandfather William Goodhugh Dawson; the *Days,* since a daughter Mary Frances Day married my grandfather William Goodhugh Dawson; the *Harris* and *Shuffill/ Sheffield* families since their daughter Florence Catherine Harris married my father William Goodhugh Dawson, and finally the *Coopers*, who married into the Harris family via Florence's sister Ivy.

Chapter 2

The Goodhughs

The Goodhughs joined the Dawson family with the marriage of Ann Goodhugh to John Dawson in 1813. They were also from Kent. Here we consider the history of this part of the family.

William Goodhugh 1

William Goodhugh 1 (WG1) was born in 1705 during the reign of Queen Ann, possibly at Sundridge near Sevenoaks, in Kent. Some years ago, I saw a record of the baptism of William Goodhugh in 1706 at Westerham Parish Church. WG1 died at Sundridge on February 20 1790 and he was buried at Westerham. His age was 84 years and 4 months old. He married Sarah French in 1729 and she died on 21 April 1794 aged about 83.

William Goodhugh 2

WG1 had three sons and one daughter. The oldest son, also named William (WG2), was born on 19 November 1730. I have two of his note books which show from his writing that he was alive in 1796. He married Sarah Burgess (recently researched) on 10 October 1758. She had been born on 30 January 1731.

One of his leather note books gives an address of Bexley, Kent (xvi). There is a hide-bound book containing twenty-five prescriptions for various illnesses (xvii). The penultimate one with perhaps an active constituent of syrup of roses was said to cure scurvy and had been effectual in curing a leg ulcer for WG2 in 1795. It reads as follows:

> *To Cure the Scurvey in the Blood*
> *Take the following Mixture Lennet*
> *of Electery 3 ounces*
> *half a ounce of Ethyops Minorols*

half a ounce of Antomoney
Two penny worth of Surrop of
Rofes mix it well together
Take a peace about the Biggefs of A
Valnut Everry Night going
To Bed for 3 Weeks or a month
This cured me of a Sore Legg When
Nothing Else would do after a long
Tryal of many other things had fail
In the year 1795 W^m. Goodhugh

The back part of this note book contains details of births, deaths and marriages, mostly of relatives. There is also a list on very old paper of the children of WG2, eight in number, the last being Ann Goodhugh 1, who was born 10 July 1776 (30). A later hand has added dates of death, the last being for Elizabeth Goodhugh on 16 June 1836. At that time, it would appear that Mary Goodhugh, born 16 June 1767, and Ann Goodhugh 1 were still alive. Other evidence suggests the family home of WG2 was in northwest Kent as a daughter, Sarah Goodhugh 2 (a sister of the same name died aged 3 months), died aged seventeen years and four months on 22 July 1782 and was buried at Plumstead.

In the note book are compositions for sky rockets and fuses containing gun-powder, saltpetre, sulphur, etc. which may give a clue to the occupation of WG2 (xvii). This notebook on the same page records the duty upon bricks - perhaps another guide to the work of WG2. His notes for 1791-1796 show a preoccupation with his weight, which hardly varied from 14 st 11 lb on 9 February 1791 to 14 st 12 lb on 20 April 1796. His note book also has entries in another hand, possibly WG4 (born 1792) dated 1838-44 (xvi).

A final note of pride on the last page of the hide-bound book records a return journey from Folkestone to Tunbridge of forty-eight miles in one day on 2 October 1780 (xvii). Whether on horseback or, less likely, on foot is not stated. He would have been fifty years old.

William Goodhugh 3

William Goodhugh 3 was born the second son of WG2 on 24 February 1761. He died on 10 September 1829 and was buried in Faversham churchyard on 15 September 1829 (31). Particulars of his life have been difficult to document.

I have a small notebook which documents family events of his children but with handwriting at first in a scholarly and later in a less practised hand (xviii). He was a saltpetre refiner and extractor mentioned in the Board of Ordinance records for 1796, and in 1802 he was rated for property at 54/61 Tanner Street (opposite The Bull). He was pensioned in 1822 and his pension in 1825 was £41 10s 8d per annum. I have his will, proven at an Ecclesiastical Court, in which he is described as 'Gentleman' (32). The account of his premises and possessions, including Bank of England Stock, suggests some prosperity (33). His wife's name was Susanna Clackett. They were married in Faversham Parish Church on 21 December 1791, and she was a widow. It appears likely that she was born Susan Hinds (Susan and Susanna were names somewhat interchangeable in those days) and had married Robert Clackett in Davington on 30 April 1780. He had been buried at the age of 34 at Faversham Parish Church on 15 February 1791. Susanna died in 1799 and William Goodhugh remarried to her sister Sarah Hinds in 1822.

William and Susanna's second surviving child, Ann married John Dawson in Faversham Parish Church on 14 August 1813. Ann was 17 and a record in the Smith Eccleston Family History says she married with her father's permission (vii). My great-grandfather WGD1 was born on 24 May 1814.

There were no further William Goodhugh's except for the eldest son of WG3 who died without issue. He was the fourth William Goodhugh, and was a collector for the Inland Revenue. I have a drawing of him dating from the wedding of WGD1 in 1845 and a very early photograph. He died in an asylum on 12 August 1858 and was buried at Ospringe by my great-grandfather. The photograph shows him dressed in country clothes. He was an executor of his father's Will, proved in 1829, so he was presumably 'compos mentis' at that time. He married Mary Rickwood at Ospringe on Christmas Day 1812. She died on 28th March 1862. The couple have an imposing tombstone just to the left of the main entrance to Ospringe church. Letters of 1864-5 from his niece

Sarah Smith née Dawson in Wisconsin, USA reproduced earlier in this book, are very concerned with a possible legacy so he may have been prosperous (19).

Ann Goodhugh (1796-1852), daughter of WG3 and his wife Susanna, who married John Dawson.

The younger son of WG3, Richard, was a watchmaker in London who married a widow named Mary Grieve on 16 May 1816. They had one daughter, Ann Goodhugh, who remained a spinster.

WG3's daughter, Ann Goodhugh, who married John Dawson may well have been strongly attached to her sister Sarah, who married the Faversham postmaster John Bunger Sharpe who is mentioned in one of Sarah Smith's letters from America. I have a silver ring with platted hair and the initials of both sisters on the inside. Another ring has hair possibly of her husband or her father.

A son of J.B. Sharpe was a medical student who sadly drowned in the Thames by Lambeth Palace. He was buried in Faversham Church graveyard. His grave was found by my nephew close to his mother's. I hope that one day a kinsman will identify his medical teaching hospital.

For further details of the Goodhughs see the family tree (34).

Chapter 3

Methodist Ministers in the Family

There were in the family at least four Ordained Methodist Ministers, descendant of John Dawson, my great-great-grandfather, and one other by marriage. This unusual number of ministers was impressed upon me as a child by my Dawson maiden aunts and I am taking this opportunity to add a short note upon each one individually in this new edition.

My records are mainly based on oral recollections and I am grateful to Mr Simon Goodhugh Dawson, grandson of Rev. Christopher Dawson for his review of this section.

The calling to Methodist ministry is still evident in the family as the brother–in-law of my daughter is shortly to be ordained a Methodist minister.

The Christian allegiance of William Dawson, father of John Dawson, had been to the Established Church. However, in later life he joined an Independent Chapel. John Dawson became a Methodist, or Wesleyan, through the influence of his sister, Sarah. His son, my great-grandfather, William Goodhugh Dawson (WGD1), married Elizabeth Fagg, descended from the Hilliers of the North Foreland Lighthouse. They followed the Swedenborg Sect and held meetings in the lighthouse.

Rev. John Wesley Dawson (1816-1885)

John Wesley Dawson was the second child of John and Anne Dawson née Goodhugh. He followed the usual life of an itinerant Wesleyan Minister. Living descendants Simon Goodhugh Dawson and Barbara LeRuez née Dawson, as well as local records in Berkshire have given me interesting insights into his life.

As a boy he travelled to Kingswood, a Methodist boarding school in the West Country, by stage-coach. A later memory was seeing the Royal Navy Fleet depart, under sail, for the Crimea. Between 1838 and 1867 he ministered in no less than 13 Circuits, mostly in southern England and South Wales, but including a period in Alnwick, Northumberland.

John Wesley Dawson had the reputation of being a kindly man, compassionate and patient with the sick, in spite of having to contend with sickness in his own family. He was forced to retire from the Wesley Church in Central Reading on account of ill-health. Later he undertook the care of a church in Rose Street, Wokingham. This church had been founded by "Other Ranks" of the Household Cavalry who had been quartered in Wokingham after the battle of Waterloo. He used his own money to enlarge the church, which is flourishing to this day. He was highly regarded and the local paper reported that his funeral was attended by the local vicar of the Established Church "who remained throughout the Service".

Rev. William Goodhugh Dawson (mid-1846-1942)

William Goodhugh Dawson was the second child of Rev. J. W. Dawson and was born at Great Farringdon.

As a young man before ordination, he was a schoolmaster at Kingswood School. There, he had the reputation of being a disciplinarian. He married Agnes Pratt in 1876, from whom he separated in middle age because of her mental illness. His career as a Circuit Minister began in 1876. He died in 1942 aged 95, the last 6 years of his life being spent in a nursing home. Until I recently exceeded his age, he was the longest-lived male Dawson ancestor of whom I have records!

Rev. Richard Goodhugh Dawson (1849-1916)

Richard Goodhugh Dawson was a younger brother of the above Rev. W. G. Dawson. I know little of his life and work as a minister. He was, however, known to have been very energetic in his calling and also a keen gardener. He was married twice and died in Swanage in 1916.

Rev. Christopher Dawson (1885-1950)

Christopher Dawson was a son of Rev. WGD and born in 1885. He worked as a missionary in India, which is where he married Beatrice

Waterhouse in 1914, in the Karur Wesleyan Chapel in Tamil Nadu. For two years in WW1, he served as an ordinary soldier in the 61st King George's Own Pioneers. This operated in British East Africa as part of the Indian Army Expeditionary Force. Later he returned to circuit ministry in England. He had a reputation as a very faithful and effective Minister of the Gospel. He died in Portsmouth in 1950 and a daughter survives.

Rev. Stephen Smith (1828-1906)

Stephen Smith was born in 1828, a son of John Smith and Elizabeth Lever, through whom he is related to the Dawson family. He received a liberal education in a private academy in Faversham before working as book-keeper and clerk at his parents' grocery store. He was licensed to preach in the Wesleyan Church Faversham in Oct.1849.

In 1855, he emigrated to America with his wife, Sarah, the sister of Rev'd John Wesley Dawson. After Sarah died, he returned and married his niece, Emily Dawson Jones, born in 1868, in Winchester. He went back to work for a few months in America before returning to help to care for Emily's aged mother, Ann Staines Jones, née Dawson, who was also sister to John Wesley Dawson.

Chapter 4

The Hilliers, Faggs, Clays, Fitchews and Days

This section looks at the history of the various families that married into the Dawson line. My great-grandfather WGD1 married Elizabeth Fagg whose mother, Elizabeth Anne Hiller, was born to John Frederick and Esther Hiller (35) in the North Foreland Lighthouse, situated at the eastern extremity of the Isle of Thanet in Kent.

There is a strong tradition that the first Hiller came to England with George I in 1714. His wife was German named Esther. These were the great-grandparents of Elizabeth Anne Hiller. My recollection as a child is that he was a royal cook (36). However, he may have been or become a farmer. Hiller is certainly a German name, for example I. Hiller was the name of a German composer of the nineteenth century.

These early Hillers had a son, John Christopher, who married Elizabeth Marsh. They in turn had a son, John Frederick Hiller, who married Esther Morgan.

John and Esther Hiller

John and Elizabeth's son John Frederick Hiller took the post of keeper of the North Foreland Lighthouse of which I had a water-colour, now donated to Margate Museum. It is dated 1809 and entitled *N. Foreland Lighthouse in 1809*, but may not have been painted until 1842. The painting is reproduced on the front cover of this book and clearly includes a steamship to the left of the lighthouse.

John Frederick Hiller's wife, Esther was widowed and allowed to remain as lighthouse keeper of the North Foreland Lighthouse - there are numerous records of women lighthouse keepers in the eighteenth century (xix). She had 15 children of whom the names of twelve are known.

Two stories have been related about Esther. On one occasion two wealthy young men from London were shown around the lighthouse. On leaving and seeing the widow had many children they each gave my great-great-great-grandmother a guinea (21 shillings) - a small fortune in those days. Now it so happened that Esther Hiller and other women friends had agreed to give any earnings that week to the chapel. After

31

much inner turmoil she discussed the matter with the Minister who advised her that she might have a dispensation and use the money for the children. On another occasion, returning from Chapel on a summer's evening, Esther realised she would not reach the lighthouse until after dark. The lantern was eventually lit and she was relieved that the absent light was not reported.

Either John Frederick Hiller or his father may have died in tragic circumstances. The evidence is ambiguous. After selling some cattle, he left an inn on horseback but never reached home. This may be why I have been unable to find evidence of the burial of John Frederick Hiller. Again, the wife of either John Frederick Hiller or his father had had the misfortune to be maid, wife, and widow in one day. She was first married at 19 and then, before she was 21, married a Mr Hiller. She was presented at Court and I have a piece of the brocade of the dress that she wore which has been dated to 1750-60. The youngest daughter of John Frederick Hiller, Elizabeth Ann, later Fagg (born 1784) had the dress made into a Christening robe for her children. Later the dress was cut up and a piece given to each daughter. I inherited the piece which had belonged to my great-grandmother Elizabeth Dawson née Fagg.

Elizabeth Ann Fagg née Hiller

Born 1784 in the North Foreland Lighthouse, married George Fagg a farmer at St Peter in Thanet on 14 May 1809, and died 14 June 1876 in Canterbury. I have her memorial card (37).

Elizabeth had eight children. A daughter Esther Fagg married Edward Fitchew and it is through this line that we have kinship with the Fitchews of today (38) (39). Esther, a daughter of Esther and Edward married Arnold Luke giving our kinship with Arnold's mother, Jemima Luke née Thompson the hymn writer (1813-1906, *I think when I read that sweet story of old)*. Jemina had married the Congregational Minister Rev. Samuel Luke in 1843 two years after she wrote the hymn. Another of Elizabeth Fagg's daughters, Georgiana, previously married to Sergeant George Bell, married George Clay as her second husband providing a relationship to the Clay family of Faversham. He was a younger brother of the John Lawson Clay, and a son of the Charles Clay already mentioned in the story of John Dawson.

My framed portrait of Elizabeth Ann Fagg née Hiller (1784-1876).

However, our family history is concerned with her second child Elizabeth Fagg, born 1811, who at the age of 34 married my great-grandfather WGD1.

Elizabeth Dawson née Fagg (1811-1900). This portrait is a companion to those of John Dawson and his wife Ann, reproduced earlier in this book.

Elizabeth Fagg spent some of her earlier childhood at the North Foreland Lighthouse and described how it was then in a letter to my Aunt Lilian Dawson written in 1897 (40). Her memories were coloured by the

Napoleonic War and she recalled her mother threatening to give her to 'Boney' (Napoleon Bonaparte 1769-1821) when she was naughty. There is a gap in my knowledge of her life from 1826 when she enrolled in the Preacher's Class - William Harvard DD commissioned 1810, died 1857 (ii) at St. Peters, Thanet - until her marriage in Rochester in 1845 (xx). I have a notebook cover of Miss Fagg, 14 Park Terrace, Regents Park (xxi). This, coupled with her name in the Ready Reckoner, suggests an early business career.

The Days (41)

This family is important to our history as Mary Frances Day married my grandfather WGD2 in 1876. I was given the nose-gay holder that my grandmother carried at her wedding, which has since been carried by my daughter Sarah, my cousin Muriel Smith née Dawson and most recently by my niece Ann Dawson, in whose possession it currently remains.

The earliest identified member of the Day family was George Day. He was a mason in County Durham and who died in 1842. We know nothing of his wife except that her Christian name was Hannah. They had four children Thomas, Hannah, Robert and John.

John Day was born on either 10 or 19 April 1815, two months before Waterloo, at Hetton-le-Hole, County Durham. He married Frances Eggleston on 17 January 1842 after Banns at St Nicholas Church, Newcastle, now Newcastle Cathedral. They were both resident in that parish.

Frances Eggleston had been born on 26 May 1819 at Cornforth, County Durham. Her father Thomas, born 1764 and died 1853, was a miller who had married Elizabeth Patterson, born in 1781. They had 12 children, of whom Frances was the tenth. It is believed that the congenital deformity of the index fingers with absence of the distal interphalangeal joints was introduced into the Dawson family by Frances Eggleston. Its occurrence has not been accurately traced, but examples are certainly found today after six generations amongst Dawson and Griffin descendants.

John Day was recorded as a mason at the time of his marriage to Frances Eggleston, following his father, but he later became a surveyor.

At some time between the birth of their eldest child Annie in 1842 in Durham and the birth of their daughter Hannah in 1849, they moved to South Wales, where he surveyed the Taff Vale Railway.

My grandmother Mary Frances Day was the fourth of their seven children. She was born on 14 October 1851, three years before the Crimean War, at Caldicot in Monmouthshire, a village on the Severn Estuary, and died on 29 April 1933. Sometime after her birth, the family moved again to Faversham, where John Day was a road surveyor and surveyed the main road from Sittingbourne to Faversham (now part of the A2).

John and Frances Day celebrated their Golden Wedding in 1892 and I have the commemorative photo. They retired to live at Minster Cottage opposite the Minster on the Isle of Sheppey, where my father and his brothers and sisters very much enjoyed holidays. John Day died suddenly at Minster on 4th October 1893 at the age of 78 after stabling the horse from his gig. Frances Day died at Faversham on 28th January 1910 aged 90. They are both buried in Faversham Churchyard in a grave adjoining that of my Dawson great grandparents and my grandfather Dawson in a somewhat neglected spot close to the shade of a clump of trees.

Two of John and Frances Days' sons emigrated. Their daughter Mary Frances Day married a Faversham man, as did her sisters Annie, Hannah and Jane.

Annie Day (1842-1924) married Benjamin Gough Berry JP, a step-brother of Sir Walter Berry. They had ten children. Some died young; others emigrated. A granddaughter Lulu, married Edgar Glanville MP for Eye, Suffolk from whom she was subsequently divorced.

Grandmother's sister Hannah Dunn, née Day (1849-1937) married Robert Dunn, the registrar of Faversham. Curiously, Robert Dunn's maternal uncles were the Smith brothers who married and emigrated with WGDl's sisters Sarah and Mary Anne (42). Lesley Smith, who wrote 'Stories of Faversham' comes from the same Smith family (43). Robert Dunn lived until 1926, long enough to give me a Christening Spoon in 1925, since given to Barry Dunn's granddaughter, Hannah who was named after my grandmother Hannah Dunn née Day. The younger daughter of Hannah and Robert Dunn, Winifred married William Fitchew as his second wife in 1919, thus making a second link with the Fitchews, first made when Esther Fagg married Edward Fitchew.

Jane Day (1858-1908) married Tom Chambers Attwater, the eldest son of the Harbour Master, Thomas Martin Attwater and his Jersey-born wife Julia Mary Chambersone. Their third son, John Post (1862-1909), was a church organist and Fellow of the Royal College of Organists (FRCO). He died young, leaving a family. A public subscription was made for their support, raising £2,000. A stained-glass window to his memory in Grafton Square Congregational Church, London was destroyed during the second World War (44). I have a photo and some of his music, which my son WGD5 found in the parish church of Leadgate, County Durham, and gave to the Faversham Society (xxii). A nephew, Donald Attwater (1892-1977) was author of the Penguin Dictionary of Saints (AP).

Chapter 5

The Harris's, Shuffills (Sheffields) and Coopers

The Harris family enter my story on account of the marriage of my mother, Florence Harris – always called 'Fluff' – to my father William Goodhugh Dawson (WDG3). There is a photograph of this event on page 21. My mother's sister Ivy married Frederick Cooper, whose antecedents led rather colourful lives during the nineteenth century.

This brief resume is largely taken from research carried out for my cousin Dr Gordon Harris of Vancouver and from more recent investigations by David Cooper, the son of my late cousin Bryan.

The Harris families (45)

My mother's ancestors can be traced reliably to my great-great-grandparents on the Harris side. In general, compared with my father's forebears on both sides they were probably less literate and came from a lower social class. A curious coincidence is that both my grandfathers were 'only' children of mothers relatively old for childbearing.

The earliest known Harris's are Thomas Harris and his wife Ann, whose names we know from the christening records of their children. The first three, all boys, were all born at Upper Hardres, a village about 5 miles south of Canterbury (46). They included my great-grandfather James Harris, born on 14 October 1825. Later, they moved to Birchington, which is where their four daughters were christened. Family history relates that one of these ladies (it is not clear which) married a man by the name of J. Care (xxiii) and that my grandfather used to visit his (J. Care's) son Fred at Tenterden. Fred had a daughter Mabel, whose husband Harold Fay and son Brian subsequently lived at Addiscombe, Surrey. However, recent investigations suggest that Fred's father was a certain William Care and that William had married into the Shoobridge family. The Cares were thus probably related through the wife of my great-grandfather James Harris, Mary-Ann Shoobridge.

Thomas Harris's occupation was stated in the records of his children's christenings as 'labourer' until 1835, when it changed to 'baker'. James Harris followed in his father's footsteps and he subsequently had a business in New Inn Yard close to the present site of Lloyds Bank in The Square at Birchington. Again, it is a coincidence that both my great-great-grandfathers on the paternal side were bakers.

James Harris married Mary Ann Shoobridge in January 1865 at Tenterden, in central Kent. Mary Ann had been baptised on 27 April 1828 in the parish of Halstow, Kent (47). Halstow is a small hamlet on the estuary of the Medway, about 25 miles from Upper Hardres.

Mary Ann Shoobridge, from a collidion positive photograph now in the possession of David Cooper.

The baptism record of Mary Ann Shoobridge names her parents as Thomas and Sarah, with Thomas' occupation shown as labourer. We can trace them back to Thomas Hunt Shoobridge, who married Sarah Wood at Strood, near Rochester on 24 October 1825. They would be my great-great-grandparents. Sarah Wood had been christened on 26 May 1799 to parents Richard and Sarah.

Mary Ann Shoobridge had a brother, Thomas who was an agricultural labourer and an executor of her will. He predeceased her in 1898. I was also told that she had two sisters who married two Kennedy brothers, both of whom were doctors. I believe that it is because of these marriages that the legend that the Shoobridges were a County family arose. There certainly was, and may still be a memorial to one of the Kennedy brothers at the Stratford Hospital, North East London. I understand that they were not welcome at my grandfather's house because of their alcoholic addiction.

By 1841, the Shoobridge family had moved to Benenden, in Kent, and were living in Feoffee Cottages. These had previously been the parish workhouse. The 1861 census shows that Mary Ann Shoobridge had moved again, and she was now living in nearby Tenterden where she was working as a servant in the house of William Mace, a solicitor. She would marry James Harris at Tenterden. He was not present at the Harris family home at Birchington at that time; perhaps he ended up in Tenterden on account of his unnamed aunt, mentioned above.

After their marriage, James Harris and his wife Mary Ann returned to Birchington, which is where their only son, my grandfather William Thomas Harris, was born on 13 February 1867.

James Harris died on 30 May 1872 (xxiv). The 1893 will of my great-grandmother describes her as a widow (48). I understand he went to Canterbury to buy yeast and walked home about 15 miles. He was soaked in heavy rain, caught cold, and subsequently died of pneumonia. My great-grandmother continued his business.

William Harris trained as a carpenter and, amongst his apprenticeships he served with Whitings of Faversham. During this time, in 1887 he carved the eaves of the windows of the Cottage Hospital. When I visited, I saw that they were still in good condition. He is also described as carpenter on his marriage certificate. He subsequently qualified as a builder and sanitary engineer, using the letters AISE after his name. He wrote a textbook 'Roofing Tables' which was widely used (xxv). My mother believed his mother Mary Ann supplied the capital to set him up in his own business. However, my cousin Colin Harris believes he was lent £100 by a Birchington man, perhaps his employer.

My grandfather married Hannah Sheffield (born as 'Shuffill') on 11 September 1891 without religious ceremony in the Thanet District Registry Office. They both gave the same address of 2 Eden Villas, Birchington, which was presumably the address of my great-grandmother. Both fathers, James Harris, baker, and Henry Sheffield were recorded as deceased (49).

The circumstances of the registry office ceremony, unwitnessed by any known relative, are unknown except to note that my grandfather had become an officer of the Salvation Army whereas my grandmother was brought up in the Established church. My grandmother had taken exception to what she perceived as a preoccupation of Salvationists with finance, so that a condition of the marriage was that as a compromise family worship should be in the Methodist church. Colin Harris tells me that Grandma also disliked spontaneous exclamations such as 'Alleluia!' during public worship.

William Thomas Harris and his wife Hannah, née Shoobridge - a wartime golden wedding photograph in 1941.

William Harris was prominent as a Methodist Local Preacher and as Chairman of the Parish Council. His lengthy sermons often lasted forty minutes and, when visiting other churches, his son Albert would be required to stay with him in the pulpit (CJH).

Before the First World War, Grandpa Harris suffered a breakdown in health from which he has not fully recovered when accompanying two of his sons, Martin and Sidney, who emigrated to Canada.

An early recollection of my mother's was of accompanying him and two workmen to set up notices for motor vehicles setting a speed limit of, I believe, 10 mph at the road approaches to Birchington.

He wrote several books published at his own expense which treated with somewhat abstruse Theology. One was titled *Under the X-Rays* (xxvi). He also wrote poems, some of which were published in the local paper. One commemorated the death of Lord Kitchener, and another was widely circulated in the family to mark my grandparents' Golden Wedding (50).

In his prime, my grandfather was a developer who built a number of houses in Birchington, including a large house in Albion Road with eight bedrooms which he named *The Homestead*. He envisaged that his family would live there for generations, but his children had other ideas and Albert fell from favour, being the first child to leave on marriage (CJH).

Grandfather retired in about 1925 when faced with local competition from his former foreman and having overlooked the relentless progress of inflation (CJH). Thenceforth he lived in some penury mainly from house rents and latterly assisted financially by my mother who bought his house for cash, and probably by his other children. Pride prevented him from accepting clerical employment. He caught cold sorting papers in the attic on a wintry day and died of pneumonia on 30 January 1945.

I was 19 when my grandfather died and could write much more fully of his life but that would destroy the balance of this history.

A Note on the Harris Sisters

According to an inscription in the Harris family Bible, my mother, Florence Catherine Harris was born on 24th August 1898, a Wednesday. However, there is some ambiguity as her mother had a recollection that the birth was on a Sunday evening when my grandfather was preaching at a local chapel.

My mother was one of four daughters of William and Hannah Harris. She was educated at the local Council School, as primary schools were then called. She had ambitions at a tender age, as she informed a school inspector that she wished to be an HM Inspector of Education! Without any encouragement she won a scholarship to the Grammar School in Dover to which she travelled daily by train from Birchington.

During the First World War she studied at Avery Hill, Teachers' Training College. Her older brother, Martin, initially serving in the 3rd Canadian Pioneers and later commissioned in the Royal Artillery, supplemented her pocket money. After two years she took a Teacher's Diploma and ended her studies without taking a degree to return home because her father was in poor health.

An early appointment took her to Faversham where her voluntary work as a Guide Captain caused her to meet my father, a Scoutmaster. My father, a bachelor of 39, was immediately attracted. She was in no hurry to marry and took a teaching appointment in London. He pursued her and successfully proposed at an arranged outing beside the

Serpentine. They were both committed Christians; although Mother did not much care for his impeccable Victorian family. She was glad that my father was a teetotaller as she had a horror of men who were drunk.

Our comfortable family life in Coulsdon was seriously damaged by the slump of 1930. Father nearly lost his job. We moved to Croydon so that my brother and I could more easily aspire to attending the Whitgift Grammar School, and Mother applied herself seriously to resuming a teaching career.

At the onset of WW2, Mother had become headmistress of a Hospital School in Ascot. We moved to Ascot the day war was declared. Later, because of enemy action by air attacks, Mother took a larger school in Sutton, to which she had been promoted, to Durham. During this period, she was seconded to take temporary charge of a girls' reformatory, Marlesford Lodge, whilst it was subject to a Parliamentary Inquiry. On a visit, Mr Herbert Morison, the Home Secretary, was impressed with her work. He suggested that she should apply after the War for an appointment to be an HMI for Education. This she did successfully in due course, thus realising her childhood ambition! From all accounts she did well. She retired from the Inspectorate at the statutory age of 60, and died aged 94 in 1993.

I will pass to Mother's older sister, Frances Eva Harris, born on 3 July 1893. The details of the birth management of my grandmother's first child, as related to me by her, are quite remarkable, as judged by present obstetric practice. Grandpa was tall and Grandma short, so the labour was difficult. It was complicated by considerable haemorrhage. After the delivery, the family doctor, Dr Worthington, persuaded Grandma to drink some of her own blood!

As the first born, Frances was given privileges, such as piano lessons, not perhaps financially possible for all the children, and which were begrudged by my mother.

In London she was employed as a seamstress by the firm of Liberty, often visiting our home in Coulsdon at weekends. She played the piano on Sunday afternoons and accompanied the family as they sang hymns. She was hospitalised with an ear infection from which she never fully recovered. She returned to her family home and later travelled daily to Canterbury undertaking sewing work for the firm of Lefevre.

On her father's death, she moved to a rented room in Herne Bay. She remained a spinster. However, she had two friendships with men who enjoyed her intelligent conversation. The first friendship, of which

Grandma had strongly disapproved, was with a married man who was a lay preacher of the Congregational church. The second was to a man deserted by his wife and known to us as Fred, as my mother entertained him. In her later years Frances had a close relationship with Fred who lived alone in a bungalow at Herne Bay. Before Fred's death Frances had moved to a care home where she died. She is buried with her father in Herne Bay cemetery.

The children of William and Hannah Harris. L to R: Frances, Albert, Sidney, Florence, Katie, Hubert and Ivy. Martin is absent.

My mother's closest relationship with a sister was with Ivy Kathleen, born on 20 February 1902, although it was said that there was always a kind of rivalry between them. Ivy had poor health as a child and suffered from anaemia. Working as a shop assistant, she met Fred Cooper who had recently inherited from an uncle, the general hardware store of Cooper and Lawrence, in Faversham.

Uncle Fred and Aunt Ivy looked after me for a prolonged period when my younger brother was born, and also around my eighth birthday, in 1933, when Martin was very seriously ill. They had three children. Bryan Walton Cooper, the oldest, died recently, on 17 December 2020 aged 92, after successful career as a Civil Engineer. Also notable was his promotion to Captain, Royal Engineers, during his National Service in Germany. Such elevation was very unusual. Having had been posted to RE Survey Branch working in the Harz Mountains, he was transferred to Bielefeld and, at just 20, was put in charge of the British Army's map depots in Germany and over 150 men, many of whom were former German soldiers who had been fighting the Allies only a few years before.

Bryan Cooper (1928-2020), eldest son of Ivy Harris, in the service dress of a subaltern, Royal Engineers. It previously was worn by my brother and is now worn by a dummy in the museum at Shere.

The younger two children are still living. Bryan is survived by his widow, a daughter and two sons. His elder son David has helped prepare this second edition.

Ivy Kathleen was prominent in Faversham public life, especially in the lay management of the local St Augustine's Geriatric Hospital. She was a strong personality. I shall always feel grateful to her for her care when I was a child. I recall that she was an excellent cook. She died on 28 December 1996 as the first edition of this book was being bound.

The youngest sister was Kathleen Miriam, born on March 2 1902 and always known as Katie. Like her older sister she embarked on a career in retail. In Herne Bay she met Christopher Pearce, also working in retail. He was a twin and slightly built. He was a kindly man and had the reputation of being the best gentleman dancer in Herne Bay. Katie sang beautifully. I recall particularly popular songs of the Victorian era such as, "The April Evening". My brother and I were page-boys at their wedding in 1930. They settled in Horsham which was accessible to my mother driving from Croydon.

Uncle Chris was just fit enough for Home Service in the Army during the Second World War and, for a while, was fortuitously billeted at our home in Croydon. Auntie Katie's career blossomed during the war and she became a buyer for a large retail firm. They had a daughter, Jean, who married Roy Terry, a music master of the Christ's Hospital School in Horsham – which Ivy's son Bryan attended. I have the honour to be Godfather of their older son.

Jean and Roy subsequently moved St George's School near St Albans, where Roy was Senior Music Master and Jean was appointed a House Matron. They were followed to St Albans by Katie and Chris. Chris died suddenly in 1990 and Katie shortly afterwards of a breast cancer, bravely born.

The Shuffills (51)

I will turn now to my grandmother's family. During the course of the nineteenth century, the original surname 'Shuffill' evolved in parts of the family to become 'Sheffield' via variations such as 'Shuffield'.

My mother spent some time trying to prove kinship with the Sheffield family of the Earls of Musgrave and, later Dukes of Buckingham. However, as the earlier spelling of Grandma, Hannah Harris's family name was Shuffill and not Sheffield I think this is unlikely. Grandma Harris also claimed some kinship with the Cook Family, but this could not be direct as the famous navigator had no children and his widow did not remarry.

The Shuffills came from Whitchurch, a small village in Buckinghamshire some 4 miles north of Aylesbury. A number of families with this surname lived in the area and records of their occupations indicate rather lowly stock. Most of the men were agricultural labourers, while many of the women were straw plaiters, braiding straw to make articles such as hats.

The earliest ancestor identified with certainty is Henry Shuffill, Grandma Harris' father. He had been born in about 1825 at Whitchurch. His parents were probably Thomas Shuffill, an agricultural labourer, and his wife Rebecca, née Cheney. In turn, Thomas's parents were John and Ann Shuffill (again there are various spellings). Henry's mother Rebecca died in early 1828 and this may be why, by 1841, the 15-year-old Henry was lodging with another family.

On my grandmother's birth certificate of 25 June 1865, her father Henry is described as a farm labourer, which was also his occupation on census returns (52). My late cousin Tessa Harris, living at nearby Halton, did research on the Shuffill families which showed Henry as a respected breeder of shire horses.

Henry Shuffill married Harriet Ann Boffin in 1847, their names being entered into the marriage register as Henry Shuffield and Harriet Baughen. Harriet came from Bloxham, near Banbury in Oxfordshire and her occupation from census records was variously a lacemaker, domestic and, in 1881 after the death of Henry, a charwoman. At some time, domestic duties brought her into contact with Baroness Orzy of "the Scarlet Pimpernel" My mother was later shocked by her low-cut dresses! Harriet's mother, Ann, appears in the records variously as Baughin and Baughen and was the daughter of an agricultural labourer. The later change to 'Boffin' may reflect a phonetic spelling. Both Henry and Harriet were illiterate at the time of their marriage, marking their names with a cross. However, a later photograph of Harriet shows her holding a book so she may have learnt to read and write (xxiii).

Harriet had been born out of wedlock in about 1828. No father is named in the record of her christening. Her mother Ann may have been pregnant again when she married Jonathan Clifton on 8 August 1833 as their daughter Caroline was christened in Bloxham on 24 December of that year. He was a stonemason; we can only speculate if he used his status as an excuse to take advantage of Ann. Ann died in 1837, aged just 27 years old. Jonathan Clifton then moved back to the home of his parents and siblings but, rather than take the children into his family, he seems to have shown scant loyalty to either Harriet or Caroline, who were looked after by Ann's parents, Edward and Elizabeth Baughen. Jonathan Clifton was named as Harriet's father on her marriage certificate, but this does not prove a biological link. It may just reflect that he later became her father through his marriage to Ann.

My grandmother used to say that she had Quaker ancestry which is interesting in view of my mother's and, later, my daughter's and her family's involvement with that sect. My brother and I were both at a Quaker boarding school and as a young man I considered joining the Society of Friends although I cannot recall actually doing so. Harriet also functioned as a local untrained village midwife. Again, many generations later, five to be precise, my brother's daughter Ann is a midwife and I have also worked in the related medical speciality of Obstetrics.

We remember an occasion when the famous American evangelists Moody and Sankey preached in the Square at Whitchurch. After the service when the square was deserted Henry Shuffield invited them home for refreshment and they enjoyed Harriet's home-made cake. Hopefully a practice of hospitality to strangers will always remain in the family. This would have been during the first visit of the evangelists to England (1870-1873) when my grandmother would have been 5-8 years old.

Henry and Harriet Shuffill had thirteen children. My grandmother Hannah was born on 25 June 1865 at Little London and was probably the seventh child of the marriage. The 1883 Ordnance Survey map of Whitchurch shows Little London as a collection of houses at the southern end of the village. It apparently once boasted a silk factory. In a letter to my mother in 1949 the Vicar of Whitchurch stated that part of the village still existed, although it is now represented only as a road name. I understand that settlements named Little London were so named as their inhabitants had fled from plague in London (BWC).

Henry died in 1877 at the age of 54. By that time, he had become a farm bailiff and the spelling of his surname name had changed to Sheffield (49). He was also described as deceased when Grandma's elder brother Caleb was married in August 1879. At this wedding bride, groom, and witnesses were all illiterate, the bridegroom even getting his age wrong, so at times genealogical evidence has been difficult to establish. Caleb had lost an arm in an accident and so was the village carrier. He was a respected local preacher. My knowledge of Henry Shuffill is almost ended with the recording that he sat up all night with a horse suffering from pneumonia and as a consequence succumbed to the same illness.

As was usual for a large family in those days, on the death of Henry Shuffill, the family provider, his widow's children were dispersed to the care of relatives. Hannah went to an aunt at Broadstairs, Kent. She received little education and was used as a parlour-maid. My mother always averred that her mother was not illiterate, although I have never seen her handwriting. However, Colin Harris recalls her giving her husband a shopping list. She had a thorough knowledge of Biblical texts and was prone to remind my grandfather that, in St. Paul's words, a man who did not provide for his family was *worse than an infidel* (1 Timothy, v.8).

It is remarkable that Hannah married a man who was highly self-educated. In later life he taught himself Greek. She was a strong personality, possessed of much common sense and wisdom in raising her large family. She had some strong prejudices, especially when she felt any of her children had been let down by the opposite sex and, when British interests were at stake, she could recite rhymes of jingoism with relish. She would sing "we don't want to fight, but by jingo if we do, we've got the men, we've got the guns, we've got the money too!" However, true to the Quaker tradition, she is remembered on her gravestone surround, recently restored by her surviving daughter and nearly all her surviving grandchildren, as a 'peacemaker'. She had a stroke at our home in Croydon in about 1948 and I carried her upstairs. She died eventually at our Hereford home on 27 February 1950. She is buried in the Municipal Cemetery.

A few further recollections should be told of Grandma's brothers and sisters. Before doing so, I will perhaps mention two other stories which I heard more than once from Grandma's lips.

She related how one of her sisters, presumably Caroline born 1856, was very distressed by a public execution, However, Grandma was born in 1865 and the Royal Commission recommended in 1866, and it was speedily carried into effect, the abolition of the public spectacle, so it is unlikely that Grandma was relying upon her own recollection. I also recall that Grandma had strict views about accepting favours from young men in whom she was not seriously interested. She used to relate with approbation that she declined an invitation from her cousin to attend the Royal Agricultural Show at Islington as 'she did not much care for him'. After her eighth child she visited the much-respected family doctor Dr Worthington. He gave her a draught of what Grandma called *very good stuff.* It was certainly effective and she had no more children *(CJH)*!

I have already mentioned Grandma's older brother Caleb. Before the last War I met one of his sons Fred at Whitchurch. He was scything thistles in a field. Another older brother, James (Jim), became manager of transport for a London Borough, Lambeth I believe. His oldest daughter, Ann, was married to the distinguished Indian Administrator, Sir Hugh Dow. Sir Hugh was Governor of Sind where he founded the Dow Medical College in association with the hospital founded earlier by the greatest of the Indian Viceroys, Lord Curzon. Later, until Indian Independence he was Governor of Bihar and Orissa. His final appointment was as the first HM Consul for Israel. James' son, Arthur, was a musician with the London Philharmonic orchestra. Another daughter Gertie, married Albert Godwin who lost a leg in the Great War.

My mother kept in touch with their daughter, Joan Godwin until her death. This branch of the family was associated with the Plymouth Brethren sect. Another cousin of my mother's, Koko, the son of Grandma's sister Elizabeth, was also a musician and was killed in the Great War. He was presumably named after the character in the Mikado.

It is remarkable that although my mother had four brothers who saw active service, the youngest in the Second World War, they all survived, although one, Albert, was severely wounded.

I once visited two of Grandma's younger sisters living at Mitcham, Surrey - Rebecca, baptised 1870 aet. 18 months, and Minnie baptised 1872 aet. 3 years. They were living in poverty and Rebecca's daughter Minnie was a young woman in the house dying of tuberculosis.

The Harris family Bible and a photo-album which contain useful references to Harris and Sheffield family history had been in the possession of my Aunt Ivy at Faversham (xxiii). They have been transferred to my cousin Colin Harris to be eventually given to the care of his grandson.

The Coopers (53)

I include this digression on the history of the Coopers by way of my aunt Ivy Harris's marriage to Frederick Walton Cooper on 22 August 1925 at Herne Bay Methodist church.

We know little about the earliest identified ancestor, William Cooper, except that he married Nancy Walton in Birmingham on 25 June 1790 and introduced the 'Walton' into the Cooper name, which continues to the present day, seven generations later. Nancy Walton may have been born in Walsall in 1763, the daughter of Benjamin Walton and his wife Ann Meeson, from the village of Gnosall in Staffordshire.

The fourth of William and Nancy's children, Benjamin (I) Cooper was baptised in Birmingham in 1797. He probably went to the Blue School in Birmingham for children from poor families before being apprenticed to a printer in Stratford. The apprenticeship was terminated abruptly in 1817 as the punishment from his prosecution for overcharging a client and pocketing the 3-shilling excess (54).

Benjamin (I) married Elizabeth Willis in 1818 in Birmingham.

She was one of eleven children of Samuel and Jane Willis, also of Birmingham. Their first child William was born there in 1821. They moved to Wrexham where they had a wine and spirits business, but this went bankrupt in 1824 (55). Benjamin (I) absconded before the final creditors' meeting, and newspaper advertisements from January 1825 offered a £20 reward for his apprehension, noting that

> *'The said Benjamin Walton Cooper is about 29 years of age, about 5 foot 6 inches high, brown hair, and blind of the right eye, and other eye is remarkably odd-formed.'*

The meeting to make the final dividend from the bankruptcy took place in July 1825, but there are no details of what was paid to creditors or of Benjamin (I)'s fate. However, the family seemed to have remained in Wrexham until at least 1828, when their second son Benjamin (II) was born. Benjamin (I) and Elizabeth then disappear from the records.

By 1841, Benjamin (II) Cooper, then aged 13, was a hawker living in Beast Market, a poor part of Wrexham, lodging with a plasterer. His brother William also became a plasterer by trade, but not Benjamin (II). He enlisted in the Army in May 1847, often an occupation of last-resort, and became a gunner and driver in the Royal Artillery (56). We can trace his progress through the Army's Pay and Muster ledgers at the National Archives. These tell us that he served first at Colchester, then in Bermuda (March 1849 to January 1854), followed by a period at Fort George near Inverness in Scotland. Here, on 29 May 1854, he married Emma Harvey. She was from a fishing family based at Brightlingsea, Essex but, by 1851, was living in Colchester. We can surmise that that may have first met there.

Benjamin (II) was promoted to bombardier as his battalion was sent to the Crimea in July 1855. He thus missed the great battles of Alma, Balaclava and Inkerman, arriving in time to be present for the final assault on Sebastopol which brought the war to an end. His was in a 'ball cartridge brigade', forming ammunition supply trains to support the field batteries. Having arrived late in the campaign, Benjamin (II) was in one of the last British units to leave the Crimea, in July 1856.

On his return, he was stationed in Ireland, variously at Waterford, Limerick and Cork, which is where his wife Emma had two children, Benjamin (III) and Flora. He was also recruiting in Belfast. By April 1858, Benjamin (II) had reached the rank of sergeant. He was then transferred to Woolwich early in 1860, but was court martialled that July and reduced back down to gunner. Entries in the Pay and Muster ledgers suggest that he went absent without leave for a couple of days. Benjamin (II) and Emma's third child Harvey William Cooper was born in 1867 at Tilbury Fort, Essex as Benjamin (II) worked his way back up the ranks to become a sergeant again.

We know little of what exactly Benjamin (II) did in the army, but there are passing references to him recruiting while based in both Colchester and Cork, him being a cook/ master cook while in Bermuda and Woolwich where he also appears variously as servant to a Colonel Ward, and working in the 'duty clothing establishment'.

Benjamin (II) was discharged from the Royal Artillery in December 1869, having served long enough to qualify for a Chelsea pension of 1s 6d a day. His discharge papers (56) noted that:

> *Conduct has been very good. He was when promoted in possession of four Good Conduct Badges. He is in possession of the Crimea Medal, with clasp for "Sebastopol", also the Turkish War Medal. He has been once convicted by Courts Martial, and, in addition his name is six times recorded in the Regimental Defaulter's Book.*

The family then moved across the Thames to Gravesend, where he was a hawker. He died in 1878.

Harvey Cooper was 11 when his father died and the family then moved to Reading. At 14 he was a stable boy, while his mother and an older sister were dressmakers. He became a plumber and married Caroline Matilda Garrett in 1888. She had been born in Southwark, in 1868, the daughter of tin plate workers. Her grandparents were both from Windsor, one a blind maker, the other a butcher. Harvey and Caroline had nine children between 1891 and 1909. Sometime between 1895 and 1898, the family relocated to Hitchin, but returned to Reading after Harvey Cooper's death in 1911.

Of their nine children, we have but snippets apart from sons John and Fred. Soon after he turned 14, Fred Cooper obtained his certified copy of the entry of his birth for the purposes of the Factory and Workshop Act 1901, proving his age to permit employment (57). He became a clerk on the railways. Both fought in WW1. John was with the 6th Battalion, Royal Berkshire Regiment. He embarked for France early in 1916 and fought at the Battle of the Somme before being killed early on 31 July 1917 while moving up to the assembly area in preparation for the opening of the Third Battle of Ypres (Passchendaele). Fred Cooper, having done his infantry training at Halton House where I was later stationed in the RAF, was in the same Brigade, in the 8th Battalion, Norfolk Regiment and passed his brother's body as he moved up towards the front. Fred had been sent to France in May 1917, and fought at Passchendaele before being transferred to the 9th Norfolks in February 1918. He was wounded soon afterwards, on 21 March, during the opening onslaught of the German Spring Offensive. He recovered and was transferred again in June 1918 to the 7th Norfolks, with whom he survived the costly battles of the 100 days offensive across northern France that led to the armistice in November 1918.

After the war, Fred Cooper moved to Faversham, where his uncle Benjamin (III) Cooper was a partner in a hardware shop styled Cooper & Laurence. Fred and his brother Robert inherited Benjamin (III)'s share in the partnership on the latter's death in 1924. The following year he married Ivy Kathleen Harris at Birchington. Fred then acquired the Laurence partnership share in 1927 and continued to run the shop until his retirement in 1968, when it was sold. He died in 1986; his wife Ivy died in 1996.

My mother's family history has now been brought to her own generation and it is appropriate to end the record at this point. Reference may be made to the family tree for basic details of date of birth of siblings (45) (51).

Chapter 6

WGD1 and WGD2: Ship-Owners

I now add a brief note on my grandfather and great-grandfather's vessels. The Dawsons' ship-owning, building and undertaking business was based at a workshop in Preston Street, Faversham, while William Goodhugh Dawson (WGD2) lived at 40 Ospringe Road, Faversham.

My father would only recall two vessels as he remembered the impact of their loss on the family as a boy. They were *Bessie Hiller* and *Pioneer* (58). I have since learnt of *Ann Goodhugh*. Finally, I had been mystified by a newspaper report of the loss of the *Pioneer* which stated that this was the last of my grandfather's *four* vessels lost over several years. However, I have found a reference to this vessel in a book on sailing barges by a Mr Child. It was strangely named *A.B.C.D.* after the first letter of the surnames of the four part-owners (xxvii).

A.B.C.D.

She was built at Faversham in 1865. 'A' was for Mary Attwater, a widow probably related to Tom Attwater, the Faversham Harbour Master whose son married Jamie Day, my grandfather's sister-in-law. 'B' was Thomas J. Beard, millwright, which strikes no chord of memory. 'C' was for Caroline Clay, widow of Charles Clay. 'D' was of course for my great-grandfather.

The Registrar of new vessels wrote after my great-grandfather's name 'miser' perhaps because he did not offer him any hospitality after the registration. Mr Child also noted in his book that William Goodhugh Dawson could well have afforded this as he was later to lament in the Faversham News of November 1893 the loss of £700 with the *Bessie Hiller*. I think that he was forgetting that WGD1 had died and WGD2 suffered the loss of the *Bessie Hiller*. Anyone reading the obituary of my grandfather in the Faversham News of 1909 would also realise that there was another view of my grandfather's character (22).

By 1884, *A.B.C.D.* was owned by J.M. Goldfinch, the Faversham barge-builder. On 4 October 1889 she stranded at Brighton en route from Swanage to Herne Bay with a cargo of stone, having been run ashore after springing a leak in heavy weather. The crew of seven were saved.

The barge broke up but some of the cargo was salvaged. On a lighter note, SGD and Thelma Dawson recall seeing on a poster in the eastern USA '*Misers make poor friends but good ancestors*' which would seem to be borne out in our family history!

Ann Goodhugh

She was built by J.M. Goldfinch (Mayor of Faversham 1875, 1877 and 1887) of Standard Quay, Faversham (1820-1905) in 1872, partly of old timber for W.G. Dawson & Co., Faversham. Her dimensions were 82.5 x 21 x 6 feet. My grandfather was only 21 in 1872 so the vessel would have belonged to my great-grandfather WGD1, who named her after his mother. The ketch was last in Register in 1879. SGD has noted in the vessel's documents that the crew's ration allowance was to be *sufficient without waste*; also that in 1872 she was trading to Antwerp and Dunkirk.

Pioneer

She was built by Goldfinch in 1876, (the year of my grandfather's marriage) and of 67 tons burthen. She was the last of the four vessels to survive and was sunk on Tuesday 27 May 1895. She was run down in a dense fog by a German steamer, the *Baron Clyde* with 2,300 tons of iron ore cargo off Shoreham, Sussex. The crew were saved although the mate was hurt (59) (60).

Bessie Hiller

She was named after my aunt whose second name in turn derived from our German ancestry. She was also built by Goldfinch in 1881 of 80 tons burthen. She was lost off the East Yorkshire coast in a great storm on 18 November 1893. She had been bound from London to Newcastle with a cargo of teak. She was seen off Flamborough head before the storm and was found capsized ashore near Aldbrough (29) (61). No trace of the crew of four was found. I understand that my grandfather had not complied with the surveyor's requirements and the insurance claim with Harwich Barge Alliance was refused. His personal loss was £700 (61).

The captain came from Essex and the mate from Uplees, and two seamen, Thomas Smith and Alfred Back were from Oare. I believe the tragedy left widows and orphans, and my grandfather made some financial provision for the dependants which was a serious strain on his resources. Those were the days before The Workman's Compensation Acts. The Faversham News of 2 December 1893 records the loss of other local vessels during the same storm, one, a new vessel worth £2,000, was also uninsured (62).

Chapter 7

Overseas Connections

There are Dawson kinsfolk in America, South Africa and Australia and this Family History would not be complete without a few words describing some aspect of their lives. I have been greatly helped by the book 'Smith-Eccleston' by Mrs Erma Swift, Seattle 1987 (ii).

Mary Anne Dawson, Sarah Dawson and their descendants

Mary Anne: born 28 April 1818, married John Lever Smith on 9 December 1841 at Faversham parish church, died 12 December 1887. Sarah: born 17 March 1827, married Rev. Stephen Smith on 2 June 1852 at Boughton Chapel, died 7 September 1902.

These two sisters of my great-grandfather Dawson WGD1 married two brothers. John Lever Smith had been born on 30 November 1815, and died 26 September 1864 and Rev. Stephen Smith, born on 11 October 1828, died in 1906. Mary and John emigrated to the USA in 1857, two years after Sarah and Stephen who left for that country in 1855. Sarah and Stephen had a daughter Clara born at Boughton, Kent in 1854 and who died in America in 1858.

Sarah and Mary Anne lived only 25 miles apart in neighbouring counties in the south east corner of Wisconsin (42). Sarah died three months after she and Stephen celebrated their Golden Wedding anniversary. He then returned to Winchester where he married Emily Dawson Jones, the twelfth child of Sarah's younger sister Ann Staines Jones née Dawson. Stephen died in 1906 and is buried at Winchester.

It is a mystery why Mary Anne and John Lever Smith emigrated with their eight children - two more were born in America (63) (64). John was a prosperous grocer like his father John before him and also Registrar of Boughton, registering his own children's births. The Census of 1851 shows three resident servants in the family home. In America he became a poor farmer and the sons went early in life to work on neighbouring farms.

Their oldest child, John Dawson Smith, trained as a teacher in England but became a farmer. He served in the Wisconsin Heavy

Artillery in the Civil War and, on returning home with a fellow soldier John Wilkinson, the latter fell in love with and consequently married John Dawson Smith's sister Mary Anne. John Dawson Smith married three times. Two of his wives predeceased him. Clifford, a son of the second marriage, was a well-known producer of prize flowers.

Clifford's grand-daughter Erma, born 1917, (Swift, by her second marriage), who visited England in 1978 and stayed with my cousin Irene Dawson at Whitstable, wrote the family history to which I have already referred. She also met Muriel, her sister, and her late husband, Eric E.F. Smith FSA, the well-known historian, who also helped me with some research into the family history.

A fourth child of Mary and John Lever Smith was William Goodhugh Smith. From humble beginnings he became a scholar and was well known in the education world of the State of Minnesota. A daughter Exine Mary, born in 1884, visited England with her maternal grandparents in 1907 and kept in touch with my paternal Aunt Alice and was sent some of the family photographs. She married a Clarence Drake who claimed decent from Devonshire forebears (xxviii). Their son, Everett corresponded with my parents.

Sarah and Rev. Stephen Smith had five children (64). The first two, both daughters, died young. The third, Ernest Stephen born 2 July 1856, was well-known to and probably visited my father. He was married twice and had four daughters. He sent my father an album of family photos for Christmas 1930. During the Second World War, he surprised my father by his strong opposition to President Roosevelt and his New Deal.

Our family have had most association with the descendants of Arthur Charles Smith, 1860-1907, the fifth child of Sarah and Rev. Stephen Smith. Of his four children, Howard, died in France in the First World War, and another, Dorothy, was a chief buyer for Marshall Field of Chicago. Dorothy, I understood from whispers in those pre-war days had been divorced from a man surnamed Ennis. She would entertain our family at 'Claridges' on her visits to London. Once I was very impressed as the Australian Prime Minister was sitting at the next table. I gave her one of my first prescriptions, which was of Gee's linctus.

I was fascinated by her glamorous daughter, Marcia, when she came to visit Europe. Marcia later married John Bradford Stevens, a U.S. Naval Officer who subsequently owned a silver-ware factory in Massachusetts. They had four children.

Other Overseas Connections

Turning to the next Dawson generation, Arthur Dawson, the eighth child of the Rev. John Wesley Dawson emigrated to Cape Town, South Africa. He returned to visit his relations including my grandfather WGD2 with his wife and two daughters in 1907 (65) (xxix).

In the next Dawson generation, my father's younger brother, Howard Day Dawson emigrated to Canada in 1911 (1). He was a surveyor and mining engineer who could not find suitable employment in this country. My grandmother's last words to him when he left for Liverpool with my father were '*Now Howard, if you had worked harder at school, you wouldn't have had to go to Canada*'. He wrote to his mother every week until she died in 1933. Such were Victorian values! Howard had one daughter, my cousin Isabel Alice born 29 July 1918, who married William Ramsey on 12 February 1941. They had four children - the oldest Tom with four daughters was manager of a Steel Corporation and living in Calgary. Isabel lived to be 100 years old.

To complete the Day family emigrations, great-grandfather John Day's sons, John and Robert went to Montreal (41). John had a daughter, Mabel born 24 May 1878, who married James Webb and my father visited them in 1955 (xxx). Great-grandfather Day's youngest son, Edward Henry, born in 1861, went to Australia while in his twenties. After an adventurous life including piloting his own aeroplane, he died on 25 May 1945, at Warnick Australia, leaving one son, W. E. Day.

To close this account of family emigrations, two of my mother's brothers, Martin and Sidney Harris went to Canada after which I had four maternal cousins in Canada (23). Sadly, most have now passed away. Since the War, my cousin Gillian (45) the daughter of my mother's sister, Ivy, married an Australian surgeon, John Aberdeen, and settled in Melbourne.

This ends a brief resume of the family who have emigrated to three continents. It is by no means exhaustive. Descendants of my grandmother's sister Annie Berry née Day also went to Australia, as did Harry Sheffield, a brother of my maternal grandmother (66) (51).

Chapter 8

Samplers

It may be of interest to record amongst family memorabilia the three samplers known to be preserved. The earliest was executed by Sarah Dawson, born 1781. The sampler is now much faded. The words read:

Tell me ye knowing and discerning where I may find a friend both firm and true who dares stand by me when in distress and then his love and friendship most express. Sarah Dawson age 9.

The sampler of my paternal great-grandmother on my father's side, Elizabeth Fagg, has been framed to form the surface of a small mahogany table in my possession. The green and gold colours are well preserved. The words read:

Virtue alone is happiness below and our best knowledge is ourselves to know. My witness is in heaven and my record is on high. Job 16.19. Elizabeth Fagg her work January 21 1822. Born 14 October 1811.

The sampler of my maternal great-grandmother on my father's side by Frances Eggleston was been reframed by the late Eric Smith FSA. The words are:

Teach O Lord a helpless youth
Always to attend to truth
Ananias I am told
Made a lie to save his gold
He a dreadful fate did meet
Falling dead at Peters feet
False Sapphira too his wife
Ended awfully her life
Suddenly behold her die
After joining in the lie
Falsehood may I never tell

Lest I be sent down to Hell
And of sins reward partake
In the ever-burning lake
Rescue from this sin and shame
From the soul tormenting flame
Save me thou God of truth
Save this praying helpless youth
Frances Eggleston her work aged 12

This is the largest of the samplers with representations of animals, Adam and Eve, and the Tree of Life, and so a considerable achievement for a little girl with two stiff fore-fingers.

Chapter 9

The North Foreland Lighthouse

Finally, I include a note on the history of the North Foreland Lighthouse, which played its part in the lives of Hiller and Fagg families. Located 57 metres above high water at 50° 22' 30" N, 1° 26' 44". With a height of 26 metres, the lighthouse stands the height of six double decker buses.

The Hillers from Hanover were the keepers successively as man and widow in the late eighteenth and early nineteenth centuries. Their daughter Elizabeth Ann Fagg née Hiller was born in the lighthouse in 1784. Their granddaughter Elizabeth Dawson née Fagg (born 1811) knew the lighthouse as a child. She married my great-grandfather WGD1.

In a letter dated 12 August 1897 Elizabeth Fagg, then aged 86, replied to a letter from her granddaughter Lillian Frances (born 1885) from Ramsgate (21). *Inter alia* Lillian's letter reported a visit to the North Foreland Lighthouse with her second cousin Eddie Fitchew (38). Remarkably this letter, according to her grandmother, was written on Wednesday afternoon and delivered the same evening. Elizabeth Fagg had childhood memories of the wooden staircase in the lighthouse with living rooms on each floor. The keepers then lived inside the lighthouse.

Unfortunately, the pre-1940 records of Trinity House Lighthouse Service were destroyed by enemy action during WW2. The Communications Officer has kindly supplied me with a fact sheet which is the main source of the following historical summary (67).

The light dates from 1499. The first lighthouse was built in 1636 and destroyed by fire in 1683. The present octagonal tower dates from 1691. In 1793 two further storeys were added and the coal fire replaced by oil lamps (xix). The plans for this renovation can be seen at The National Archives (xxxi).

In 1890, a lantern house was built on top of the tower and the light was electrified in 1920. There are 5 red and white flashes every 20 seconds. The light is of 175,000 candela with a range of 21 nautical miles. A radio beacon transmits the signal NF in Morse Code (_. .._.).

The date of the disappearance of John Frederick Hiller has not yet been established. Very little is known about him. Like his Sovereign, he would have had to learn English to carry out his duties. However, it is clear that either he or his widow, Esther, my great-great-great-grandmother, would have lit the oil lantern that welcomed at least part of the victorious English fleet limping back to Chatham Dockyard in 1805 after Trafalgar.

The water-colour of the North Foreland Lighthouse now donated to Margate Museum is inscribed *North Foreland Lighthouse in 1809*, but also attributed in typescript to P Wareham 1842. Hence the painting may date from 1842, particularly as one of the sailing ships depicted in the background appears to have a tall funnel.

This history begins with a representation of the North Foreland Lighthouse taken from this picture. It seems fitting that this incomplete family history should conclude with an account of the light which, in the words of the motto of the Trinity Light House Service, has been 'Serving the Mariner' for nearly 500 years.

Appendices

APPENDIX 1: Abbreviations

WG   William Goodhugh (1, 2, 3, 4)
WGD   William Goodhugh Dawson (1, 2, 3, 4, 5)
SGD   Simon Goodhugh Dawson
AP   Arthur Percival
MHD   Martin Harris Dawson
AMD   Alice Mary Dawson
CJH   Colin James Harris
BWC   Bryan Walton Cooper
PW   Penny Ward

APPENDIX 2: Sources

1.   William Dawson tree
2.   Unconfirmed internet research, SGD
3.   Reference to family tradition of residence in Norway of William Dawson on old Goodhugh-Dawson tree, probably writing of WGD2
4.   Descendants of John Dawson, SGD
5.   Antecedents of Susanna Presley, SGD
6.   Gravestone of John Dawson and other family members, 1850
7.   Burial Register of St. Mary of Charity, Faversham, Susanna Dawson, 21 April 1822
8.   Annie Staines Jones tree
9.   Letter of William Dawson to John Dawson, 28 March 1814
10.   Will of William Dawson, 18 March 1802
11.   Memorandum of John Dawson, probably by WGD1
12.   Sampler of Sarah Dawson aged 9, 1781 (in possession of Sarah Margaret Griffin née Dawson)
13.   Burial Register of St. Mary of Charity, Faversham, John Dawson, 2 October 1850
14.   Election poster of John Dawson and others as Liberal Candidates for Faversham Council (28 October 1835) and petition with his name concerning Faversham Creek improvement, 23 December

1811 (John Dawson moved to Faversham in the spring of 1810)

15. Will of John Dawson, made 29 May 1850, proved 19 March 1851
16. Insurance premia for listed properties of the late John Dawson, 1852
17. Gravestone inscription of WGD1 and other family members, 1884-1909
18. Agreement for the lease of Drill Hall Cottage to WGD1, 25 March 1851 from AP
19. Letters from America from Sarah Smith née Dawson to WGD1, 1864-5
20. Letter-card AMD to WGD3, 15 May 1940
21. Letter from WGD2 to WGD3 acknowledging loan
22. *Faversham & North East Kent Advertiser,* announcement and obituary 30 June 1909, funeral and memorial service 7 July 1909. *North East Kent News,* announcement and obituary 3 July 1909, funeral and memorial service 10 July 1909.
23. Copy of letter from Rev. John Wesley (currently mislaid)
24. PC from Major General Dudgeon OC 46 Division to Private 512408 W.G. Dawson, 11 December 1917
25. Letter of Mrs WGD2 to Miss A.M. Dawson, 3 Jan 1918
26. Note of despatch ribbon MM to Private Dawson from QMS H Stevens, 26 December 1917
27. Faversham and North East Kent News, 12 January 1918
28. Army discharge of Private 512408 W.G. Dawson by OC 2/3 London Field Ambulance Lieutenant Colonel Ducat, 14 February 1919
29. Presentation to WGD3 on leaving the Scout Movement, Faversham local paper 1923
30. Ancient manuscript showing the children of WG2
31. Burial Register of St. Mary of Charity, Faversham, WG3, 15 September 1829
32. Will of WG3, 30 November 1822
33. Inventory of the home of the late WG3, 28 September 1829
34. William Goodhugh tree
35. Fagg-Hiller tree
36. Record of Hiller in Royal Catering Household of George I in my father's tree for American kinsmen. Also refers to William Dawson coming from Norway
37. Memorial Card Elizabeth Ann Fagg née Hiller died 14 June 1876

38. Hiller-Fitchew tree
39. Records to 1915 of Birth/Baptism, Marriage and Death Certificates given by the late Geoffrey Fitchew
40. Letter from Elizabeth Dawson née Fagg to grandchild Lilian Dawson, 12 August 1897
41. Day tree
42. Lever-Smith tree
43. Letter from Barry Dunn, 8 March 1975
44. E.E.F. Smith FSA, Clapham Antiquarian Society, Occasional Sheet - September 1980 and letter 10 November 1981
45. Harris tree
46. Manuscript record listing the births and dates of baptism of George 1824), James (1825) and Henry (1828) Harris, and their parents' names. Handwriting indicates it is broadly contemporaneous. Held by David Cooper
47. Abstract from the Baptismal Register for the Parish of Halstow, Mary Ann Shoobridge by Vicar E.R. Olive, 28 September 1909
48. Will of Mary Ann Harris née Shoobridge, 27 September 1893
49. Marriage Certificate of Hannah Harris née Sheffield, 11 September 1891
50. *The Year of Jubilee,* poem by W.T. Harris written for Golden Wedding, September 1941
51. Shuffill (Sheffield) tree
52. Birth Certificate of Hannah Harris née Shuffill, born 25 June 1865
53. Cooper Tree, research mainly from David Cooper
54. James Ward (Printer) v Benjamin Walton Cooper, Stratford upon Avon, 1817, file ER11/14/21 at The Shakespeare Trust, Stratford-upon-Avon
55. Notices in 'The Law Advertiser', Vol II (1824), publ. J.W. Paget, London, p.341, 347 and 372. Also, newspaper notices – www.britishnewspaperarchive.co.uk searching for Benjamin Walton Cooper
56. National Archives Pay and Muster ledgers for 2 Company 6 Battalion Royal Artillery, then 7 Company 6 Battalion, then 10 Battery 4 Brigade, then 2 Division Depot Brigade, then 19 battery 4 Division Deport Brigade, and finally to 9 Division Coast Brigade, bookended by his discharge papers which detail his joining and leaving (National Archives WO 97/1315). Unfortunately, the record of his Court Martial has not been

preserved
57. Certificate held by David Cooper
58. Mercantile Navy List 1887
59. The loss of *Pionéer*, Faversham local paper, 27 May 1895. Also cutting 75 *Years Ago*
60. Wreck Inquiry *Collision Between Channel Steamers*, 30 May 1908
61. The loss of the *Bessie Hiller* on 18 November 1893, *Kent Journal*, 2 December 1893
62. Idem, *Faversham News*, 9 December 1893
63. John Lever Smith and Mary Anne Smith née Dawson tree, on same sheet as (33) and descendants of John Lever tree (SGD)
64. Rev. Stephen Smith and Sarah Smith née Dawson tree, on same sheet as (33) and descendants of John Lever tree (SGD)
65. Rev. John Wesley Dawson tree
66. Berry tree
67. Trinity House Lighthouse Service, North Foreland Lighthouse Fact Sheet

APPENDIX 3: References

(References marked with an asterisk are not in my possession)
i.   Stories of my Canadian Pioneers, Edith Norine Harris, 2nd edition
ii.   Alphabetical Arrangement of Wesleyan Ministers, 1892
iii.   The Origin and Progress of Methodism in Margate*, Rev. F.F. Bretherton. This book refers to many records seen in 1911 but now lost.
iv.   Hawley Square Wesleyan Church, Margate 1811-1911*
v.   Wesley Chapel Magazine, recording gifts of Methodist Magazine and map of Methodism 1824, April 1934
vi.   Some Clays and other Ancestors, Ruth Clay, 1985
vii.   Smith-Eccleston, Erma Swift, 1978
viii.   Diary, WGD2, 1868
ix.   Wesley's Journal - abridged, 1902
x.   Diary, WGD3, 1895
xi.   Diary, WGD3, 1898
xii.   Thomas Hankey and Co. Three Hundred Years' Trade with the

West Indies, M Hughes
xiii. The 56th Division, Dudley- Ward, 1921
xiv. 2/3 City of London Field Ambulance, 1914-1918, London Soldiers - Unarmed Comrades, Arthur Atkinson, 1969
xv. War Diary*, OC 2/3 London Field Ambulance RAMC TF 1915-19 (PRO)
xvi. Leather notebook, WG2
xvii. Hide-bound notebook, WG2
xviii. Notebook, WG3 dated 1777
xix. History of Lighthouses, P. Beaver
xx. Wesley's Hymns: belonged to Elizabeth Fagg (signed 1831) with Methodist Society membership card (1826) attached
xxi. Notebook cover, Miss Fagg, 14 Park Terrace, Regents Park
xxii. Postlude in F, J.P. Attwater, September 1901
xxiii. Harris Family Photo Album*, photo of Mary Anne Harris - née Shoobridge, and of Mr & Mrs Care
xxiv. Harris Family Bible*
xxv. Roofing Tables, W.T. Harris AISE
xxvi. Under the X-Rays, W.T. Harris, (mislaid at present)
xxvii. Rochester Sailing Barges of the Victorian Era, B. Childs, pp 112, 133
xxviii. Clarence Drake Family History at page 93, 1979
xxix. Yesterday Our Ancestry*, Leonard Webster Pratt, 1929
xxx. Holiday to Canada, WGD3, 1955
xxxi. Plan and Elevation NFLH*, J. Yenn (1756-1821) 19 May 1792. Formerly at the Public Record Office (PRO ADM8063165). Plans and elevations of the North and South Foreland Lighthouses are now held at The National Archives, reference MPI 1/455/1-3 and 6-12and 14-16.

APPENDIX 4 – Family Trees

These family trees show graphically the relationships between some of the people mentioned in this history. Any name sufficed by an asterisk requires further validating.

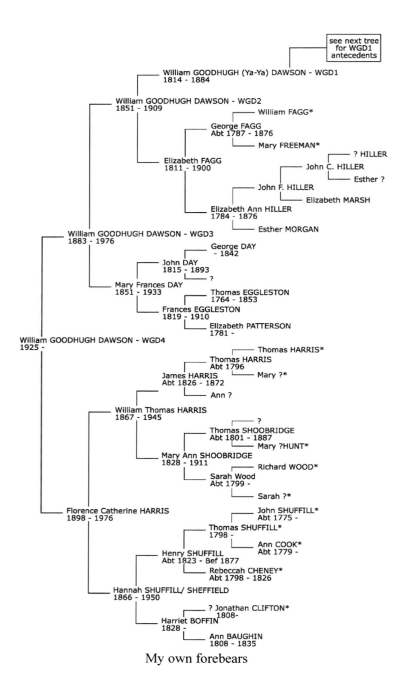

see next tree for WGD1 antecedents

William GOODHUGH (Ya-Ya) DAWSON - WGD1
1814 - 1884

William GOODHUGH DAWSON - WGD2
1851 - 1909

William FAGG*

George FAGG
Abt 1787 - 1876

Mary FREEMAN*

Elizabeth FAGG
1811 - 1900

? HILLER

John C. HILLER

Esther ?

John F. HILLER

Elizabeth MARSH

Elizabeth Ann HILLER
1784 - 1876

Esther MORGAN

William GOODHUGH DAWSON - WGD3
1883 - 1976

George DAY
- 1842

John DAY
1815 - 1893

?

Mary Frances DAY
1851 - 1933

Thomas EGGLESTON
1764 - 1853

Frances EGGLESTON
1819 - 1910

Elizabeth PATTERSON
1781 -

William GOODHUGH DAWSON - WGD4
1925 -

Thomas HARRIS*

Thomas HARRIS
Abt 1796

Mary ?*

James HARRIS
Abt 1826 - 1872

Ann ?

William Thomas HARRIS
1867 - 1945

?

Thomas SHOOBRIDGE
Abt 1801 - 1887

Mary ?HUNT*

Mary Ann SHOOBRIDGE
1828 - 1911

Richard WOOD*

Sarah Wood
Abt 1799 -

Sarah ?*

Florence Catherine HARRIS
1898 - 1976

John SHUFFILL*
Abt 1775 -

Thomas SHUFFILL*
1798 -

Ann COOK*
Abt 1779 -

Henry SHUFFILL
Abt 1823 - Bef 1877

Rebeccah CHENEY*
Abt 1798 - 1826

Hannah SHUFFILL/ SHEFFIELD
1866 - 1950

? Jonathan CLIFTON*
1808-

Harriet BOFFIN
1828 -

Ann BAUGHIN
1808 - 1835

My own forebears

69

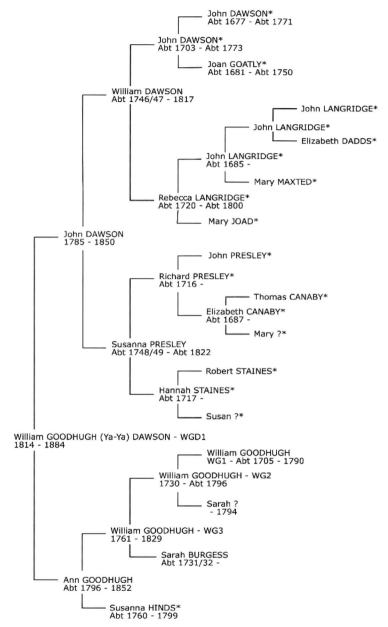

Forebears of William Goodhugh DAWSON (WGD1)

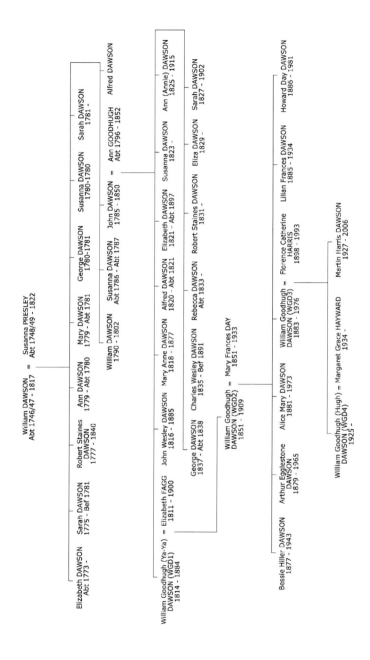

Descendants of William DAWSON (abt 1746/47 - 1817) and his wife Susanna PRESLEY showings siblings and the link with HARRIS

71

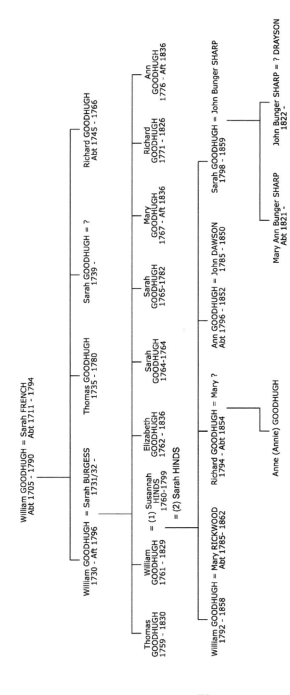

Direct descendants including siblings from William GOODHUGH (abt 1705-1790) and his wife Sarah to Ann GOODHUGH (1769-1852), and the link with DAWSON

72

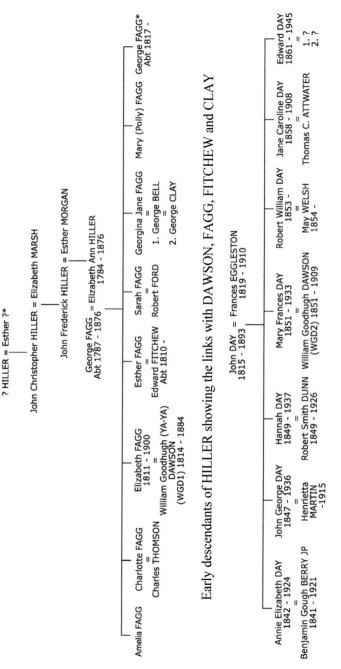

? HILLER = Esther ?*

John Christopher HILLER = Elizabeth MARSH

John Frederick HILLER = Esther MORGAN

George FAGG = Elizabeth Ann HILLER
Abt 1787 - 1876   1784 - 1876

Amelia FAGG

Charlotte FAGG
=
Charles THOMSON

Elizabeth FAGG
1811 - 1900
=
William Goodhugh (YA-YA) DAWSON
(WGD1) 1814 - 1884

Esther FAGG
=
Edward FITCHEW
Abt 1810 -

Sarah FAGG
=
Robert FORD

Georgina Jane FAGG
=
1. George BELL
2. George CLAY

Mary (Polly) FAGG

George FAGG*
Abt 1817 -

Early descendants of HILLER showing the links with DAWSON, FAGG, FITCHEW and CLAY

John DAY = Frances EGGLESTON
1815 - 1893   1819 - 1910

Annie Elizabeth DAY
1842 - 1924
=
Benjamin Gough BERRY JP
1841 - 1921

John George DAY
1847 - 1936
=
Henrietta MARTIN
-1915

Hannah DAY
1849 - 1937
=
Robert Smith DUNN
1849 - 1926

Mary Frances DAY
1851 - 1933
=
William Goodhugh DAWSON
(WGD2) 1851 - 1909

Robert William DAY
1853 -
=
May WELSH
1854 -

Jane Caroline DAY
1858 - 1908
=
Thomas C. ATTWATER

Edward DAY
1861 - 1945
=
1. ?
2. ?

Descendants of John DAY (1815-1893) and Frances EGGLESTON (1819-1910) showing the links with BERRY and DUNN

73

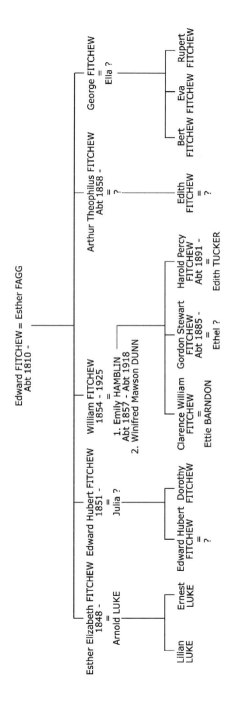

Early descendants of Edward FITCHEW (1810-) and Esther FAGG showing the link with LUKE

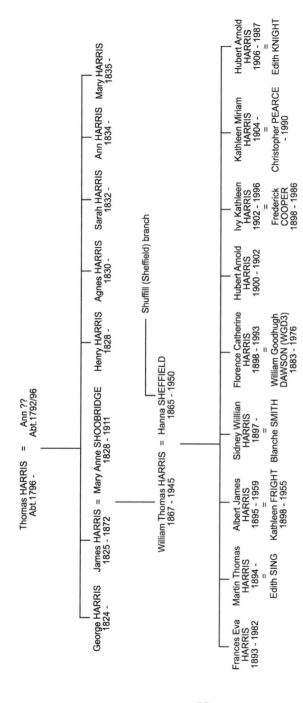

Descendants of Thomas HARRIS (abt.1796-) and his wife Ann showing the link with SHEFFIELD (SHUFFILL), DAWSON and COOPER

75

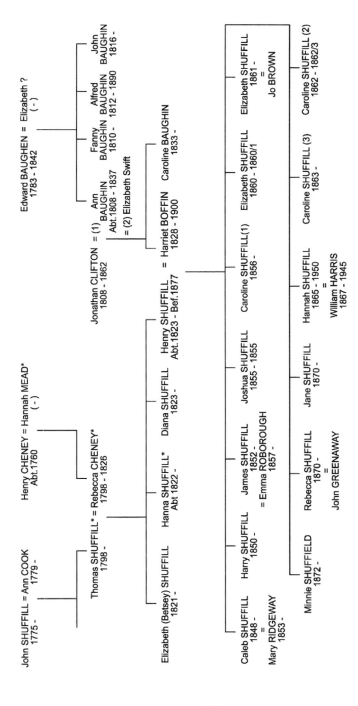

The SHUFFILL (SHEFFIELD) and BAUGHIN (BOFFIN) branches, showing the link with HARRIS. Many of Hannah's generation changed their surname to Sheffield during the later 19th Century

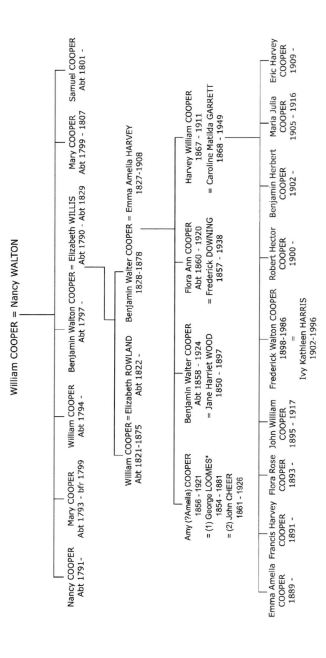

Descendants of William COOPER and Nancy WALTON, showing the link with HARRIS. Ivy Harris's sister Florence married William Goodhugh DAWSON (WGD3)

APPENDIX 5: Outline Trees

These trees contain the names of many more relatives of the people mentioned in this history. Any name suffixed by an asterisk requires further validating. Many people appear in more than one of these trees. To preserve the privacy of individuals and ensure compliance with data protection regulations, the trees omit details of relatives that may still be living at the time of writing.

DAWSON

1. **John DAWSON** * (c. 1677-c. 1771). Born: c. 1677, St Laurence, Ramsgate, Kent. Marr: Joan GOATLY * 18 Oct 1702, St Laurence, Ramsgate, Kent. Died: c. Jul 1771, St Laurence, Ramsgate, Kent. Buried: 21 Jul 1771, St Laurence, Ramsgate, Kent.
= Joan GOATLY * (c. 1681-c. 1750). Born: c. 1681. Died: c. Jun 1750. Buried: 1 Jul 1750, St Laurence, Ramsgate, Kent.
  2. **John DAWSON** (c. 1703-c. 1773). Born: c. 1703, St Laurence, Ramsgate, Kent. Bap: 18 Jul 1703, St Laurence, Ramsgate, Kent. Marr: Ann MOVERLY 29 Jun 1731, St Laurence, Ramsgate, Kent. Marr: Rebecca LANGRIDGE 21 Sep 1746, St Laurence, Ramsgate, Kent. Died: c. Aug 1773. Buried: 26 Aug 1773, St Laurence, Ramsgate, Kent.
  = Ann MOVERLY (c. 1702-c. 1740), dau. of Jeremy MOVERLY (-) and Jane UNDERDOWN (c. 1672-). Born: c. 1702. Bap: 20 Sep 1702, St Laurence, Ramsgate, Kent. Died: c. Aug 1740. Buried: 27 Aug 1740, St Laurence, Ramsgate, Kent.
    3. **John DAWSON** (c. 1732-c. 1732). Born: c. 1732. Bap: 14 May 1732, St Laurence, Ramsgate, Kent. Died: c. Jul 1732. Buried: 27 Jul 1732, St Laurence, Ramsgate, Kent.
    3. **Ann DAWSON** (c. 1733-c. 1760). Born: c. Jun 1733. Bap: 17 Jun 1733, St Laurence, Ramsgate, Kent. Died: c. Dec 1760. Buried: 11 Dec 1760, St Laurence, Ramsgate, Kent.
    3. **Richard DAWSON** (c. 1736-). Born: c. Aug 1736. Bap: 16 Aug 1736, St Laurence, Ramsgate, Kent. Marr: Sarah MARSHALL 14 Feb 1765, St Laurence, Ramsgate, Kent.
    = Sarah MARSHALL (c. 1742-c. 1806), dau. of Robert MARSHALL (1710-1755) and Dorothy HEWITT (c. 1714-1789). Born: c. 1742, St Laurence, Ramsgate, Kent. Died: c. Oct 1806. Buried: c. 26 Oct 1806, Aged 64.

4. **John DAWSON** (c. 1765-c. 1828). Born: c. 1765. Bap: 1 Dec 1765, St Laurence, Ramsgate, Kent. Marr: Ann CRAMP 29 Nov 1791, St Laurence, Ramsgate, Kent. Died: c. Oct 1828, Ramsgate, Kent. Buried: 9 Oct 1828, Protestant Dissenters Burying Ground, Ramsgate, Kent.
= Ann CRAMP (-).
  5. **Mary Ann DAWSON** * (1792-). Born: 16 Oct 1792. Bap: 18 Nov 1792, Ebenezer Independent Chapel, Ramsgate, Kent.
  5. **Catherine DAWSON** * (1794-bef1797). Born: 7 Sep 1794, Ramsgate, Kent. Bap: 20 Sep 1794, Ebenezer Independent Chapel, Ramsgate, Kent. Died: bef Nov 1797, Ramsgate, Kent.
  5. **Sarah DAWSON** * (1795-). Born: 9 Dec 1795. Bap: 1 Jan 1796, Ebenezer Independent Chapel, Ramsgate, Kent.
  5. **Catherine DAWSON** * (1797-). Born: 24 Nov 1797. Bap: 24 Dec 1797, Ebenezer Independent Chapel, Ramsgate, Kent.
  5. **Ann DAWSON** * (1818-). Born: 15 Dec 1818. Bap: 24 Jan 1819, Ebenezer Independent Chapel, Ramsgate, Kent.
  5. **John Marshall DAWSON** * (1821-). Born: 22 Aug 1821. Bap: 16 Sep 1821, Ebenezer Independent Chapel, Ramsgate, Kent.[7]
4. **Anna DAWSON** (c. 1768-). Born: c. 1768. Bap: 29 May 1768, St Laurence, Ramsgate, Kent. Marr: Thomas LUMLEY * 16 Sep 1787, St Laurence, Ramsgate, Kent.
= Thomas LUMLEY * (-).
4. **Richard DAWSON** (c. 1772-). Born: c. 1772. Bap: 20 Sep 1772, St Laurence, Ramsgate, Kent. Marr: Elizabeth WEST * 14 Nov 1797, St. Mary, Minster on Thanet, Kent. Marr: Elizabeth FOX * 13 Oct 1808, St. Mary, Minster on Thanet, Kent.
= Elizabeth WEST * (-).
  5. **Sarah Ann DAWSON** * (1799-). Born: 19 Aug 1799. Bap: 29 Sep 1799, Ebenezer Independent Chapel, Ramsgate, Kent.
  5. **John DAWSON** * (c. 1801-). Born: c. 1801. Bap: 13 Dec 1801, St Laurence, Ramsgate, Kent.
  5. **Richard DAWSON** * (c. 1808-). Born: c. 1808. Bap: 13 Mar 1808, St Laurence, Ramsgate, Kent.
  = Elizabeth FOX * (-).
  5. **William DAWSON** * (c. 1810-). Born: c. 1810. Bap: 18 Aug 1810, St. Mary, Minster on Thanet, Kent.
  5. **Elizabeth DAWSON** * (c. 1811-). Born: c. 1811. Bap: 22 Sep 1811, St. Mary, Minster on Thanet, Kent.
3. **Jane DAWSON** (c. 1738-). Born: c. Sep 1738. Bap: 1 Oct 1738, St Laurence, Ramsgate, Kent. Marr: John MORRIS 9 May 1768, St Laurence, Ramsgate, Kent.
= John MORRIS (-).
3. **John DAWSON** (c. 1740-c. 1740). Born: c. Jul 1740. Bap: 13 Jul 1740, St Laurence, Ramsgate, Kent. Died: c. Aug 1740. Buried: 10 Aug 1740, St Laurence, Ramsgate, Kent.
= Rebecca LANGRIDGE (c. 1720-c. 1800), dau. of John LANGRIDGE * (c. 1685-) and Mary JOAD * (-). Born: c. 1720. Bap: 10 Jul 1720, St Laurence, Ramsgate, Kent. Died: 13 Jan 1800, St Laurence, Ramsgate, Kent. Buried: 13 Jan 1800, St Laurence, Ramsgate, Kent.
3. **William DAWSON** (c. 1747-1817). Born: c. Jan 1746/47. Bap: 8 Feb 1746/47, St Laurence, Ramsgate, Kent. Marr: Susanna PRESLEY 12

Nov 1772, St Laurence, Ramsgate, Kent. Died: Dec 1817, Margate, Kent. Buried: 2 Jan 1818, St John in Thanet, Margate, Kent.

= Susanna PRESLEY (c. 1749-c. 1822), dau. of Richard PRESLEY (c. 1716-) and Hannah STAINES (c. 1717-). Born: c. Jan 1748/49, Thanet, Kent. Bap: 4 Feb 1748/49, St Laurence, Ramsgate, Kent. Died: c. Apr 1822, Faversham, Kent. Buried: 21 Apr 1822, Faversham, Kent.

4. **Elizabeth DAWSON** (c. 1773-). Born: c. 1773, Sandwich, Kent. Bap: 30 Oct 1773, St. Marys, Sandwich, Kent. Marr: James DIXON 28 Mar 1795, St. John the Baptist, Thanet, Kent.

= James DIXON (c. 1768-), son of James DIXON (-aft1832). Born: c. 1768. Bap: 4 Dec 1768, St. John the Baptist, Thanet, Kent.

  5. **Sarah DIXON** * (-). Marr: Thomas HAWKINGS 20 Jun 1827, St. John the Baptist, Thanet, Kent.

  = Thomas HAWKINGS (-).

4. **Sarah DAWSON** (1775-bef1781). Born: 1775, Margate, Kent. Died: bef Nov 1781.

4. **Robert Staines DAWSON** (1777-1840). Born: Jun 1777. Bap: 27 Jul 1777, St. Marys, Sandwich, Kent. Marr: Mary SANDWELL 17 Dec 1801, St Peter-in-Thanet, Broadstairs, Kent. Died: 11 May 1840, Broadstairs, Kent. Buried: St. Peters Baptist Burial Ground, Thanet, Kent.

= Mary SANDWELL (1781-1868), dau. of Mockett SANDWELL (-) and Sarah WADE (-). Born: 27 Mar 1781. Bap: 22 Apr 1781, St Peter-in-Thanet, Broadstairs, Kent. Died: 1868.

  5. **William Sandwell DAWSON** (1802-1873). Born: 10 Aug 1802, Broadstairs, Kent. Bap: 12 Sep 1802, St Peter-in-Thanet, Broadstairs, Kent. Marr: Sarah ROBERTS 12 Jun 1827, St. Mary of Charity, Faversham, Kent. Marr: Mary RICHARDSON 18 Feb 1868, Bethel Baptist Chapel, Maidstone, Kent. Died: 1873, Maidstone, Kent.

  = Sarah ROBERTS (c. 1804-1864), dau. of John ROBERTS (1780-c. 1865) and Sarah SPILLETT (1785-1869). Born: c. 1804, Faversham, Kent. Died: 3 Feb 1864, 18 Kingsley Road, Maidstone.

    6. **Sarah DAWSON** (c. 1828-1859). Born: c. Mar 1828, Thanet, Kent. Bap: 20 Apr 1828, St Peter-in-Thanet, Broadstairs, Kent. Died: 16 Mar 1859.

    = BOLLINGER (-).

      7. **Alice BOLLINGER** (-1859). Died: 18 Mar 1859.

    6. **Susannah DAWSON** (c. 1835-). Born: c. 1835. Bap: Maidstone, Kent.

    6. **Mary Ann DAWSON** (c. 1835-). Born: c. 1835. Bap: Maidstone, Kent.

    6. **George Henry DAWSON** (1838-1923). Born: 26 Aug 1838, Maidstone, Kent. Marr: Louisa DAVIS 24 Aug 1862, East Malling, Kent. Died: 3 Mar 1923, Indianapolis, Indiana, USA. Buried: Crown Hill Cemetery, Indianapolis, Indiana, USA.

    = Louisa DAVIS (1842-1923), dau. of William DAVIS (c. 1813-) and Elizabeth GARDNER (c. 1811-). Born: 29 Nov 1842, Bearstead, Kent. Died: 2 Mar 1923. Buried: Crown Hill Cemetery, Indianapolis, Indiana, USA.

      7. **Louisa DAWSON** (1863-1863). Born: 18 May 1863. Died: 15 Jun 1863.

      7. **Louisa DAWSON** (1864-1896). Born: May 1864, Maidstone, Kent. Marr: Ned ENDFIELD 6 Nov 1889. Died: 23

Dec 1896, Texas, USA. Buried: Dec 1896.
= Ned ENDFIELD (-).
    8. **Wilbur ENDFIELD** (-).
    8. **Winnifred ENDFIELD** (-).
7. **William Alfred DAWSON** (c. 1866-1870). Born: c. Aug 1866. Died: 13 Jul 1870, 16 Kingsley Road, Maidstone, Kent.
7. **Percy DAWSON** (1867-1874). Born: 1867, Maidstone, Kent. Died: 1874, At sea on the emigration ship. Buried: "At sea?".
7. **George Henry DAWSON** (1869-1952). Born: 8 Jan 1869, 16 Kingsley Road, Maidstone, Kent. Marr: Ida May GROSS 6 May 1896, Indianapolis, Indiana, USA. Died: 9 Feb 1952, Jefferson City, Missouri, USA. Buried: Feb 1952, Crown Hill Cemetery, Indianapolis, Indiana, USA.
= Ida May GROSS (-1939). Died: 2 Mar 1939, Moberly, Missouri, USA. Buried: Crown Hill Cemetery, Indianapolis, Indiana, USA.
    8. **Royce Herbert DAWSON** (1909-1981). Born: 16 Jan 1909, Indianapolis, Indiana, USA. Marr: Carita Dysart MILLER 26 May 1934, Independence, Missouri, USA. Died: 8 Feb 1981, St. Simons Island, Georgia, USA. Buried: 13 Feb 1981, Oglethrope Cemetery, St. Simons Island, Georgia, USA.
    = Carita Dysart MILLER (-1998). Died: 13 Mar 1998, St. Simons Island, Georgia, USA. Buried: Oglethrope Cemetery, St. Simons Island, Georgia, USA.
        9. **Lida Anne DAWSON** (1938-2011). Born: 19 Jan 1938, Jefferson City, Missouri, USA. Died: 10 Sep 2011.
        = M PRICE.
            10. **M PRICE**.
            10. **F PRICE**.
            10. **F PRICE**.
            10. **F PRICE**.
                11. **F**.
                11. **F**.
        9. **F DAWSON**.
        = Scott LaCoaste RODGERS.
            10. **F RODGERS**.
                11. **M**.

10. **M RODGERS**.

7. **Herbert Owen DAWSON** (1871-1954). Born: 23 Apr 1871, 16 Kingsley Road, Maidstone, Kent. Died: 29 Jan 1954, Canton, Ohio, USA.
= [unnamed person] (-).

   8. **Bertha DAWSON** (1892-1972). Born: 22 Dec 1892, Indianapolis, Indiana, USA. Died: 10 Oct 1972, Indianapolis, Indiana, USA. Buried: Oct 1972, Crown Hill Cemetery, Indianapolis, Indiana, USA.
   = Dennis GREGORY (-).
   = [unnamed person] (-).

   8. **Nellie Mae DAWSON**. (1912-). Born: 1912, Indianapolis, Indiana, USA. Died: Canton, Ohio USA.

   8. **Herbert Owen DAWSON** (1912-1983). Born: 15 Mar 1912, Indianapolis, Indiana, USA. Died: 2 Mar 1983, Indianapolis, Indiana, USA.

      9. **F DAWSON**.
      = M HABERER.
         10. **M HABERER**.

   8. **George Richard DAWSON**. (1919-). Born: 29 May 1919, Indianapolis, Indiana, USA

      9. **F DAWSON**.
      = M OGDEN.
         10. **M OGDEN**.
            11. **M OGDEN**.
         10. **F OGDEN**.
         10. **F OGDEN**.
         = M SHINN.
            11. **M SHINN**.
            11. **F SHINN**.
         10. **F OGDEN**.

      9. **M DAWSON**.
         10. **M DAWSON**.
         10. **F DAWSON**.

      9. **Teresa DAWSON** (1958-1990). Born: 1958, Canton, Ohio, USA. Died: 1990, Canton, Ohio, USA.
      = M PELLEGRENE.

10. **F PELLEGRENE.**
   = M KESTAL.
      11. **F KESTAL.**
   10. **F PELLEGRENE.**
8. **Marie DAWSON** (-).
   = [unnamed person] (-).
8. **Nellie Mae DAWSON** (-).
7. **Winnifred DAWSON** (1875-1924). Born: 1875, Indianapolis, Indiana, USA. Died: 1924, Indianapolis, Indiana, USA.
   = Charles W. CARTER (-).
8. **Dorothy CARTER** (-).
8. **Winnifred CARTER** (-). Born: "4 APR".
7. **William Alfred DAWSON** (1878-1931). Born: 18 Jun 1878, Indianapolis, Indiana, USA. Marr: Susie Bailey PULLIAM 1901, Indianapolis, Indiana, USA. Died: 19 Mar 1931, Indianapolis, Indiana, USA. Buried: Crown Hill Cemetery, Indianapolis, Indiana, USA.
   = Susie Bailey PULLIAM (-).
8. **Nellie Elizabeth DAWSON** (1908-1996). Born: 16 Dec 1908, Indianapolis, Indiana, USA. Died: Dec 1996, Indianapolis, Indiana, USA.
   = Lester Merle BOLLANDER.
9. **M BOLLANDER.**
   = F.
      10. **M BOLLANDER.**
      10. **M BOLLANDER.**
   = F GUFFY.
8. **Carl Alfred DAWSON** (1917-1994). Born: 19 Jan 1917, Indianapolis, Indiana, USA. Died: 7 Jun 1994, Indianapolis, Indiana, USA. Buried: Memorial Park Cemetery, Indianapolis, Indiana, USA.
   = Virginia Leona HEDRICK (1921-2006). Born: 18 Jan 1921, Harrison, Arkansas. Died: 28 Jun 2006. Buried: Memorial Park Cemetery, Indianapolis, Indiana, USA.
9. **Robert Carl DAWSON** (1948-2004). Born: 28 Sep 1948, Indianapolis, Indiana, USA. Died: 28 May 2004. Buried: 5 Jun 2004, Memorial Park Cemetery, Indianapolis, Indiana, USA.
   = F TRASK.

10. **M DAWSON**.
10. **F DAWSON**.
   11. **M**.
10. **M DAWSON**.
10. **F DAWSON**.
   11. **F**.
   11. **M**.
9. **Michael William DAWSON** (1950-2007). Born: 24 Jun 1950, Indianapolis, Indiana, USA. Died: 27 Aug 2007, San Diego, California. Buried: National Military Cemetery in San Diego, California.
= F FRONTERAS.
10. **M DAWSON**.
10. **F DAWSON**.
10. **F DAWSON**.
= F LOGAN.
   11. **Michael LOGAN**.
9. **M DAWSON**.
= F TIMMONS.
10. **M DAWSON**.
= F.
   11. **F DAWSON**.
   11. **F DAWSON**.
10. **F DAWSON**.
= M HESS.
   11. **F HESS**.
   11. **M HESS**.
10. **M DAWSON**.
= F BROWN.
= F DORY.
10. **M DAWSON**.
= F JENSEN.

9. **M DAWSON.**
= F RAISIS.
   10. **M DAWSON.**
   10. **M DAWSON.**
   10. **M DAWSON.**

7. **Nellie Mae DAWSON** (1883-1980). Born: 15 Jun 1883, Indianapolis, Indiana, USA. Marr: Turner Dexter BOTTOME 1920. Died: 8 Nov 1980. Buried: Crown Hill Cemetery, Indianapolis, Indiana, USA.
= Turner Dexter BOTTOME (-).
   8. **BOTTOME** (1924-1924). Born: 1924. Died: 1924.

6. **Alfred DAWSON** (c. 1841-1927). Born: c. 1841. Bap: Maidstone, Kent. Marr: Una Marie England. Died: 12 Feb 1927, Indianapolis, Indiana, USA. Buried: Feb 1927, Crown Hill Cemetery, Indianapolis, Indiana, USA.
= Una Marie (-).
   7. **Charles Wilfred DAWSON** (c. 1870-). Born: c. 1870.
   = Mary RICHARDSON (c. 1807-). Born: c. 1807, Sussex.

5. **Mary Ann DAWSON** (1803-1847). Born: 21 Sep 1803. Bap: 20 Nov 1803, St Peter-in-Thanet, Broadstairs, Kent. Marr: Robert Minter COCK 2 Mar 1837, St Peter-in-Thanet, Broadstairs, Kent. Died: 1 Feb 1847, Broadstairs, Kent. Buried: Feb 1847, St Peter-in-Thanet, Broadstairs, Kent.
= Robert Minter COCK (-).
   6. **George Dawson COCK** * (-).
   6. **Robert Minter COCK** (bap. c. 1840, d.1863). Bap: c. 1840, St Peter-in-Thanet, Broadstairs, Kent. Died: 14 May 1863, Broadstairs, Kent. Buried: May 1863, St Peter-in-Thanet, Broadstairs, Kent.

5. **Robert Staines DAWSON** (1805-1884). Born: 24 Aug 1805, Broadstairs, Kent. Bap: 29 Sep 1805, St Peter-in-Thanet, Broadstairs, Kent. Marr: Elizabeth Ann COCK 6 Dec 1838, St Peter-in-Thanet, Broadstairs, Kent. Died: 6 May 1884. Buried: May 1884, St. Peter's Baptist churchyard, Thanet, Kent.
= Elizabeth Ann COCK (c. 1810-aft1881), dau. of Robert COCK (-) and [unnamed person] (-). Born: c. 1810, Broadstairs, Kent. Died: aft Mar 1881.
   6. **Robert Staines DAWSON** (c. 1840-c. 1923). Born: c. Oct 1840. Bap: 20 Oct 1845, Broadstairs, Kent. Marr: Norah CLARK 2 Jan 1866, St. George, Hanover Square. Died: c. 1923, Broadstairs, Kent.
   = Norah CLARK (-), dau. of Thomas CLARK (-).
   6. **Elizabeth A. DAWSON** (c. 1841-1927). Born: c. 1841, Broadstairs, Kent. Died: 22 Jan 1927, Broadstairs, Kent. Buried: 1927, Broadstairs, Kent.

6. **Mary Sandwell DAWSON** (c. 1844-1937). Born: c. 1844, Broadstairs, Kent. Died: 10 Mar 1937, Broadstairs, Kent. Buried: 1937, Broadstairs, Kent.

6. **Sarah DAWSON** (c. 1855-). Born: c. 1855, Broadstairs, Kent.

6. **George D. DAWSON** (-). Born: Broadstairs, Kent.

6. **John DAWSON** (-).

5. **George DAWSON** (1807-1839). Born: 19 Jul 1807, Broadstairs, Kent. Bap: 16 Aug 1807, St Peter-in-Thanet, Broadstairs, Kent. Died: 22 Apr 1839, St Peter-in-Thanet, Broadstairs, Kent. Buried: St. Peters Baptist Burial Ground, Thanet, Kent.

5. **Sarah DAWSON** (1810-1864). Born: 7 May 1810, Broadstairs, Kent. Bap: 3 Jun 1810, St Peter-in-Thanet, Broadstairs, Kent. Died: 14 Jun 1864. Buried: Jun 1864, St. Peter's Baptist churchyard, Thanet, Kent.

5. **Elizabeth DAWSON** (1812-1883). Born: 14 Apr 1812, Broadstairs, Kent. Bap: 24 May 1812, St Peter-in-Thanet, Broadstairs, Kent. Died: 1883, Broadstairs, Kent. Buried: 1883, St. Peter's Baptist churchyard, Thanet, Kent.

5. **Susanna DAWSON** (c. 1814-1834). Born: c. 1814, Broadstairs, Kent. Bap: 13 Feb 1814, St Peter-in-Thanet, Broadstairs, Kent. Died: 15 Feb 1834, Broadstairs, Kent. Buried: 1834, St. Peters Baptist Burial Ground, Thanet, Kent.

5. **John DAWSON** (1817-1867). Born: 22 Mar 1817, Broadstairs, Kent. Bap: 22 Mar 1817, St. Peters Isle of Thanet, Particular Baptist, Kent. Died: 23 Mar 1867, Dumpton, Kent. Buried: Mar 1867, St. Peter's Baptist churchyard, Thanet, Kent.
= Mary Ann MINTER (1824-1864). Born: 1824. Died: 17 Dec 1864, Dumpton, Kent.

6. **John Minter DAWSON** (1854-1873). Born: 1854, Broadstairs, Kent. Died: 11 Nov 1873, Dumpton, Kent.

6. **Alexander George DAWSON** (1854-1866). Born: 1854, Broadstairs, Kent. Died: 1866, Dumpton, Kent.

6. **William Henry Minter DAWSON** (c. 1856-1864). Born: c. 1856, Dumpton, Kent. Died: 20 Oct 1864, Dumpton, Kent.

6. **Mary Ann DAWSON** (1863-1864). Born: 1863, Dumpton, Kent. Died: 1864, Dumpton, Kent.

6. **George Ernst Dawson DAWSON** (1863-1867). Born: 1863, Dumpton, Kent. Died: 15 Mar 1867, Dumpton, Kent.

4. **Ann DAWSON** (1779-c. 1780). Born: 27 Oct 1779. Bap: 12 Dec 1779, St. John the Baptist, Thanet, Kent. Died: c. Sep 1780. Buried: 6 Sep 1780, St. John the Baptist, Thanet, Kent.

4. **Mary DAWSON** (1779-c. 1781). Born: 27 Oct 1779. Died: c. Oct 1779. Buried: 9 Oct 1781. St. John the Baptist, Thanet, Kent.

4. **George DAWSON** (1780-1781). Born: 26 Nov 1780. Died: Sep 1781. Buried: 2 Oct 1781. St. John the Baptist, Thanet, Kent.

4. **Susannah DAWSON** (1780-1780). Born: 26 Nov 1780. Bap: 30 Nov 1780, St. John in Thanet, Kent. Died: 4 Dec 1780. Buried: 8 Dec 1780, St. John the Baptist, Thanet, Kent.

4. **Sarah DAWSON** (1781-). Born: 4 Nov 1781, Margate, Kent. Bap: 25 Dec 1781, St. John the Baptist, Thanet, Kent. Marr: John GOUGER 6 Nov 1838, St.John the Baptist, Thanet, Kent.
= John GOUGER (1759-aft1851), son of John GOUGER (c. 1725-c. 1809) and Mary SMALL (-). Born: 5 Nov 1759, Ramsgate, Kent. Bap: 9 Dec 1759, Ebenezer Independ. Chapel, Ramsgate, Kent. Marr: Mary WILKINSON 1 Dec 1783, Birchington, Kent. Died: aft 1851.

4. **Alfred DAWSON** (-). Born:

4. **John DAWSON** (1785-1850). Born: 20 Apr 1785. Marr: Ann GOODHUGH 14 Aug 1813, St. Mary of Charity, Faversham, Kent. Died: 3 Oct 1850. Buried: Faversham, Kent, NE corner of churchyard.

= Ann GOODHUGH (c. 1796-1852), dau. of William GOODHUGH (1761-1829) and Susannah HINDS (c. 1760-1799). Born: c. Jun 1796. Bap: 24 Jul 1796, St. Mary of Charity, Faversham, Kent. Died: 21 Apr 1852.

    5. **William Goodhugh DAWSON** (1814-1884). Born: 24 May 1814, Faversham, Kent. Bap: 5 Jun 1814, Wesleyan Chapel, Faversham, Kent. Marr: Elizabeth FAGG 11 Jul 1845, Wesleyan Bethal Chapel, Rochester, Kent. Died: 5 Apr 1884, Faversham, Kent. Buried: Faversham churchyard, Kent.

    = Elizabeth FAGG (1811-1900), dau. of George FAGG (c. 1787-1876) and Elizabeth Ann HILLER (1784-1876). Born: 1811, St Peter-in-Thanet, Broadstairs, Kent. Bap: 17 Nov 1811, St Peter-in-Thanet, Broadstairs, Kent. Died: 17 Jan 1900. Buried: Faversham churchyard, Kent.

        6. **William Goodhugh DAWSON** (1851-1909). Born: 12 Dec 1851, Faversham, Kent. Marr: Mary Frances DAY 8 Jun 1876. Died: 25 Jun 1909. Buried: Faversham churchyard, Kent.

        = Mary Frances DAY (1851-1933), dau. of John DAY (1815-1893) and Frances EGGLESTON (1819-1910). Born: 14 Oct 1851, Caldicot, Monmouthshire. Died: 29 Apr 1933.

            7. **Bessie Hiller DAWSON** (1877-1943). Born: 15 Jul 1877, Faversham, Kent. Marr: Thomas J. THOMAS 1 Jun 1921. Died: 23 Aug 1943.

            = Thomas J. THOMAS (-1953). Died: 5 Mar 1953.

            7. **Arthur Egglestone DAWSON** (1879-1965). Born: 7 Jan 1879, Faversham, Kent. Marr: Elsie Tillotson JARMAN 22 Jan 1916. Died: 6 May 1965.

            = Elsie Tillotson JARMAN (1886-). Born: 1 Sep 1886.

                8. **Irene Mary DAWSON** (1917-2017). Born: 6 Feb 1917. Died: 10 Aug 2017. Abbeyfield Society, 11 Maitland Rd, Reading RG1 6NL.

                8. **Muriel Frances DAWSON**.

                = Eric E. F. SMITH (1907-1990).

            7. **Alice Mary DAWSON** (1881-1973). Born: 20 Feb 1881. Died: 8 Apr 1973.

            7. **William Goodhugh DAWSON** (1883-1976). Born: 17 May 1883. Marr: Florence Catherine HARRIS 9 Apr 1923. Died: 25 Sep 1976.

            = Florence Catherine HARRIS (1898-1993), dau. of William Thomas HARRIS (1867-1945) and Hannah SHEFFIELD (1865-1950). Born: 24 Aug 1898. Died: 17 Apr 1993.

8. **William Goodhugh DAWSON**.
= Margaret Grace HAYWARD.
   9. **William Goodhugh DAWSON**.
   = Andrea Lynne THOMPSON.
   9. **Sarah Margaret DAWSON**.
   = Philip James GRIFFIN.
      10. **Anna Elizabeth GRIFFIN**.
      10. **Owen James GRIFFIN**.
      10. **Bethany Rachel GRIFFIN**.

8. **Martin Harris DAWSON** (1927-2006). Born: 18 Feb 1927. Marr: Shirley GREY 2 Jul 1955. Died: 29 Nov 2006, Norfolk. Buried: 11 Dec 2006.
= Shirley GREY (1936-2005). Born: 21 May 1936. Died: 15 Mar 2005.
   9. **M DAWSON**.
   = F HARVEY.
      10. **M DAWSON**.
      10. **F DAWSON**.
      10. **M DAWSON**.
      = F DIBLEY.
   9. **M DAWSON**.
   = F MCRAE.
      10. **M DAWSON**.
      10. **M DAWSON**.
      10. **M DAWSON**.
      10. **M DAWSON**.
   9. **M DAWSON**.
   9. **M DAWSON**.
   = F.
   = F SINCLAIRE.
      10. **M DAWSON**.
      = F.
      10. **F DAWSON**.

9. **F DAWSON**.
= M LINES.
    10. **M LINES**.
9. **M DAWSON**.
= F DENNIS.
    10. **M DAWSON**.
    = [unnamed person].
7. **Lilian Frances DAWSON** (1885-1934). Born: 9 Jan 1885. Died: 20 Nov 1934.
7. **Howard Day DAWSON** (1886-1981). Born: 2 Jun 1886. Marr: Daisy Hilda RATCLIFFE 24 Jan 1914. Marr: Fran aft 1918. Died: 6 Apr 1981.
= Daisy Hilda RATCLIFFE (1886-1966). Born: 1886. Died: 3 Jan 1966.
8. **Isabel Alice DAWSON** (1918-2019). Born: 29 Jul 1918. Marr: William Simmons RAMSAY 12 Feb 1941. Died: 7 Mar 2019, Nelson, British Columbia, Canada.
= William Simmons RAMSAY (1915-2001). Born: 3 Oct 1915. Died: 4 Nov 2001.
9. **M RAMSAY**.
= F SIMPSON.
    10. **F RAMSAY**.
    10. **F RAMSAY**.
    10. **F RAMSAY**.
    10. **F RAMSAY**.
9. **F RAMSAY**.
= M MARTIN.
    10. **Jason William MARTIN** (1969-1997). Born: 30 Dec 1969. Died: Jun 1997.
    10. **F MARTIN**.
    10. **M MARTIN**.
9. **F RAMSAY**.
= M HAGEL.
    10. **F HAGEL**.
    10. **M HAGEL**.
    10. **F HAGEL**.

9. **M RAMSAY**.
= F CULLEN.
   10. **M RAMSAY**.
   10. **F RAMSAY**.
   10. **F RAMSAY**.
   = F TRIMBOLI.
   10. **M RAMSAY**.
= Fran (-1978). Died: Dec 1978.

5. **John Wesley DAWSON** (1816-1885). Born: 17 Aug 1816, Faversham, Kent. Bap: 18 Sep 1816, Wesleyan Chapel, Faversham, Kent. Marr: Anne Proctor GROOMBRIDGE 17 Aug 1843, St. Peter's Street Methodist Chapel, Canterbury, Kent. Died: 15 Feb 1885, Wokingham, Berkshire.
= Anne Proctor GROOMBRIDGE (1818-1897), dau. of James GROOMBRIDGE (c. 1785-bef1839) and Ann PARNUM (c. 1788-1862). Born: 19 Jul 1818. St. Mary Bredin, Canterbury, Kent. Bap: 28 Oct 1818, Union Chapel, Canterbury, Kent. Died: 17 Oct 1897, Wellington, Shropshire. Buried: 21 Oct 1897, St Paul, Wokingham, Berkshire.

6. **John Wesley DAWSON** (1845-). Born: 10 Mar 1845, Farringdon, Berkshire. Bap: 25 Jun 1845, Wesleyan Chapel, Swindon, Wiltshire. Marr: Fanny SCORE c. Nov 1868, Yeovil, Somerset.
= Fanny SCORE (c. 1843-), dau. of John SCORE (c. 1808-) and Marianna (c. 1816-). Born: c. 1843, Powerstock, Dorset.

7. **John Wesley Score DAWSON** (1870-1954). Born: 22 May 1870, St. Anns Road, Edmonton. Marr: Alice Maud M TENNANT c. Aug 1895, Edmonton, Middlesex. Died: 1954.
= Alice Maud M TENNANT (c. 1872-). Born: c. 1872, Wood Green, Middlesex.

8. **John Lancelot DAWSON** (c. 1899-c. 1976). Born: c. Nov 1899, Tottenham, Middlesex. Marr: Mary J ROUQUET* c. May 1920, Edmonton, Middlesex. Died: c. Nov 1976, Brighton, Sussex.
= Mary J ROUQUET* (-).

8. **Francis Lloyd DAWSON** (1906-c. 1985). Born: 31 Dec 1906, Shoreditch, Middlesex. Marr: Pauline A HANSFORD c. Aug 1930, Southwark, Middlesex. Died: c. Nov 1985, Winchester, Hampshire.
= Pauline A HANSFORD (-).

7. **Fanny Caroline DAWSON** (1872-). Born: 6 Feb 1872, St. Pancras, London.

7. **Annie Marian DAWSON** (1878-). Born: 26 Jan 1878, Powerstock, Dorset.
= [unnamed person] (-).

8. **[unnamed person]** (-).

7. **Leonard DAWSON** (c. 1880-). Born: c. 1880, St. Pancras, London.

7. **Herbert M. DAWSON** (c. 1882-). Born: c. 1882, Tottenham, Middlesex.

7. **DAWSON** (-).

6. **William Goodhugh DAWSON** (1846-1942). Born: 4 Jun 1846, Great Faringdon, Berkshire. Bap: 26 Jul 1846, Wesleyan Chapel, Swindon, Wiltshire. Marr: Agnes PRATT 16 Aug 1876, Eastbrook Chapel, Bradford. Died: 15 Jan 1942, St. Albans, Herfordshire.

= Agnes PRATT (1850-c. 1922), dau. of Christopher PRATT (1819-1903) and Jane CHEESEBROUGH (1821-1898). Born: 10 Jun 1850. Died: c. Feb 1922, Mental Hospital, Burley-in-Wharfdale.

7. **Percival William DAWSON** (1878-1938). Born: 29 Oct 1878. Marr: Jane Elizabeth CARSON c. 1912. Died: 1938.

= Jane Elizabeth CARSON (c. 1876-1961), dau. of Robert CARSON (-) and Elizabeth Jane WOOD (-). Born: c. 1876, Belmullet, Ireland. Died: 3 May 1961. Buried: Kilglass Church of Ireland Cemetery, Ireland.

8. **Robert Carson DAWSON** (1914-1977). Born: 23 Jan 1914. Died: 30 Apr 1977. Buried: Kilglass Church of Ireland Cemetery, Ireland.

= Sylvia Eleanor Margaret SHAW. Born: 9 Feb 1916. Died: 4 Jul 2011.

    9. **M DAWSON.**

        = F RUSSELL (-).

        10. **F DAWSON.**

        10. **F DAWSON.**

            = M KELLY (-).

            11. **M KELLY.**

            11. **M KELLY.**

            11. **F KELLY.**

        10. **F DAWSON.**

            = M HARRISON (-).

            11. **M HARRISON.**

            11. **F HARRISON.**

    9. **F DAWSON.**

        = Neville BAKER (-2015).

        10. **F Norah BAKER.**

            = M LE BOUSQUET.

            11. **M LE BOUSQUET.**

            11. **M LE BOUSQUET.**

10. **M BAKER**.
10. **F BAKER**.
= M JONES (-).
11. **M JONES**.
11. **F JONES**.
9. **F DAWSON**.
= M POLYDOROU (-).
10. **F POLYDOROU**.
10. **M POLYDOROU**.
9. **M DAWSON**.
= F LOUW (-).
10. **M DAWSON**.
= F RYAN.

7. **William Goodhugh DAWSON** (1880-1937). Born: 12 Aug 1880, Ramsey, Isle of Man. Died: 26 Aug 1937.
= Margaret Emily GLEDHILL (-).
8. **Winifred Margaret DAWSON** (1907-1999). Born: 1907. Marr: Wilfred Mills CRAVEN c. Oct 1932. Died: 18 Nov 1999.
= Wilfred Mills CRAVEN (1905-1987). Born: 1905. Died: 1987.
9. **F CRAVEN**.
= M DIGGLE.
9. **M CRAVEN**.
= F RAINES.
10. **CRAVEN**.
10. **CRAVEN**.
10. **CRAVEN**.
9. **M CRAVEN**.
= F WOOD-WOLFE.
8. **Josephine Mary DAWSON** (1909-1954). Born: 28 Aug 1909. Marr: John Walker ROBERTS 1935, Tanfield, nr. Ripon, Yorkshire. Died: 22 Sep 1954.
= John Walker ROBERTS (1904-1995). Born: 1904. Died: 1995.
9. **F ROBERTS**.

= M RICKER.
    10. **RICKER.**
    10. **RICKER.**
    10. **RICKER.**
  9. **Stephen ROBERTS** (1945-1945). Born: 1945. Died: 1945.
  9. **F ROBERTS.**
  = [unnamed person].
  9. **M ROBERTS.**
7. **Winifred Agnes DAWSON** (1882-1965). Born: 21 Apr 1882. Marr: Harold Felvus WALKER 1904. Died: 1965.
= Harold Felvus WALKER (1878-1952), son of Richard Felvus WALKER (1843-) and Ann Elizabeth WALKER (-). Born: 1878, 4 Spring Mount, Laisteridge Lane, Bradford, Yorkshire. Died: 1952.
  8. **Agnes Elise WALKER** (1905-1997). Born: 1905. Died: May 1997.
  8. **Richard Felvus WALKER** (1906-1938). Born: 1906. Marr: Died: 1938.
  = [unnamed person] (-).
  8. **William Dawson WALKER** (1908-1987). Born: 1908. Died: 1987.
  = Dorothy H. SCHIACH (-1989). Died: 1989.
    9. **Phillipa Jane WALKER.**
    = Michael.
      10. **M.**
      10. **F.**
    9. **M WALKER.**
    = F.
      10. **M WALKER.**
      10. **M WALKER.**
      10. **F WALKER.**
  8. **Winifred Ruth WALKER** (1912-1985). Born: 1912. Marr: Thomas Hearn CLEGHORN 1939. Died: 1985.
= Thomas Hearn CLEGHORN (1911-1989), son of Arthur William CLEGHORN (c. 1868-1954) and Edith DAVIES (-1923). Born: 1911. Died: 1989.
  9. **M CLEGHORN.**
  = F HUNT.
    10. **F CLEGHORN.**

          10. **F CLEGHORN.**
          10. **M CLEGHORN.**
      9. **M CLEGHORN.**
      = F SMITH.
          10. **M CLEGHORN.**
          10. **M CLEGHORN.**
          10. **F CLEGHORN.**
          10. **F CLEGHORN.**
      9. **M CLEGHORN.**
      = Susan Mary HORREX, dau. of William George HORREX and Irene SHIPLEE (-bef1976).
          10. **M CLEGHORN.**
          10. **F CLEGHORN.**
          10. **F CLEGHORN.**
8. **Leonard Geoffrey WALKER** (1915-1992). Born: 1915. Marr: Rosemary SALAMAN c. 1948. Died: 20 Jun 1992.
= Rosemary SALAMAN (-).
      9. **M WALKER.**
      = F.
      9. **M WALKER.**
      = F SKULL.
          10. **F WALKER.**
      9. **M WALKER.**
      = F.
      9. **M WALKER.**
7. **Christopher DAWSON** (1885-1950). Born: 15 Sep 1885, Hunmanby, Yorkshire. Marr: Beatrice Maud WATERHOUSE 23 Nov 1914, Karur Wesleyan Chapel, India. Marr: Norah Anne Marjory DYKE 6 Dec 1949. Died: 24 Mar 1950, Portsmouth, Hampshire.
= Beatrice Maud WATERHOUSE (1884-1948), dau. of Thomas Holmes WATERHOUSE (1848-1902) and Eliza Sarah SANDERS (1844-1895). Born: 27 Dec 1884, Holywell, Flintshire. Died: 7 Dec 1948, Portsmouth, Hampshire.
= Norah Anne Marjory DYKE (-) Marr: 6 Dec 1949.

8. **Eileen Mary DAWSON** (1915-1949). Born: 16 Oct 1915, Karur, Tamil Nadu, India. Died: 12 Oct 1949, Dorchester.

8. **Robert Goodhugh DAWSON** (1921-2012). Born: 10 Oct 1921, Holywell, Flintshire. Marr: Marthe MARTHALER 19 Mar 1949. Died: 19 Dec 2012, Wollaston, Northamptonshire.
= Marthe MARTHALER (1920-2009). Born: 17 Jun 1920, Berne, Switzerland. Died: 21 Sep 2009, Wollaston, Northamptonshire.
   9. **F DAWSON**.
   9. **F DAWSON**.
     10. **M DAWSON**.

8. **Peter Goodhugh DAWSON** (1923-2007). Born: 26 Dec 1923, Holywell, Flintshire. Marr: Margaret Snowdon STEWART 1 Jan 1948, Swanage Methodist Church. Died: 5 Oct 2007, Castle Hill Hospital, Cottingham, East Yorkshire.
= Margaret Snowdon STEWART (1924-1999), dau. of James STEWART (1893-1935) and Margaret Winifred WHITEHEAD (1899-1969). Born: 20 Apr 1924, Edgbaston. Died: 29 Oct 1999, Dove House Hospice, Chamberlain Road, Kingston upon Hull.
   9. **M DAWSON**.
   = F CORNISH
   9. **M DAWSON**.
   = F WILSON, dau. of Percy Everett CAMPBELL (1926-1994).
     10. **M DAWSON**.
     10. **F DAWSON**.
     = M PETTY (-).
       11. **F PETTY**.
       11. **M PETTY**.

8. **F DAWSON**.
= Arthur Stanley LE RUEZ (1929-2021).
   9. **F LE RUEZ**.
   = M UPTON.
   9. **F LE RUEZ**.
   = M MCCRUDDEN.
     10. **F MCCRUDDEN**.

10. **F MCCRUDDEN**.

10. **M MCCRUDDEN**.

   = Norah Anne Marjory DYKE (1889-c. 1974). Born: 14 Mar 1889. Died: c. Jul 1974.

7. **Leonard Goodhugh DAWSON** (1887-). Born: 21 Apr 1887. Marr: Freda HOLLIS c. 1912.

   = Freda HOLLIS (-), dau. of Charles T. HOLLIS (-) and Jennie CHEESEBROUGH (1857-).

    8. **Richard Leonard Goodhugh DAWSON** (1916-1992). Born: 24 Aug 1916. Died: 21 Jun 1992.

      = Betty Marie FREEMAN-MATHEWS.

        9. **M DAWSON**.

        9. **M DAWSON**.

    8. **Ruth DAWSON**.

      = Ilay MARTIN.

        9. **M MARTIN**.

    8. **Molly DAWSON**.

      = Hugh MARTIN.

        9. **F MARTIN**.

        9. **M MARTIN**.

        9. **M MARTIN**.

6. **Frederick Groombridge DAWSON** (1847-1932). Born: 21 Nov 1847, Alnwick, Northumberland. Marr: Emily Willson BULEY c. Nov 1872. Marr: Eleanor Jane ELTON c. May 1901, Peterborough Registration District. Died: 17 Dec 1932.

   = Emily Willson BULEY (1850-1895), dau. of Amos BULEY (1816-1894) and Maria MACPHERSON (1817-bef1894). Born: 18 Jan 1850, Gravesend, Kent. Died: 10 Dec 1895.

    7. **Frederick Groombridge DAWSON** (c. 1873-c. 1873). Born: c. Feb 1873. Died: c. May 1873.

    7. **Arthur Buley DAWSON** (1874-). Born: 20 Jun 1874, Holloway, Middlesex. Bap: 29 Mar 1875, by Rev. John Wesley Dawson.

      = Marjory Maud READ (1876-). Born: 1876, Gravesend.

        8. **Ralph Buley DAWSON** (1905-). Born: 4 Feb 1905.

        8. **Mollie DAWSON** (1908-). Born: 1908.

    7. **Frank DAWSON** (1877-). Born: 3 Feb 1877, London. Bap: 6 Aug 1877, In a private house.

    7. **Harold Groombridge DAWSON** (1878-1950). Born: 14 Sep 1878, Hackney, Middlesex. Died: 7 Oct 1950.

   = Amy Gertrude ESLICK (1880-1963), dau. of ESLICK (-). Born: 2 Aug 1880, Bangalore, India. Died: 15 May 1963.

8. **Cyril Groombridge DAWSON** (1907-1978). Born: 19 Jan 1907. Marr: Muriel Gertrude MUNNS 15 Aug 1931. Died: 18 Mar 1978.
= Muriel Gertrude MUNNS (1907-1979), dau. of Walter John MUNNS (1870-1950) and Nellie Gertrude HOLLINGHAM (1874-1946). Born: 3 Jan 1907. Died: 10 Nov 1979.
    9. **M DAWSON**.
    = F JEARY.
        10. **M DAWSON**.
        10. **F DAWSON**.
        = M MITCHELL.
            11. **M MITCHELL**.
            11. **M MITCHELL**.
    9. **F DAWSON**.
    = M OSTIME.
        10. **M OSTIME**.
        = F NILI.
        10. **F OSTIME**.
        = M WOOD.

8. **Alan Buley DAWSON** (1916-1998). Born: 8 Jun 1916, Gravesend, Kent. Died: 6 May 1998, Blackwater, Surrey.
= Yvonne Margaret BALCAM, dau. of Henry Charles BALCAM (-1957) and Ellen Mathilda EARL (-1957). Born: 9 Dec 1925, Hastings, Sussex.
    9. **F DAWSON**.
    9. **M DAWSON**.

7. **Emily Ethel DAWSON** (1880-). Born: 26 Sep 1880, Hackney, Middlesex. Bap: 16 Oct 1880, At a private house, London, by Rev. John Wesley Dawson.
= Arthur John LODGE (1878-1975). Born: 30 Jul 1878. Died: 19 Mar 1975.
    8. **Donald Arthur LODGE** (1906-2002). Born: 24 Jul 1906. Died: 24 May 2002, Tadworth, Surrey.
    = Beatrice Lucy Rosemary SPENCER (-).
        9. **M LODGE**.
        = F ANSELL.

10. **F LODGE.**
= M STILL.
    11. **M STILL.**
        10. **F LODGE.** (1881-). Born: 1881.

7. **Alec DAWSON** (1881-). Born: 1881.
7. **Elsie Rachel DAWSON** (1882-1883). Born: 5 Jun 1882, Gravesend, Kent. Bap: 18 Oct 1882. At a private house, Gravesend, by Rev. John Wesley Dawson. Died: 29 Jan 1883.
7. **Maria Nelly DAWSON** (1886-). Born: 15 Jan 1886, Gravesend, Kent.
7. **Stanley Edward DAWSON** (1888-1888). Born: Mar 1888. Died: 15 Aug 1888.
7. **Howard MacKenzie DAWSON** (1890-1965). Born: 10 Apr 1890, Gravesend, Kent. Marr: Norah Lucy MANN 29 Nov 1924. Died: 25 Jun 1965.
= Norah Lucy MANN (1892-1985). Born: 22 May 1892. Died: 5 Jun 1985.
    8. **F DAWSON.**
    = Eleanor Jane ELTON (1872-1948), dau. of John Pratt ELTON (-). Born: 8 Jun 1872. Died: 30 Jun 1948.
7. **Kathleen Edith DAWSON** (1902-1981). Born: 19 Sep 1902. Died: 14 Jan 1981.
= Eric COLEBY (1889-). Born: 12 May 1889.
    8. **F COLEBY.**
    = M HUDSON (-).
        9. **M HUDSON.**
        9. **F HUDSON.**
        = M NORDIN, son of NORDIN (-).
    8. **F COLEBY.**
    = M GOLDSMITH.
    8. **M COLEBY.**
    = F WOOLHEAD.
        9. **F COLEBY.**
        9. **F COLEBY.**
7. **Gladys Eleanor DAWSON** (1905-1987). Born: 21 Jun 1905. Died: 24 Aug 1987.
= John Selwyn DUNN (1895-1978). Born: 17 Mar 1895. Died: 11 Dec 1978.
7. **Alec Elton DAWSON** (1909-1918). Born: 31 Jul 1909. Died: 9 May 1918.
6. **Florence DAWSON** (1848-). Born: 1848.

6. **Richard Goodhugh DAWSON** (1849-1916). Born: 1849, Tenterden, Kent. Marr: Maria BALLARD c. Aug 1878, Chichester, Sussex. Marr: Sarah MOORE c. Aug 1886, West Ham, Essex. Died: 21 Nov 1916, Swanage, Dorset.

= Maria BALLARD (c. 1846-c. 1883). Born: c. 1846, Chichester, Sussex. Died: c. 1883.

   7. **Ruth Croswellen DAWSON** (1881-). Born: 12 Mar 1881, Maidstone, Kent. Died: c. Aug 1972, Weston super Mare, Somerset.

      8. **DAWSON.**

   7. **Richard DAWSON** (1882-). Born: 1882.

   7. **Maria Ballard DAWSON** (1882-). Born: 31 May 1882, Maidstone, Kent. Died: c. May 1968, Bournemouth, Dorset

   = Oliver MARSH (-).

   7. **Adolphus William DAWSON** (c. 1883-1883). Born: c. May 1883. Died: 2 Sep 1883.

   = Sarah MOORE (c. 1838-). Born: c. 1838, St. George's, Middlesex.

   7. **DAWSON** (-).

   7. **DAWSON** (-).

6. **Annie Goodhugh DAWSON** (c. 1850-). Born: c. Aug 1850, Tenterden, Kent.

6. **Benjamin DAWSON** (1851-c. 1899). Born: 16 Sep 1851, Tenterden, Kent. Died: c. Feb 1899, Wellington, Shropshire.

= Edith (-).

6. **Arthur James DAWSON** (1853-). Born: 1853, Dover, Kent.

= Hannie (-).

   7. **Florence DAWSON** (-).

   7. **Edith DAWSON** (-).

      8. **DAWSON** * (-).

   7. **Lilian Proctor DAWSON** (1877-). Born: 14 Dec 1877.

   7. **Arthur James DAWSON** (-).

6. **Samuel Wesley DAWSON** (1854-1933). Born: 10 Dec 1854, Wimbourne, Dorset. Marr: Isabella BIGG c. Nov 1879, Milton Registration District, Kent. Died: 30 Dec 1933.

= Isabella BIGG (c. 1855-). Born: c. 1855, Sittingbourne, Kent.

5. **Mary Anne DAWSON** (1818-1877). Born: 28 Apr 1818, Faversham, Kent. Bap: 17 Jun 1818, Wesleyan Chapel, Faversham, Kent. Marr: John Lever SMITH 9 Dec 1841, St Mary of Charity, Faversham, Kent. Died: 12 Dec 1877, Yorkville, Wisconsin. Buried: Union Grove Cemetery, Yorkville, Wisconsin.

= John Lever SMITH (1815-1864), son of John SMITH (1777-1858) and Elizabeth LEVER (1789-1873). Born: 30 Nov 1815,

99

Faversham, Kent. Bap: St. Mary of Charity, Faversham, Kent. Died: 26 Sep 1864, Yorkville, Wisconsin. Buried: Union Grove Cemetery, Racine County, Wisconsin.

6. **John Dawson SMITH** (1842-1920). Born: 29 Sep 1842, Boughton, Kent. Marr: Lucy Hannah BACKHUS 2 Oct 1868, Union Grove, Wisconsin, USA. Marr: Elizabeth CARTER 19 Mar 1879, Osage, Iowa. Marr: Frances Louise FRENCH 19 May 1897. Died: 24 Jun 1920, Austin, Minnesota. Buried: Oak Grove Cemetery, Mitchell, Iowa.
= Lucy Hannah BACKHUS (1847-1877), dau. of John BACKHUS (-) and Olivia Harriet LOCKWOOD (-). Born: 2 Oct 1847, Yorkville, Wisconsin. Bap: 14 Sep 1858, Yorkville United Methodist Church. Died: 6 Oct 1877, Mitchell, Iowa. Buried: Oak Grove Cemetery, Mitchell, Iowa.

7. **Clifford Henry SMITH** (1869-1939). Born: 25 Nov 1869, Union Grove, Wisconsin. Marr: Ethel Constance ECCLESTON 3 Sep 1894, Ethel's home, Austin, Minnesota. Died: 15 Jul 1939, St. Lucas Hospital, Faribault, Minnesota. Buried: Oak Ridge Cemetery, Faribault, Minnesota.
= Ethel Constance ECCLESTON (1866-1949). Born: 13 Sep 1866, Kankakee, Illinois. Died: 1 Oct 1949, St. Lucas Hospital, Faribault, Minnesota. Buried: Oak Ridge Cemetery, Faribault, Minnesota.

8. **Maurice Clifford SMITH** (1895-1972). Born: 8 Jun 1895, Carver, Minnesota. Marr: Alma Josephine Ethelyn LUNDSTOM 26 Jun 1922, Minneapolis, Minnesota. Died: 15 Mar 1972, Minneapolis, Minnesota. Buried: Sunset Memorial Park, Minneapolis, Minnesota.
= Alma Josephine Ethelyn LUNDSTOM (-).

9. **Kenneth Maurice SMITH** (1927-1978). Born: 20 Feb 1927, Minneapolis, Minnesota. Died: 17 Sep 1978, Minneapolis, Minnesota.
= F.

10. **F SMITH**.
= M JANIKOWSKI.
11. **M JANIKOWSKI**.
11. **M JANIKOWSKI**.

10. **Robert SMITH** (1951-1953). Born: 14 May 1951, Minneapolis, Minnesota. Died: 9 Feb 1953, Minneapolis, Minnesota.

8. **Lucy Constance SMITH** (1896-1960). Born: 22 Nov 1896, Carver, Minnesota. Marr: John Paul CHAPMAN 29 Jan 1916, Faribault, Minnesota. Died: 27 Nov 1960, Rochester, Minnesota. Buried: Grandview Gardens Cemetery, Rochester, Minnesota.
= John Paul CHAPMAN (-).

9. **F CHAPMAN**.
= M NIETULA.
= M L SWIFT.
  10. **F SWIFT** (-).
  = M HICKS (-).
    11. **F HICKS**.
    = M JONES (-).
      12. **M JONES**.
      12. **F JONES**.
    11. **M HICKS**.
    = F HARRELL (-).
      12. **M HICKS**.
      = NIETULA (-).

9. **M CHAPMAN**.
9. **F CHAPMAN**.
9. **F CHAPMAN**.
9. **F CHAPMAN**.
9. **M CHAPMAN**.
9. **M CHAPMAN**.
9. **F CHAPMAN**.

8. **Allegra Winifred SMITH** (1901-1982). Born: 4 Dec 1901, Woodlake, Minnesota. Died: 25 Feb 1982. Buried: Columbus, Indiana.
= Joseph Luell COOK.
  9. **M COOK**.
  = [unnamed person].
    10. **COOK**.
    = [unnamed person].
  9. **F COOK**.
  9. **M COOK**.
  = F.
    10. **M COOK**.

10. **F COOK**.

10. **M COOK**.

8. **Dorene Hazel SMITH**.

= Melville HOOVER.

7. **Howard Allison SMITH** (1871-1960). Born: 8 Oct 1871, Union Grove, Wisconsin, USA. Marr: Lenore HEWITT 24 Nov 1904. Died: 1960.

= Lenore HEWITT (-).

7. **Arthur Ellison SMITH** (1873-1965). Born: 26 Oct 1873, Union Grove, Wisconsin, USA. Marr: Mabel DICKINSON 4 Nov 1903. Died: 1965.

= Mabel DICKINSON (-).

7. **Stella May SMITH** (1876-1878). Born: 30 Nov 1876, Iowa. Died: 11 Jan 1878, Mitchell, Iowa. Buried: Oak Grove Cemetery, Mitchell, Iowa.

= Elizabeth CARTER (1853-1889). Born: 10 Jul 1853. Died: 28 Feb 1889, Mitchell, Iowa. Buried: Oak Grove Cemetery, Mitchell, Iowa.

= Frances Louise FRENCH (1859-1932). dau. of John FRENCH (-) and Mary (-). Born: 18 Mar 1859, Onieda County, New York. Died: 30 Mar 1932, Austin, Minnesota. Buried: Oakwood Cemetery, Austin, Minnesota.

7. **Mary Aileen SMITH** (1901-). Born: 7 Sep 1901, Austin, Minnesota.

= Clarence LARSON (-).

6. **Mary Anne SMITH** (1844-1904). Born: 2 Jul 1844, Boughton, Kent. Marr: John WILKINSON 13 Sep 1866. Died: 26 Jan 1904. At home, Milford, Iowa. Buried: 30 Jan 1904, Milford Cemetery, Wisconsin.

= John WILKINSON (-1887). Died: 1887.

7. **Luella Eliza WILKINSON** (1867-). Born: 4 Jul 1867. Marr: William L. G. WILKINSON 3 Sep 1888.

= William L. G. WILKINSON (-).

7. **Edith Mary WILKINSON** (1873-). Born: 5 Jul 1873. Marr: George P. WOODS 7 Dec 1899.

= George P. WOODS (-).

7. **Laurence John WILKINSON** (1877-). Born: 12 Feb 1877. Marr: Ann E. MILLER 24 Feb 1907.

= Ann E. MILLER (-).

7. **WILKINSON** (-c. 1902). Died: c. 1902.

= FITCH (-).

6. **Helen Elizabeth SMITH** (1845-1898). Born: 28 Dec 1845, Boughton, Kent. Marr: James H. JONES 3 Oct 1872. Died: 26 Aug 1898.

= James H. JONES (-aft1898). Died: aft Aug 1898.

7. **Walter Henry JONES** (1873-). Born: 16 Dec 1873. Marr: Esabel BURNSIDE 10 Jun 1905.

= Esabel BURNSIDE (-).

8. **Margaret Elizabeth JONES** (1906-). Born: 26 Jun 1906.

7. **Ernest Stephen JONES** (1877-). Born: 8 Jul 1877.

7. **Sarah Grace JONES** (1882-). Born: 18 Aug 1882.

6. **William Goodhugh SMITH** (1847-1922). Born: 15 Apr 1847, Boughton, Kent. Marr: Eleanor May STOCK 14 Nov 1877. Died: 1922.

= Eleanor May STOCK (-).

7. **Elmo Vincent SMITH** (1879-). Born: 16 Jan 1879. Marr: Palma HARTIS 28 Dec 1904.

= Palma HARTIS (-).

8. **William B. SMITH** (1907-). Born: 12 Dec 1907.

= Althis CLARK (-).

7. **Exine Mary SMITH** (1883-). Born: 2 Jan 1883. Marr: Clarence Everett DRAKE 10 Jun 1908, Mitchell, Iowa, USA.

= Clarence Everett DRAKE (-), son of Everett E DRAKE (-) and Emma KNOULTON (-). Born:

8. **Everett Almos DRAKE** (1909-). Born: 20 Mar 1909. Marr: Ruth E. DICKSON 25 May 1935.

= Ruth E. DICKSON (1910-2004), Born: 25 Jan 1910. Died: 4 May 2004. Buried: 10 May 2004.

9. **F DRAKE**.

= M HORTON.

10. **F HORTON**.

= M COLLINS.

11. **F COLLINS**.

10. **M HORTON**.

= F PAULIS.

11. **F HORTON**.

10. **F HORTON**.

= M MOESLEIN.

11. **M MOESLEIN**.

10. **M HORTON**.

9. **M DRAKE**.
= F CHENG.
10. **M DRAKE**.
= F MCLAUGHLIN (-).
11. **M DRAKE-MCLAUGHLIN**.
11. **M DRAKE-MCLAUGHLIN**.
6. **Walter Thomas SMITH** (1848-1925). Born: 1 Nov 1848, Boughton, Kent. Marr: Cynthia Ann CHAPPELL 1 Jan 1874. Died: 8 Jan 1925, Hartley Hospital, Battle Creek, Iowa.
= Cynthia Ann CHAPPELL (-).
7. **Aida May SMITH** (1875-). Born: 6 Apr 1875.
7. **Alfred Burton SMITH** (1877-1953). Born: 18 Feb 1877, Battle Creek, Iowa. Marr: Flora BURKHARDT 28 May 1904. Died: 1 Oct 1953, Battle Creek, Iowa.
= Flora BURKHARDT (-).
8. **Walter B. SMITH** (1905-1908). Born: 19 Apr 1905. Died: 28 Aug 1908.
8. **Florence Dawson SMITH** (1907-). Born: 18 Dec 1907.
= SIFFERD (-).
6. **Alfred Dawson SMITH** (1850-1936). Born: 29 Jan 1850, Boughton, Kent. Marr: Ida A. CHAMBERS 12 Jan 1882, Mitchell, Iowa. Died: 23 Feb 1936, at home, 817 Nicholas Street, Fulton, Missouri. Buried: Mitchell, Iowa.
= Ida A. CHAMBERS (-1931). Died: 1 Oct 1931. Buried: Mitchell, Iowa.
7. **Harriet Olive SMITH** (-). Marr: Raymond SCHAFFER 1 Sep 1935.
= Raymond SCHAFFER (-).
6. **Lever Charles SMITH** (1851-1864). Born: 10 Oct 1851, Boughton, Kent. Died: 26 Sep 1864.
6. **Sarah Dawson SMITH** (1854-aft1916). Born: 14 Feb 1854, Boughton, Kent. Marr: William Henry HELMS 14 Mar 1884. Died: aft Jul 1916.
= William Henry HELMS (-).
7. **Lillian Annanora HELMS** (1888-). Born: Jun 1888. Marr: George Francis TAYLOR, Jnr. 31 Jul 1917.
= George Francis TAYLOR, Jnr. (-).
8. **F TAYLOR**.
= M GOSHORN.
9. **M GOSHORN** (1943-1991). Born: 1943. Died: 1991, Washington DC, USA.
= F CARRIER.

10. **F GOSHORN.**
= M CLARKSON.
   11. **M CLARKSON.**
   11. **M CLARKSON.**
   11. **F CLARKSON.**
   11. **M CLARKSON.**
10. **F GOSHORN.**
   11. **F.**

9. **F GOSHORN.**
= M FRUCTER.
   10. **M FRUCTER** (-1992), Died: 1992.

8. **F TAYLOR.**

6. **Mary Jane SMITH** (1855-1902). Born: 21 Nov 1855, Boughton, Kent. Marr: Clarence Augustus OSBORNE 5 Apr 1883, Minneapolis, Minnesota, USA. Died: 1902, Bancroft, Cuming County, Nebraska, USA. Buried: Bancroft Cemetery.
= Clarence Augustus OSBORNE (1852-1936). Born: 26 May 1852, Cattaragus, New York, USA. Marr: Edith HUDSON 25 Nov 1913, Eureka, California, USA. Died: 25 Aug 1936, Canon City, Colorado, USA.

7. **Ella Mildred OSBORNE** (1884-1977). Born: 8 Feb 1884, Milford, Dickenson County, Iowa, USA. Marr: William Lourie JACOBS c. 1903. Died: 17 Jan 1977, Omaha, Douglas County, Nebraska, USA. Buried: 20 Jan 1977, Evergreen Cemetery, Omaha, Douglas County, Nebraska, USA.
= William Lourie JACOBS (1879-1943). Born: 26 Apr 1879, Champion, Marquette County, Michigan, USA. Died: 19 May 1943.

8. **Florence Lourie JACOBS** (1905-1985). Born: 6 May 1905, Bancroft, Cuming County, Nebraska, USA. Marr: Theodore E CARLSON c. 1924, Council Bluffs, Pottawattamie County, Iowa, USA. Died: 15 Mar 1985, Omaha, Douglas County, Nebraska, USA. Buried: Mar 1985, Evergreen Cemetery, Omaha, Douglas County, Nebraska, USA.
= Theodore E CARLSON (1900-1976). Born: 2 Oct 1900, Oakland, Burt County, Nebraska, USA. Died: 31 Oct 1976, Omaha, Douglas County, Nebraska, USA.

9. **Richard James CARLSON** (1925-1997). Born: 9 Mar 1925, Omaha, Douglas County, Nebraska, USA. Marr: Elizabeth WISELISEN 11 Aug 1951, Blair, Washington County, Nebraska, USA. Died: 9 Dec 1997, Rogers, Arkansas, USA. Buried: Cremated and buried by his mother in Evergreen Cemetery, Omaha, Douglas County, Nebraska, USA.

= Elizabeth WISELISEN (1918-1998). Born: 8 Nov 1918. Died: 8 Aug 1998, Rogers, Arkansas, USA. Buried: cremated and buried by her husband in Evergreen Cemetery, Omaha, Douglas County, Nebraska, USA.

8. **James Lourie JACOBS** (1907-1985). Born: 4 Jan 1907, Bancroft, Cuming County, Nebraska, USA. Marr: Helen SANKO 5 May 1932. Died: 17 Jul 1985, Elkhorn, Douglas County, Nebraska, USA. Buried: Cremated and buried with spouse at a later date.

= Helen SANKO (1912-1997). Born: 18 Feb 1912, Omaha, Douglas County, Nebraska, USA. Died: 12 Jun 1997, Omaha, Douglas County, Nebraska, USA. Buried: 14 Jun 1997, Prospect Hill Cemetery, Elkhorn, Douglas County, Nebraska, USA.

    9. **F JACOBS**.
    = M GOTTSCH.
        10. **M GOTTSCH**.
        10. **M GOTTSCH**.
        10. **Jerry Jeffrey GOTTSCH**.

7. **Morton Henry OSBORNE** (1885-). Born: 1 Aug 1885, Milford, Dickenson County, Iowa, USA. Buried: Montana.
= Georgia MAUN (-).
    8. **Lawrence OSBORNE**.

7. **Emily Lucille OSBORNE** (1890-1974). Born: 3 Jan 1890, Milford, Dickenson County, Iowa, USA. Died: Nov 1974, Detroit, Michigan, USA. Buried: Michigan, USA.
= [unnamed person] (-).
    8. **[unnamed person]** (-).
    = Robert HERTEN (-). Born: South Dakota, USA. Died: Detroit, Michigan, USA.
    8. **Roland HERTEN** (1910-1996). Born: 29 Aug 1910, Presho, Lyman County, South Dakota, USA. Died: 15 Oct 1996, Titusville, Florida, USA.
    8. **Ruth Elizabeth HERTEN**.
    = Kermit Otto LAGMAN (-).
        9. **LAGMAN** (-).
        = [unnamed person] (-).
        9. **LAGMAN** (-).
        9. **LAGMAN** (-).
    8. **Beryl HERTEN** (1919-1968). Born: 14 Mar 1919. Died: 31 May 1968, Detroit, Michigan, USA.

8. **Phyllis HERTEN** (1925-c. 2002). Born: 9 Apr 1925. Died: c. 2002, Detroit, Michigan, USA.

8. **Clara Augusta OSBORNE** (1893-). Born: 10 Feb 1893, Flandreau, Moody County, South Dakota, USA.
= Floyd CORKILL (-).
   8. **M CORKILL**.
   8. **F CORKILL**.

7. **Russell S OSBORNE** (1897-1972). Born: 1 May 1897, Flandreau, Moody County, South Dakota, USA. Died: 27 Jun 1972, Greenville, Michigan, USA.
= Lucille (-1976). Died: Mar 1976.

6. **Susannah Dawson SMITH** (1859-1916). Born: 20 Feb 1859, Yorkville, Racine County, Wisconsin. Marr: Fred B. SHANCKS 30 Sep 1879, West Mitchell, Iowa. Died: 4 Jul 1916, Red Oak, Iowa. Buried: 6 Jul 1916, Mitchell, Iowa.
= Fred B. SHANCKS (-1916). Died: 4 Jul 1916, 924 Highland Avenue, Red Oak, Iowa.
   7. **Naomi Dorothy SHANCKS** (-aft1916). Died: aft Jul 1916.
   7. **Courtland W. SHANCKS** (-aft1916). Died: aft Jul 1916.
   7. **Ellsworth SHANCKS** (-).

5. **Alfred DAWSON** (1820-c. 1821). Born: 1820, Faversham, Kent. Died: c. Oct 1821, Faversham, Kent. Buried: 24 Oct 1821, Faversham churchyard, Kent.

5. **Elizabeth Dixon DAWSON** (1821-c. 1897). Born: 13 Oct 1821, Faversham, Kent. Bap: 4 Dec 1821, Wesleyan Chapel, Faversham, Kent. Marr: John STICKALS 8 Oct 1842. Marr: George WHITE c. Feb 1856, Islington, Middlesex. Died: c. May 1897, Winchester, Hampshire.
= John STICKALS (c. 1819-), son of Henry STICKALS (-) and [unnamed person] (-). Born: c. 1819, Kent.
= George WHITE (-).

5. **Susanna DAWSON** (1823-). Born: 8 Aug 1823, Faversham, Kent. Bap: 28 Sep 1823, Wesleyan Chapel, Faversham, Kent.

5. **Ann Staines DAWSON** (1825-1915). Born: 6 Jun 1825, Faversham, Kent. Bap: 23 Feb 1826, Wesleyan Chapel, Faversham, Kent. Marr: John JONES May 1846, Faversham, Kent. Died: 1915, Winchester, Hampshire.
= John JONES (c. 1820-c. 1904), son of John JONES (1777-) and HOWARD (-). Born: c. 1820, Faversham, Kent.[10] Died: c. May 1904.
   6. **John Dawson JONES** (c. 1848-). Born: c. May 1848. Died:
   6. **Annie JONES** (c. 1850-1926). Born: c. May 1850, Winchester, Hampshire. Died: 1926.
   = Joseph CLARK (-).
      7. **Annie Staines CLARK** (-).
      = Alfred Liddington JACKSON (-).

7. **Elsie Mary CLARK** (1883-). Born: 23 May 1883. Marr: John Edward DIXON-SPAIN ,
FRIBA 23 Aug 1905, St Oswald, Rand, Lincolnshire.
= John Edward DIXON-SPAIN, FRIBA (1878-1955), son of Thomas DIXON-SPAIN (-). Born: 1878, Long Sutton,
Lincolnshire. Died: 7 May 1955, Graveley, Hertfordshire.
    8. **Mary Monica DIXON-SPAIN** (c. 1908-). Born: c. May 1908, Hendon.
    8. **Barbara J. DIXON-SPAIN** (1913-). Born: 7 Oct 1913.
    8. **Mary Beatrice DIXON-SPAIN** (1916-). Born: 11 May 1916.
7. **Wilfred CLARK** (-).
= Sydney (-).
    8. **Rosemary CLARK** (-).
7. **Margaret CLARK** (-).
= Alan DRUMMOND (-).

6. **Arthur JONES** (c. 1852-). Born: c. May 1852, Winchester, Hampshire.
7. **Flossie JONES** (-).
    8. **JONES** (-).
7. **Edith JONES** (-).
    8. **JONES** (-).

6. **Sarah JONES** (c. 1855-). Born: c. 1855, Winchester, Hampshire. Marr: Arthur BROWN c. Feb 1880, Winchester,
Hampshire.
= Arthur BROWN (c. 1856-). Born: c. 1856, Winchester, Hampshire.
7. **Mary BROWN** (-).
= DOWDEN (-).
    8. **DOWDEN** (-).
7. **Winnie BROWN** (-).
    8. **BROWN** (-).
    8. **BROWN** (-).
7. **Bernard BROWN** (-).
    8. **BROWN** (-).
7. **Effie BROWN** (-).
7. **Theo BROWN** (-).

6. **Ernest JONES** (c. 1856-). Born: c. 1856, Winchester, Hampshire.

7. **JONES** (-).
7. **Kate JONES** (-).
7. **Ted JONES** (-).
6. **Eliza JONES** (c. 1859-). Born: c. May 1859, Winchester, Hampshire.
= Fred SEYMOUR (-).
7. **Nellie SEYMOUR** (-).
= H. CLARK (-).
7. **Frank SEYMOUR** (-).
8. **SEYMOUR** (-).
7. **Percy SEYMOUR** (-).
6. **Alice Rebekah JONES** (1860-). Born: 12 Jan 1860, Eastgate Street, Winchester, Hampshire. Marr: William Talbot NEWMAN 6 Oct 1880, Wesleyan Chapel, Winchester, Hampshire.
= William Talbot NEWMAN (-).
7. **Annie Eliza NEWMAN** (c. 1881-). Born: c. Nov 1881, Wandsworth, Middlesex.
7. **Ernest Talbot NEWMAN** (-).
= Isobel (-).
7. **Dora Helen NEWMAN** (c. 1884-). Born: c. Nov 1884, Wandsworth, Middlesex.
7. **Olive Gwendoline NEWMAN** (-).
= Josiah Birkett SWAIN (-).
8. **John Goodhugh SWAIN** (1920-1943). Born: 1920. Died: 26 Feb 1943.
7. **Hilda Mary NEWMAN** (-).
= James BISHOP (-).
8. **Margaret BISHOP** (-).
7. **Arthur Cecil NEWMAN** (c. 1890-1917). Born: c. Aug 1890, Wandsworth, Middlesex. Died: 20 Sep 1917, Ypres, Belgium.
7. **Harold Winton NEWMAN** (c. 1892-). Born: c. May 1892, Wandsworth, Middlesex.
= Dolly POLKINGHORNE (-).
8. **Francis T. NEWMAN**.
= Dorothy (-).
8. **Phyllis NEWMAN**.
8. **Paul NEWMAN**.

7. **William Edwin NEWMAN** (1895-1975). Born: 5 Mar 1895. Died: Sep 1975.
= Violet Louise WILLMOTT (1894-1966). Born: 23 Sep 1894. Died: Feb 1966.
   8. **June Louise NEWMAN** (1920-2005). Born: 28 Mar 1920. Marr: William Alfred WILTSHIRE 3 Sep 1950,
     Chorleywood, Hertfordshire. Died: 29 Jan 2005.
   = William Alfred WILTSHIRE (1923-1995). Born: 16 Jun 1923. Died: 2 Dec 1995.
      9. **F WILTSHIRE**.
      = M BOWN.
         10. **M BOWN**.
            11. **M BOWN**.
         10. **M BOWN**.
      9. **M WILTSHIRE**.
      9. **F WILTSHIRE**.
      = M JENKINS.
         10. **F JENKINS**.
         10. **M JENKINS**.
   8. **F NEWMAN**.
   = M KELYNACK.
   8. **M** (-1931). Died: 1931.
   8. **M NEWMAN**.
   = F BRENTNALL.
      9. **M NEWMAN**.
      = F MARRIOTT.
         10. **M NEWMAN**.
         10. **F NEWMAN**.
      9. **M NEWMAN**.
      = F OLIVER.
         10. **M NEWMAN**.
         10. **F NEWMAN**.
      9. **M NEWMAN**.
      9. **M NEWMAN**.
      = F GIBBONS.

10. **M NEWMAN**.
10. **M NEWMAN**.
10. **F NEWMAN**.

7. **Irene NEWMAN** (-).
= Charles HALL (-).
8. **F HALL** (-).
8. **F HALL** (-).

7. **Margery NEWMAN** (-).

6. **Henry William JONES** (c. 1862-c. 1947). Born: c. Feb 1862, Winchester, Hampshire. Marr: Ellen NEVILLE c. Feb 1888, Lewisham. Died: c. 1947.
= Ellen NEVILLE (c. 1866-). Born: c. 1866, Onger, Essex.

7. **Alice JONES** (c. 1889-c. 1918). Born: c. 1889, Brentwood, Essex. Died: c. 1918.

7. **Annette JONES** (c. 1891-c. 1955) Born: c. 1891, Brentwood, Essex. Died: c. 1955.

7. **Henry Neville JONES** (c. 1895-). Born: c. May 1895, Camberwell, Surrey.
8. **M JONES**.
= F (-).
9. **F JONES**.
10. **F**
10. **M**
10. **[unnamed person]**.
10. **[unnamed person]**.
9. **M JONES**.
9. **M JONES**.
9. **F JONES**.
9. **F JONES**.

7. **John Dawson JONES** (1897-1971). Born: 4 Apr 1897. Marr: Audrey Ada Maud NEWTON 20 Jun 1926. Died: 29 Jul 1971.
= Audrey Ada Maud NEWTON (c. 1904-). Born: c. Aug 1904, London.
8. **F JONES**.
= M JAMES.

111

9. **F JAMES.**
= M GRIFFITHS.
9. **M JAMES.**
= F.
    10. **M JAMES.**
    10. **F JAMES.**
    10. **M JAMES.**
9. **M JAMES.**
= F
    10. **F JAMES.**
    10. **M JAMES.**
    10. **F JAMES.**
    = M STRAIGHT.
9. **F STRAIGHT.**
= M HOBBS.
    10. **F HOBBS.**
    10. **M HOBBS.**
    10. **F HOBBS.**
    10. **M HOBBS.**
8. **F JONES.**
= [unnamed person].
= [unnamed person].
= [unnamed person].
8. **M DAWSON-JONES.**
= F MANN.
9. **F DAWSON-JONES.**
9. **M DAWSON-JONES.**
= F BRAMMAR.
    10. **M DAWSON-JONES.**
9. **M DAWSON-JONES.**
= F MAPP.

10. **M DAWSON-JONES.**
10. **F DAWSON-JONES.**
9. **F DAWSON-JONES.**
9. **F DAWSON-JONES.**
= M SPILLER.
10. **F SPILLER.**
7. **Stanley Howard JONES** (c. 1899-1918). Born: c. Feb 1899, Camberwell, Surrey. Died: 21 Mar 1918, Arras, France.
7. **Gilbert Arthur JONES** (c. 1903-1907). Born: c. May 1903, Bromley, Kent. Died: 1907.
7. **Ernest Ronald JONES** (-).
7. **Philip Leonard JONES** (-to1960). Died: frm 1950 to 1960.
= Kathleen SNELL (-2004). Died: 2004.
8. **M JONES.**
= F.
9. **F JONES.**
10. **[unnamed person].**
10. **[unnamed person].**
10. **[unnamed person].**
9. **M JONES.**
9. **F JONES.**
6. **Helen JONES** (c. 1864-). Born: c. Aug 1864, Winchester, Hampshire.
= M. GILBERT (-).
7. **Marion GILBERT** (-).
7. **Donald GILBERT** (-).
7. **Seymour GILBERT** (-).
6. **Florence L. JONES** (c. 1866-). Born: c. Feb 1866, Winchester, Hampshire.
= A. COLES (-).
7. **COLES** (-).
7. **COLES** (-).
7. **COLES** (-).

6. **Emily Dawson JONES** (c. 1868-). Born: c. Feb 1868, Winchester, Hampshire. Marr: Stephen SMITH aft Sep 1902. Marr: PAYNE aft 7 Sep 1902.

= Stephen SMITH (1828-1906), son of John SMITH (1777-1858) and Elizabeth LEVER (1789-1873). Born: 11 Oct 1828, Preston, Faversham, Kent. Bap: 7 Nov 1828, St. Mary of Charity, Faversham, Kent. Marr: Sarah DAWSON 2 Jun 1852, Boughton Chapel, Kent. Died: 12 Dec 1906, Winchester, Hampshire. Buried: Winchester.

= PAYNE (-).

5. **Sarah DAWSON** (1827-1902). Born: 17 Mar 1827, Faversham, Kent. Bap: 29 Apr 1827, Wesleyan Chapel, Faversham, Kent. Marr: Stephen SMITH 2 Jun 1852, Boughton Chapel, Kent. Died: 7 Sep 1902. Buried: River View cemetery, Oshkosh, Wisconsin.

= Stephen SMITH (1828-1906), son of John SMITH (1777-1858) and Elizabeth LEVER (1789-1873). Born: 11 Oct 1828, Preston, Faversham, Kent. Bap: 7 Nov 1828, St. Mary of Charity, Faversham, Kent. Marr: Emily Dawson JONES aft Sep 1902. Died: 12 Dec 1906, Winchester, Hampshire. Buried: Winchester.

6. **Annie Dawson SMITH** (1853-bef1855). Born: 1853. Died: bef 1855. Buried: Boughton chapel yard, Kent.

6. **Clara Elizabeth SMITH** (1854-1858). Born: 1854, Boughton, Kent. Died: 1858, Elkhorn, Wisconsin.

6. **Ernest Stephen SMITH** (1856-1941). Born: 2 Jul 1856, Elk Grove, Illinois. Marr: Ida May VANDERPOOL 8 Oct 1879, Mitchell, Iowa. Marr: Luelia THOMPSON 6 Dec 1910, Little Rock, Arkansas. Died: 17 Jun 1941.

= Ida May VANDERPOOL (-).

7. **Emily Dawson SMITH** (1880-). Born: 20 Oct 1880, Mitchell, Iowa. Marr: Charles Robert PAYNE c. May 1910, Winchester, Hampshire.

= John S. VEGGENER (1876-). Born: 12 Nov 1876.

= Charles Robert PAYNE (-).

7. **Florence Gertrude SMITH** (1882-). Born: 2 Feb 1882.

7. **Marjorie Lucille SMITH** (1888-1945). Born: 18 Aug 1888. Marr: Clement MACMAHON 22 Jun 1910. Died: Jun 1945.

= Clement MACMAHON (1871-1930). Born: 24 Oct 1871. Died: Feb 1930.

    8. **Ida Jane MACMAHON.**

7. **Caroline May SMITH** (1894-). Born: 20 Dec 1894. Marr: Donald B. CAMPBELL 2 Nov 1918.

= Donald B. CAMPBELL (1898-). Born: Nov 1898.

    8. **Betsy May CAMPBELL.**

    8. **Bob CAMPBELL.**

= Luelia THOMPSON (1871-). Born: 25 May 1871.

6. **Clarence Dawson SMITH** (1859-1926). Born: 23 Jan 1859, Sharon, Wisconsin. Died: 1926.
= Georgia SANFORD (-).
   7. **Doris SANFORD** (-).
     = William HOSKINS (-).
6. **Arthur Charles SMITH** (1860-1907). Born: 25 Nov 1860, Sharon, Wisconsin. Marr: Martha WILBOR Oshkosh, Wisconsin. Died: 1907.
= Martha WILBOR (-).
   7. **Carlton Wilbor SMITH** (1890-). Born: 1890.
     = Jeanette HAWES (-).
       8. **Jane SMITH**. Born: 1916
         = James Dockray TUVERSON.
           9. **M TUVERSON.**
             = F BRUCE (-).
               10. **F TUVERSON.**
                 = SINCLAIR.
               10. **F TUVERSON.**
                 = DAGOSTIN.
               10. **M TUVERSON.**
                 = Kim (-).
               10. **M TUVERSON.**
           9. **M TUVERSON.**
             = F SKELTON, dau. of Obie Kirk SKELTON (-) and Bessie May WHITEHEAD (-).
               10. **F TUVERSON.**
                 = M WILEY.
                   11. **F SISCO.**
                     = M SISCO.
                   11. **M SISCO.**
               10. **M TUVERSON.**
                 = F ROSE.
                   11. **F TUVERSON.**
                   11. **F TUVERSON.**

9. **F TUVERSON.**
   = PERKINS (-).
8. **Shirley SMITH.**
   = Buzz KELCH.
   9. **M KELCH.**
8. **Frances SMITH.**
   = JUNK.
8. **Marilyn SMITH** (-).
   = GRAEF (-).
7. **Howard Lowell SMITH** (1892-1918). Born: 1892. Died: 1918, France.
7. **Dorothy Dawson SMITH** (1896-). Born: 1896.
   = Robert H ENNIS (-).
8. **Marcia ENNIS.**
   = John Bradford STEVENS, son of Evarts C. STEVENS (-).
   9. **M STEVENS.**
      = F RIESS.
         10. **F STEVENS.**
         10. **M STEVENS.**
            = Alexis Carol SIDORAK.
   9. **F STEVENS.**
      = M AKIN.
         10. **M STEVENS.**
   9. **M STEVENS.**
      = F CALHOUN.
         10. **M STEVENS.**
         10. **F STEVENS.**
   9. **F STEVENS.**
      = M WILSON.
         10. **M WILSON.**
         10. **M WILSON.**

116

7. **Marshall Henry SMITH** (1900-). Born: 1900. Marr: Charlotte PRADT Warsaw, Wisconsin.
= Charlotte PRADT (-).
    8. **F SMITH**.
    = [unnamed person].
        9. **M**.
    8. **M SMITH**.
    8. **M SMITH**.
5. **Eliza DAWSON** (1829-). Born: 10 Apr 1829, Faversham, Kent. Bap: 10 May 1829, Wesleyan Chapel, Faversham, Kent.
5. **Robert Staines DAWSON** (1831-). Born: 7 Jun 1831, Faversham, Kent. Bap: 6 May 1832, Wesleyan Chapel, Faversham, Kent.
5. **Rebecca DAWSON** (c. 1833-). Born: c. 1833, Faversham, Kent.
5. **Charles Wesley DAWSON** (1835-bef1891). Born: 24 Mar 1835, Faversham, Kent. Bap: 7 Jun 1835, Wesleyan Chapel, Faversham, Kent. Marr: Emily Elizabeth MURRELL c. Nov 1867, Winchester, Hampshire. Died: bef 1891.
= Emily Elizabeth MURRELL (c. 1843-). Born: c. 1843, London.
    6. **Charles G. DAWSON** (c. 1869-). Born: c. 1869, Sherborne, Dorset.
    6. **Emily Murrell DAWSON** (c. 1871-). Born: c. Aug 1871, Sherborne, Dorset.
    6. **Helen Mary DAWSON** (c. 1873-). Born: c. 1873, Sherborne, Dorset.
    6. **Annie Jones DAWSON** (c. 1874-). Born: c. Nov 1874, Sherborne, Dorset.
    6. **Herbert Frank DAWSON** (c. 1878-). Born: c. Feb 1878, Sherborne, Dorset.
5. **George DAWSON** (1837-c. 1838). Born: 11 Mar 1837, Faversham, Kent. Bap: 21 May 1837. Died: c. Mar 1838, Faversham, Kent. Buried: 28 Mar 1838, St. Mary of Charity, Faversham, Kent.
4. **Susanna DAWSON** (c. 1786-c. 1787). Born: c. Aug 1786. Bap: Died: c. Aug 1787. Buried: 2 Sep 1787, St. John the Baptist, Thanet, Kent.
4. **William DAWSON** (1790-1802). Born: 16 Apr 1790. Bap: 17 May 1790, St. Johns, Margate, Kent. Died: 19 Aug 1802, Margate, Kent.
2. **Jane DAWSON** (c. 1708-c. 1756). Born: c. 1708. Bap: 24 Jul 1708, St Laurence, Ramsgate, Kent. Died: c. Aug 1756. Buried: 7 Aug 1756, St Laurence, Ramsgate, Kent.

GOODHUGH

1. **William GOODHUGH** (c. 1705-1790). Born: c. Oct 1705, Sundridge?, Kent. Bap: Westerham, Kent. Marr: Sarah FRENCH 22 Oct 1729, St Nicholas, Sevenoaks, Kent. Died: 20 Feb 1790, Sundridge, Kent. Buried: Westerham churchyard, Kent.
= Sarah FRENCH (c. 1711-1794), dau. of Adam FRENCH (-). Born: c. 1711. Bap: 6 May 1711, St Nicholas, Sevenoaks, Kent. Died: 21 Apr 1794.

  2. **William GOODHUGH** (1730-aft1796). Born: 19 Nov 1730. Marr: Sarah BURGESS 10 Oct 1758, St Nicholas, Sevenoaks, Kent. Died: aft 1796.
  = Sarah BURGESS (1731-c. 1809), dau. of Richard BURGESS (-1766) and Mary (-). Born: 20 Jan 1731, Old Meeting House (Baptist), Bessells Green, Kent. Died: c. Apr 1809, Faversham, Kent. Buried: 11 Apr 1809, St. Mary of Charity, Faversham, Kent.

    3. **Thomas GOODHUGH** (1759-1830). Born: 14 Aug 1759. Died: 19 Sep 1830.

    3. **William GOODHUGH** (1761-1829). Born: 24 Feb 1761. Marr: (i) Susanna HINDS 21 Dec 1791, St. Mary of Charity, Faversham, Kent. Marr: (ii) Sarah HINDS 31 Oct 1822, St. Mary of Charity, Faversham, Kent. Died: 10 Sep 1829. Buried: 15 Sep 1829, Faversham churchyard, Kent.
    = Susanna HINDS (c. 1760-1799), dau. of Richard HINDS (-) and Sarah (1733-c. 1821). Born: c. 1760. Marr: Robert CLACKETT 30 Apr 1780, Davington, Kent. Died: 21 May 1799. Buried: 26 May 1799, Faversham churchyard, Kent.

      4. **William GOODHUGH** (1792-1858). Born: 20 Oct 1792. Marr: Mary RICKWOOD 25 Dec 1812, Ospringe church, Kent. Died: 12 Apr 1858. Buried: Apr 1858, Ospringe churchyard, Kent.
      = Mary RICKWOOD (c. 1785-1862), dau. of John RICKWOOD (-) and SUSANNA (-). Born: c. 1785. Bap: 9 Oct 1785, Ospringe church, Kent. Died: 28 Mar 1862. Buried: with her husband.

      4. **Richard GOODHUGH** (1794-c. 1857). Born: 1794. Bap: 5 Oct 1794, St Mary of Charity, Faversham, Kent. Marr: Mary 16 May 1816, London. Died: c. Nov 1857.
      = Mary (-).

        5. **Ann GOODHUGH** (-).
        = Eleanor (-c. 1851). Died: c. Jul 1851.

        5. **Ann GOODHUGH** (-).

      4. **Ann GOODHUGH** (c. 1796-1852). Born: c. Jun 1796. Bap: 24 Jul 1796, St. Mary of Charity, Faversham, Kent. Marr: John DAWSON 14 Aug 1813, St. Mary of Charity, Faversham, Kent. Died: 21 Apr 1852.
      = John DAWSON (1785-1850), son of William DAWSON (c. 1747-1817) and Susanna PRESLEY (c. 1749-c. 1822). Born: 20 Apr 1785. Died: 3 Oct 1850. Buried: Faversham, Kent, NE corner of churchyard.

SEE DAWSON TREE FOR DESCENDANTS OF ANN GOODHUGH AND JOHN DAWSON

4. **Sarah GOODHUGH** (1798-1859). Born: 1798. Marr: John Bunger SHARP 21 May 1818, Faversham church, Kent. Died: 28 Jun 1859.

= John Bunger SHARP (c. 1796-). Born: c. 1796.

  5. **Mary Ann Bunger SHARP** (c. 1821-). Born: c. 1821.

  5. **John Bunger SHARP** (1822-). Born: 17 Sep 1822, Faversham, Kent. Bap: 11 Oct 1822, Faversham Wesleyan Chapel, Kent.

  = DRAYSON (-).

    6. **E. E. SHARP** (-).

    6. **E. M. SHARP** (-1938). Died: 1938.

  5. **Frederick SHARP** (1825-). Born: 2 Jan 1825, Faversham, Kent. Bap: 13 Feb 1825, Faversham Wesleyan Chapel, Kent.

  = Sarah HINDS (c. 1761-1838), dau. of Richard HINDS (-) and Sarah (1733-c. 1821). Born: c. 1761. Bap: 4 Oct 1761, St. Mary of Charity, Faversham, Kent. Died: Jun 1838. Buried: 8 Jun 1838, Faversham churchyard, Kent.

3. **Elizabeth GOODHUGH** (1762-1836). Born: 4 Aug 1762. Died: 16 Jul 1836. Buried: 20 Jul 1836, St. Mary of Charity, Faversham, Kent.

3. **Sarah GOODHUGH** (1764-1764). Born: 23 Mar 1764. Died: Jun 1764.

3. **Sarah GOODHUGH** (1765-1782). Born: 5 Mar 1765. Died: 22 Jul 1782. Buried: 1782, Plumstead.

3. **Mary GOODHUGH** (1767-aft1836). Born: 16 Jun 1767. Died: aft Jun 1836.

3. **Richard GOODHUGH** (1771-1826). Born: 20 Sep 1771. Marr: Elizabeth EDWARDS * 31 Aug 1796, St. Marylebone, London. Died: 20 Apr 1826.

= Elizabeth EDWARDS * (-), dau. of Thomas EDWARDS * (-).

  4. **Mary Ann GOODHUGH** (1796-). Born: 27 Nov 1796, Paddington St, Marylebone, London. Bap: 17 Mar 1797, St. Marylebone, London. Marr: Ebenezer FOX 15 Feb 1815, Westminster, London.

  = Ebenezer FOX (-). Born: Bourton-on-the-Water, Gloucestershire.

    5. **Isabella Charlotte FOX** (1818-c. 1855). Born: 1818. Marr: Andrew MUIR 1844, Greenock, Renfrewshire. Died: c. 1855.

    = KENNEDY (-).

    = Andrew MUIR (1781-c. 1849). Born: 1781. Died: c. 1849.

      6. **Isabella Charlotte MUIR** (1846-1912). Born: 1846. Marr: Robert BLYTH 1873, Holloway Chapel, London. Died: 1912.

      = Robert BLYTH (-). Born: Glasgow, Lanarkshire. Buried: Glasgow Necropolis, Lanarkshire.

        7. **Alice BLYTH** (1874-1948). Born: 1874. Died: 1948.

        7. **Lucy BLYTH** (1876-1948). Born: 1876. Died: 1948.

        7. **Margaret Dorothy BLYTH** (1879-1916). Born: 1879. Died: 1916.

        7. **Robert Oswald BLYTH** (1883-1980). Born: 1883. Marr: Caroline Anna REDDIE 1919, Halifax Parish Church, Yorkshire. Died: 1980.

= Caroline Anna REDDIE (1888-1944). Born: 1888. Died: 1944.

    8. **F BLYTH.**

    8. **Robert BLYTH** (1922-1944). Born: 1922. Died: 1944.

    8. **M BLYTH.**

    = F WEBBER.

        9. **F BLYTH.**

        9. **F BLYTH.**

        9. **M BLYTH.**

        9. **F BLYTH.**

    8. **M BLYTH.**

    = F ANDERSON.

5. **Edwin FOX** (c. 1821-). Born: c. 1821.

5. **Alfred FOX** (c. 1822-). Born: c. 1822.

5. **Henry Frederick FOX** (1824-1911). Born: 9 Aug 1824, Soho, London. Bap: 29 Aug 1824, St Anne, Soho, Westminster, London. Marr: Ellen Maria WATSON 1862, Rock Ferry, Cheshire. Died: 1911, Liverpool, Lancashire.

= Ellen Maria WATSON (-).

    6. **Arthur Sinclair FOX** (c. 1863-1892). Born: c. Aug 1863, Birkenhead, Cheshire. Died: 26 Apr 1892, Lima, Peru.

    6. **Rosa FOX** (1884-). Born: 1884. Marr: José LOSTAUNAU

    = José LOSTAUNAU (c. 1870-). Born: c. 1870.

        8. **Rosa LOSTAUNAU** (1912-). Born: 9 Jun 1912, Lima, Peru.

    6. **Ellen Amelia FOX** (c. 1867-). Born: c. 1867.

    6. **Ethel Henrietta FOX** (c. 1869-). Born: c. 1869.

5. **Charlotte FOX** (c. 1826-). Born: c. 1826.

5. **Eliza Catherine FOX** (c. 1829-). Born: c. 1829.

= HOCOMBE (-).

5. **Nathaniel FOX** (c. 1832-). Born: c. 1832.

5. **Ann F FOX** (c. 1839-). Born: c. 1839.

5. **Charles James FOX** (1816-). Born: 1816.

4. **William GOODHUGH** (1797-1842). Born: 2 Sep 1797, Blandford Street, London. Bap: 31 May 1799, St. Marylebone, London. Marr: Sarah ROSE 20 Jan 1822, St Marylebone, London. Died: 23 May 1842, 11 South Parade, Chelsea, London.

= Sarah ROSE (-1842). Died: 1842.

5. **William Smith GOODHUGH** (1824-1908). Born: 11 May 1824. Bap: 13 Oct 1824, Saint Mary-St Marylebone Road, Saint Marylebone, London. Marr: Eliza Proudfoot GARIE 1854, Victoria, Australia. Marr: Mary Steele POWELL 1878, Montreal, Canada. Died: 1908, Montreal, Canada.
= Eliza Proudfoot GARIE (-1876). Born: Perth, Scotland. Died: 1876, Montreal, Canada.
    6. **William Garie GOODHUGH** (-). Marr: 1886.
       = [unnamed person] (-).
    6. **Minnie Eliza GOODHUGH** (-).
    6. **Nellie GOODHUGH** (-).
    6. **GOODHUGH** (-).
       = Mary Steele POWELL (-1908). Died: 1908, Montreal, Canada.
    6. **GOODHUGH** (-).
    6. **GOODHUGH** (-1904). Died: 1904, Montreal, Canada.
5. **Sarah Rose GOODHUGH** (1825-1912). Born: 1825, London. Died: 1912, Canterbury, Kent. Buried: St Martin's churchyard, Canterbury, Kent.
4. **Richard GOODHUGH** (1799-). Born: 20 Oct 1799, Blandford St, Marylebone, London.
= Eleanor * (-).
    5. **Anne GOODHUGH** * (c. 1833-). Born: c. 1833. Bap: 12 Jul 1833, St. James, Paddington.
4. **Sarah GOODHUGH** (1801-). Born: 6 Aug 1801.
4. **Hannah GOODHUGH** (1802-). Born: 27 Sep 1802, Blandford St, Marylebone, London.
4. **Thomas GOODHUGH** (1804-). Born: 27 Oct 1804.
3. **Ann GOODHUGH** (1776-aft1836). Born: 10 Jul 1776. Died: aft Jun 1836.
2. **Thomas GOODHUGH** (1735-1780). Born: 22 Jul 1735. Died: 23 Jul 1780. Buried: Chiddingstone, Kent.
2. **Sarah GOODHUGH** (1739-). Born: 26 Mar 1739, Of Westerham. Marr: James JONES 13 Oct 1772.
= James JONES (-). Born: Of Westerham.
2. **Richard GOODHUGH** (c. 1745-1766). Born: c. 1745. Died: 3 Nov 1766.

121

FAGG

1. **William FAGG** * (-). Born: Marr: Mary FREEMAN * 24 Apr 1786, St. John the Baptist, Thanet, Kent.
= Mary FREEMAN * (-). Born:
  2. **George FAGG** (c. 1787-1876). Born: c. 1787. Bap: 6 Jan 1788, St Peter-in-Thanet, Broadstairs, Kent. Marr: Elizabeth Ann HILLER 14 May 1809, St Peter-in-Thanet, Broadstairs, Kent. Died: 14 Jun 1876.
  = Elizabeth Ann HILLER (1784-1876), dau. of John Frederick HILLER (1742-1816) and Esther MORGAN (c. 1742-1818). Born: 1784. Bap: 17 Oct 1784, St Peter-in-Thanet, Broadstairs, Kent. Died: 14 Jun 1876, Canterbury, Kent.
    3. **Amelia FAGG** (-).
    3. **Elizabeth FAGG** (1811-1900). Born: 1811, St Peter-in-Thanet, Broadstairs, Kent. Bap: 17 Nov 1811, St Peter-in-Thanet, Broadstairs, Kent. Marr: William Goodhugh DAWSON 11 Jul 1845, Wesleyan Bethal Chapel, Rochester, Kent. Died: 17 Jan 1900. Buried: Faversham churchyard, Kent.
    = William Goodhugh DAWSON (1814-1884), son of John DAWSON (1785-1850) and Ann GOODHUGH (c. 1796-1852). Born: 24 May 1814, Faversham, Kent. Bap: 5 Jun 1814, Wesleyan Chapel, Faversham, Kent. Died: 5 Apr 1884, Faversham, Kent. Buried: Faversham churchyard, Kent.
      4. **William Goodhugh DAWSON** (1851-1909). Born: 12 Dec 1851, Faversham, Kent. Marr: Mary Frances DAY 8 Jun 1876. Died: 25 Jun 1909. Buried: Faversham churchyard, Kent.
      = Mary Frances DAY (1851-1933), dau. of John DAY (1815-1893) and Frances EGGLESTON (1819-1910). Born: 14 Oct 1851, Caldicot, Monmouthshire. Died: 29 Apr 1933.
        5. **Bessie Hiller DAWSON** (1877-1943). Born: 15 Jul 1877, Faversham, Kent. Marr: Thomas J. THOMAS 1 Jun 1921. Died: 23 Aug 1943.
        = Thomas J. THOMAS (-1953). Died: 5 Mar 1953.
        5. **Arthur Egglestone DAWSON** (1879-1965). Born: 7 Jan 1879, Faversham, Kent. Marr: Elsie Tillotson JARMAN 22 Jan 1916. Died: 6 May 1965.
        = Elsie Tillotson JARMAN (1886-). Born: 1 Sep 1886.
          6. **Irene Mary DAWSON** (1917-2017). Born: 6 Feb 1917. Died: 10 Aug 2017, Abbeyfield Society, 11 Maitland Rd, Reading RG1 6NL.
          6. **Muriel Frances DAWSON**.
          = Eric E. F. SMITH (1907-1990).
        5. **Alice Mary DAWSON** (1881-1973). Born: 20 Feb 1881. Died: 8 Apr 1973.
        5. **William Goodhugh DAWSON** (1883-1976). Born: 17 May 1883. Marr: Florence Catherine HARRIS 9 Apr 1923. Died: 25 Sep

1976.

= Florence Catherine HARRIS (1898-1993), dau. of William Thomas HARRIS (1867-1945) and Hannah SHEFFIELD (1865-1950). Born: 24 Aug 1898. Died: 17 Apr 1993.

    6. **William Goodhugh DAWSON.**
    = Margaret Grace HAYWARD.
        7. **William Goodhugh DAWSON.**
        = Andrea Lynne THOMPSON.
        7. **Sarah Margaret DAWSON.**
        = Philip James GRIFFIN.
            8. **Anna Elizabeth GRIFFIN.**
            8. **Owen James GRIFFIN.**
            8. **Bethany Rachel GRIFFIN.**

6. **Martin Harris DAWSON** (1927-2006). Born: 18 Feb 1927. Marr: Shirley GREY 2 Jul 1955. Died: 29 Nov 2006, Norfolk. Buried: 11 Dec 2006.

= Shirley GREY (1936-2005). Born: 21 May 1936. Died: 15 Mar 2005.

        7. **M DAWSON.**
        = F HARVEY.
            8. **M DAWSON.**
            8. **F DAWSON.**
            8. **M DAWSON.**
            = Cathryn DIBLEY.
        7. **M DAWSON.**
        = F MCRAE.
            8. **M DAWSON.**
            8. **M DAWSON.**
            8. **M DAWSON.**
            8. **M DAWSON.**
        7. **M DAWSON.**
        7. **M DAWSON.**
        = F.
        = F.

8. **M DAWSON**.
    = F.
       8. **F DAWSON**.
7. **F DAWSON**.
   = M LINES.
       8. **M LINES**.
7. **M DAWSON**.
   = F DENNIS.
       8. **M DAWSON**.
          = [unnamed person].
5. **Lilian Frances** DAWSON (1885-1934). Born: 9 Jan 1885. Died: 20 Nov 1934.
5. **Howard Day** DAWSON (1886-1981). Born: 2 Jun 1886. Marr: Daisy Hilda RATCLIFFE 24 Jan 1914. Marr: Fran aft 1918. Died: 6 Apr 1981.
   = Daisy Hilda RATCLIFFE (1886-1966). Born: 1886. Died: 3 Jan 1966.
   6. **Isabel Alice** DAWSON (1918-2019). Born: 29 Jul 1918. Marr: William Simmons RAMSAY 12 Feb 1941. Died: 7 Mar 2019, Nelson, British Columbia, Canada.
      = William Simmons RAMSAY (1915-2001). Born: 3 Oct 1915. Died: 4 Nov 2001.
      7. **M RAMSAY**.
         = F SIMPSON, dau. of [unnamed person] (-).
             8. **F RAMSAY**.
             8. **F RAMSAY**.
             8. **F RAMSAY**.
             8. **F RAMSAY**.
      7. **F RAMSAY**.
         = M MARTIN.
             8. **M MARTIN** (1969-1997). Born: 30 Dec 1969. Died: Jun 1997.
             8. **F MARTIN**.
             8. **M MARTIN**.
      7. **F RAMSAY**.
         = M E. HAGEL.
             8. **F HAGEL**.

8. **M HAGEL.**
8. **F HAGEL.**
7. **M RAMSAY.**
= F CULLEN.
   8. **M RAMSAY.**
   8. **F RAMSAY.**
   8. **F RAMSAY.**
   = F TRIMBOLI.
   8. **M RAMSAY.**
   = Fran (-1978). Died: Dec 1978.

3. **Charlotte FAGG** (-).
= Charles THOMSON (-).
   4. **Charlotte THOMSON** (-).
   4. **Lizzie THOMSON** (-).
   4. **Duncan THOMSON** (-).
   4. **Edith THOMSON** (-).
   = BARNES (-).
3. **Esther FAGG** (-). Marr: Edward FITCHEW 22 Jun 1846, St. Peter's St. Wesleyan Methodist Chapel, Canterbury, Kent.
= Edward FITCHEW (c. 1810-), son of John William FITCHEW (c. 1775-1857) and Elizabeth (c. 1777-1846). Born: c. 1810. Bap: 19 Jul 1810, St. George the Martyr, Southwark.
   4. **Esther Elizabeth FITCHEW** (1848-). Born: 19 Jul 1848. St. Peter, Brighthelmston, Sussex.
   = Arnold LUKE (-), son of Samuel LUKE (-) and Jemima THOMPSON (1813-1906).
      5. **Lilian LUKE** (-).
      5. **Ernest LUKE** (-).
   4. **Edward Hubert FITCHEW** (c. 1851-). Born: c. 1851, St. Peter, Brighthelmston, Sussex. Bap: 7 Dec 1851.
   = Julia (-).
      5. **Edward Hubert FITCHEW** (-).
      = [unnamed person] (-).
         6. **Peter FITCHEW** (-).
      5. **Dorothy FITCHEW** (-).
   4. **William FITCHEW** (1854-1925). Born: 1854. Marr: Emily Anne HAMBLIN c. Feb 1881, Wandsworth, Middlesex. Marr: Winifred

Mawson DUNN c. May 1919, Faversham, Kent. Died: Aug 1925.
= Emily Anne HAMBLIN (c. 1857-c. 1918). Born: c. Feb 1857, Wandsworth, Middlesex. Died: c. Feb 1918, Croydon, Surrey.
  5. **Clarence William FITCHEW** (c. 1882-). Born: c. Feb 1882, Wandsworth, Middlesex.
    = Ettie BARNDON (-).
      6. **Marjorie FITCHEW** (-).
        = Marcus COLLINS (-).
          7. **F COLLINS** (-).
            = M MAUNSELL (-).
          7. **M COLLINS** (-).
            = F (-).
              8. **M COLLINS** (-).
              8. **F COLLINS** (-).
      6. **Geoffrey FITCHEW**.
        = Leonor SHALLIS.
          7. **F FITCHEW**.
            = M RISDON (-).
              8. **M RISDON**.
              8. **M RISDON**.
          7. **M FITCHEW**.
      6. **David FITCHEW** (-1941). Died: 1941.
  5. **Gordon Stewart FITCHEW** (c. 1885-). Born: c. May 1885, Croydon, Surrey.
    = ETHEL (-).
      6. **Gladys FITCHEW** (-).
        = Eric ORAM (-).
  5. **Harold Percy FITCHEW** (c. 1891-). Born: c. Aug 1891, Croydon, Surrey.
    = Edith TUCKER (-).
      6. **Mary FITCHEW** (-).
      6. **Desmond FITCHEW** (-).
        = Doris (-).
      6. **Jean FITCHEW** (-).
    = Winifred Mawson DUNN (1876-1947), dau. of Robert Smith DUNN (1849-1926) and Hannah DAY (1849-1937). Born:

16 Oct 1876. Died: 6 Aug 1947.
4. **Arthur Theophilus FITCHEW** (c. 1858-). Born: c. 1858. Bap: 7 Dec 1858, Wesleyan Methodist Chapel, Brighton, Sussex.
= [unnamed person] (-).
  5. **Edith FITCHEW** (-).
  = [unnamed person] (-).
    6. **Charles** (-).
    = [unnamed person] (-).
      7. **M** (-).
      = [unnamed person] (-).
        8. **F** (-).
4. **George FITCHEW** (-).
= Ella (-).
  5. **Bert FITCHEW** (-).
  5. **Eva FITCHEW** (-).
  5. **Rupert FITCHEW** (-).
3. **Mary FAGG** (-).
3. **Sarah FAGG** (-).
= Robert FORD (-).
  4. **Emmeline FORD** (-).
  = George BAILEY (-).
  = Sydney WOOLCOT (-).
3. **George FAGG** * (c. 1817-). Born: c. 1817. Bap: 8 Jun 1817, St Peter-in-Thanet, Broadstairs, Kent.
3. **Georgiana Jane FAGG** (c. 1824-). Born: c. 1824.
= George BELL (-).
= George CLAY (-), son of Charles CLAY (-).

DAY

1. **George DAY** (-1842). Died: 1842.
   = Hannah (-).
   2. **Thomas DAY** (-).
      3. **Anna Maria DAY** * (-).
         = SMILES * (-).
   2. **Hannah DAY** (-).
   2. **Robert DAY** (c. 1810-). Born: c. 1810.
      = Ann (c. 1810-). Born: c. 1810.
         3. **Isabella DAY** (c. 1834-). Born: c. 1834. Bap: 20 Apr 1834, Hetton-Le-Hole.
         3. **Eleanor DAY** (c. 1837-). Born: c. 1837.
         3. **Hannah DAY** (c. 1840-). Born: c. 1840.
   2. **John DAY** (1815-1893). Born: 10 Apr 1815, Hetton-le-Hole, Durham. Bap: 21 May 1815, Houghton-Le-Spring, Durham. Marr: Frances EGGLESTON 17 Jan 1842, St. Nicholas, Newcastle upon Tyne. Died: 4 Oct 1893, Minster, Sheppy, Kent.
      = Frances EGGLESTON (1819-1910), dau. of Thomas EGGLESTON (1764-1853) and Elizabeth PATTERSON (1781-). Born: 26 May 1819, Cornforth, Durham. Died: 28 Jan 1910, Faversham, Kent.
         3. **Annie Elizabeth DAY** (1842-1924). Born: 8 Apr 1842, Durham. Marr: Benjamin Gough BERRY c. Aug 1868. Died: Dec 1924, Faversham, Kent. Buried: Hernhill, Kent.
            = Benjamin Gough BERRY (1841-1921), son of Thomas BERRY (1805-) and Elizabeth PARTON (-). Born: 25 Dec 1841. Died: 23 Apr 1921.
               4. **Stanley Egglestone BERRY** (1869-c. 1926). Born: 14 Jun 1869. Died: c. 1926, Margate, Kent.
               4. **Annie Gough BERRY** (1872-). Born: 1872.
                  = J. Martin DELBRIDGE (-).
                     5. **Max DELBRIDGE** (-).
                     5. **Christine DELBRIDGE** (-).
                        = Stewart COURTNAY (-).
                           6. **Pamela COURTNAY** (-).
                              = COWLEY (-).
                                 7. **Ronny COWLEY** (-).
                                 7. **Yvonne COWLEY** (-).

6. **Peter COURTNAY** (-).
= DEPLEDGE (-).
    7. **Christopher COURTNAY** (-).
    7. **Martin COURTNAY** (-).
    = [unnamed person] (-).
6. **Geoffrey COURTNAY** (-).
= Andrea (-).
    7. **Stewart COURTNAY** (-).
4. **Percy Turnbull BERRY** (-1930). Died: 2 Oct 1930.
= Lydia BERRY (-), dau. of Henry BERRY (1836-) and DELBRIDGE (-).
    5. **Percival BERRY** (-).
    5. **Louise BERRY** (-).
    = Edgar GLANVILLE (-).
4. **Elizabeth Parton BERRY** (-).
4. **Alice BERRY** (-).
4. **Kate Delbridge BERRY** (1876-). Born: Jul 1876.
= Clarence HARVARD (-).
    5. **Betty HARVARD** (-).
4. **Gertrude Mary BERRY** (-).
4. **Grace Eggleston BERRY** (-).
4. **Newton Day BERRY** (-).
= Edith HARTLEY (-).
    5. **Barbara BERRY** (-).
    5. **Constance BERRY** (-).
    5. **Christopher BERRY** (-).
4. **Hilda Frances BERRY** (1884-). Born: 28 Nov 1884.
3. **John George DAY** (1847-c. 1936). Born: 29 Jun 1847. Died: c. Jul 1936.
= Henrietta MARTIN (-1915). Died: 25 Mar 1915.
4. **Mabel DAY** (1878-). Born: 24 May 1878, Montreal.
= James H. WEBB (-). Born: Ireland.
    5. **Melbourne WEBB** (1904-1914). Born: 29 Apr 1904. Died: 27 Aug 1914.

5. **John WEBB** (1911-). Born: 14 Jul 1911.
= Jean.
    6. **M WEBB.**
    6. **M WEBB.**
    6. **F WEBB.**
5. **Eleanor Ruth WEBB.**
4. **Edward M. DAY** (1882-1934). Born: 14 May 1882. Died: 17 Apr 1934, Wellington, Ontario.
= Charlotte KEMP (1877-). Born: 1877, Montreal.
  5. **Stanley DAY** (1904-). Born: 1904. Marr: Mary Carlotta MCGAW 1929.
  = Mary Carlotta MCGAW (1910-). Born: 1910, Canada.
  5. **Donald DAY** (-).
  5. **Margaret DAY** (1909-). Born: 9 Nov 1909.
  5. **Eleanor DAY** (1911-). Born: 8 Jul 1911.
  = BRADFORD.
  5. **Phyllis DAY.**
  = HACK.
    6. **HACK.**
    6. **HACK.**
4. **Charles DAY** (-).
3. **Hannah DAY** (1849-1937). Born: 10 Nov 1849, Monmouthshire. Marr: Robert Smith DUNN 1873, Faversham, Kent. Died: 19 Mar 1937.
= Robert Smith DUNN (1849-1926), son of James DUNN (1816-1872) and Frances SMITH (1817-1874). Born: 1849. Died: 24 Feb 1926.
  4. **Marion Frances Eggleston DUNN** (1874-1955). Born: 18 Oct 1874. Died: 30 Jan 1955.
  4. **Winifred Mawson DUNN** (1876-1947). Born: 16 Oct 1876. Marr: William FITCHEW c. May 1919, Faversham, Kent. Died: 6 Aug 1947.
  = William FITCHEW (1854-1925), son of Edward FITCHEW (c. 1810-) and Esther FAGG (-). Born: 1854. Marr: Emily Anne HAMBLIN c. Feb 1881, Wandsworth, Middlesex. Died: Aug 1925.
3. **Mary Frances DAY** (1851-1933). Born: 14 Oct 1851, Caldicot, Monmouthshire. Marr: William Goodhugh DAWSON 8 Jun 1876. Died: 29 Apr 1933.
= William Goodhugh DAWSON (1851-1909), son of William Goodhugh DAWSON (1814-1884) and Elizabeth FAGG (1811-1900). Born: 12 Dec 1851, Faversham, Kent. Died: 25 Jun 1909. Buried: Faversham churchyard, Kent.

4. **Bessie Hiller DAWSON** (1877-1943). Born: 15 Jul 1877, Faversham, Kent. Marr: Thomas J. THOMAS 1 Jun 1921. Died: 23 Aug 1943.
= Thomas J. THOMAS (-1953). Died: 5 Mar 1953.

4. **Arthur Egglestone DAWSON** (1879-1965). Born: 7 Jan 1879, Faversham, Kent. Marr: Elsie Tillotson JARMAN 22 Jan 1916. Died: 6 May 1965.
= Elsie Tillotson JARMAN (1886-). Born: 1 Sep 1886.

  5. **Irene Mary DAWSON** (1917-2017). Born: 6 Feb 1917. Died: 10 Aug 2017. Abbeyfield Society, 11 Maitland Rd, Reading RG1 6NL.

  5. **Muriel Frances DAWSON**.
  = Eric E. F. SMITH (1907-1990).

4. **Alice Mary DAWSON** (1881-1973). Born: 20 Feb 1881. Died: 8 Apr 1973.

4. **William Goodhugh DAWSON** (1883-1976). Born: 17 May 1883. Marr: Florence Catherine HARRIS 9 Apr 1923. Died: 25 Sep 1976.
= Florence Catherine HARRIS (1898-1993), dau. of William Thomas HARRIS (1867-1945) and Hannah SHEFFIELD (1865-1950). Born: 24 Aug 1898. Died: 17 Apr 1993.

  5. **William Goodhugh DAWSON**.
  = Margaret Grace HAYWARD.

    6. **William Goodhugh DAWSON**.
    = Andrea Lynne THOMPSON.

    6. **Sarah Margaret DAWSON**.
    = Philip James GRIFFIN.

      7. **Anna Elizabeth GRIFFIN**.
      7. **Owen James GRIFFIN**.
      7. **Bethany Rachel GRIFFIN**.

  5. **Martin Harris DAWSON** (1927-2006). Born: 18 Feb 1927. Marr: Shirley GREY 2 Jul 1955. Died: 29 Nov 2006, Norfolk. Buried: 11 Dec 2006.
= Shirley GREY (1936-2005). Born: 21 May 1936. Died: 15 Mar 2005.

    6. **M DAWSON**.
    = F HARVEY.

      7. **M DAWSON**.
      7. **F DAWSON**.

7. **M DAWSON**.
= F DIBLEY.
6. **M DAWSON**.
= F MCRAE.
7. **M DAWSON**.
7. **M DAWSON**.
7. **M DAWSON**.
7. **M DAWSON**.
6. **M DAWSON**.
6. **M DAWSON**.
= F.
= F SINCLAIRE.
7. **M DAWSON**.
= F.
7. **F DAWSON**.
6. **F DAWSON**.
= M LINES.
7. **M LINES**.
6. **M DAWSON**.
= F DENNIS.
7. **M DAWSON**.
= [unnamed person].
4. **Lilian Frances DAWSON** (1885-1934). Born: 9 Jan 1885. Died: 20 Nov 1934.
4. **Howard Day DAWSON** (1886-1981). Born: 2 Jun 1886. Marr: Daisy Hilda RATCLIFFE 24 Jan 1914. Marr: Fran aft 1918. Died: 6 Apr 1981.
= Daisy Hilda RATCLIFFE (1886-1966). Born: 1886. Died: 3 Jan 1966.
5. **Isabel Alice DAWSON** (1918-2019). Born: 29 Jul 1918. Marr: William Simmons RAMSAY 12 Feb 1941. Died: 7 Mar 2019, Nelson, British Columbia, Canada.
= William Simmons RAMSAY (1915-2001). Born: 3 Oct 1915. Died: 4 Nov 2001.
6. **M RAMSAY**.
= F SIMPSON, dau. of [unnamed person] (-).

132

7. **F RAMSAY**.
7. **F RAMSAY**.
7. **F RAMSAY**.
7. **F RAMSAY**.
6. **Sheila Joan RAMSAY**.
= M MARTIN.
   7. **M MARTIN** (1969-1997). Born: 30 Dec 1969. Died: Jun 1997.
   7. **F MARTIN**.
   7. **M MARTIN**.
6. **F RAMSAY**.
= M HAGEL.
   7. **F HAGEL**.
   7. **M HAGEL**.
   7. **F HAGEL**.
6. **M RAMSAY**.
= F CULLEN.
   7. **M RAMSAY**.
   7. **F RAMSAY**.
   7. **F RAMSAY**.
   = F TRIMBOLI.
   7. **M RAMSAY**.
   = Fran (-1978). Died: Dec 1978.
3. **Robert William DAY** (1853-). Born: 27 Dec 1853, Breconshire.
= May WELSH (1854-). Born: 28 Aug 1854.
   4. **Mabel DAY** (1878-). Born: 24 Mar 1878.
   4. **Robert DAY** (1882-). Born: 14 May 1882.
3. **Jane Caroline DAY** (1858-1908). Born: 7 Nov 1858, Pontypridd, Glamorgan. Marr: Thomas Chambers ATTWATER 6 Feb 1884, Minster, Sheppy, Kent. Died: 21 Jan 1908, Widnes.
= Thomas Chambers ATTWATER (c. 1858-), son of Thomas Martin ATTWATER (1828-) and Julia Mary CHAMBERS (1831-). Born: c. Dec 1858, Faversham, Kent.
   4. **J.P. ATTWATER** (-).

4. **Florence ATTWATER** (-).
4. **Harold ATTWATER** (-).
4. **Dorothy ATTWATER** (-).
3. **Edward Henry DAY** (1861-1945). Born: 6 Jul 1861, Glamorgan. Died: 25 May 1945, Warnick, Australia.
= [unnamed person] (-).
    4. **W. E. DAY** (-).
    = [unnamed person] (-).

LEVER, SMITH

1. **John LEVER** (1752-). Born: 22 Dec 1752, Ebbsbourne, Wiltshire. Marr: Eleanor PITHER (-).
= Eleanor PITHER (1759-), dau. of David PITHER (-) and Mary ROGERS (-). Born: 16 Jan 1759, Binfield, Berkshire.
  2. **Mary LEVER** (1778-). Born: 4 Dec 1778, Wokingham, Berkshire.
  2. **Sarah LEVER** (1780-). Born: 8 Feb 1780, Halstead, Essex.
  2. **Susannah LEVER** (-).
  2. **Elizabeth LEVER** (1789-1873). Born: 2 Apr 1789, St. Mary Magdalene, Southwark, London. Marr: John SMITH 10 May 1813, St. Mary of Charity, Faversham, Kent. Died: 24 Dec 1873. Buried: Faversham churchyard, Kent.
  = John SMITH (1777-1858). Born: 26 Jul 1777, Doddington, Kent. Died: 12 Nov 1858.
    3. **Ellen SMITH** (1814-1871). Born: 7 Sep 1814. Died: 1871.
    = William Bryham MAWSON (-1889). Died: 1889.
      4. **Ellen Lonsdale MAWSON** (1844-1909). Born: 1844. Died: 1909.
      = Harold Arthur DOLLY (-1883). Died: 1883.
        5. **Arthur Lonsdale DOLLY** (-).
      4. **Alice Louisa Lever MAWSON** (1846-). Born: 20 May 1846. Marr: Julius Carl FRIEDBERGER 1865.
      = Julius Carl FRIEDBERGER (1838-). Born: 1838.
        5. **William FRIEDBERGER** (1866-1916). Born: 1866. Died: 1916.
        5. **Henry FRIEDBERGER** (-).

5. **Carl FRIEDBERGER** (1869-). Born: 1869.

= Mildred CRAKE (-).

5. **Rosa FRIEDBERGER** (-).

= Edgar CRAKE (-).

5. **Maurice Bryham FRIEDBERGER** (-).

5. **Marie FRIEDBERGER** (-).

= Richard SIMPSON (-).

3. **John Lever SMITH** (1815-1864). Born: 30 Nov 1815, Faversham, Kent. Bap: St. Mary of Charity, Faversham, Kent. Marr: Mary Anne DAWSON 9 Dec 1841, St Mary of Charity, Faversham, Kent. Died: 26 Sep 1864, Yorkville, Wisconsin. Buried: Union Grove Cemetery, Racine County, Wisconsin.

= Mary Anne DAWSON (1818-1877), dau. of John DAWSON (1785-1850) and Ann GOODHUGH (c. 1796-1852). Born: 28 Apr 1818, Faversham, Kent. Bap: 17 Jun 1818, Wesleyan Chapel, Faversham, Kent. Died: 12 Dec 1877, Yorkville, Wisconsin. Buried: Union Grove Cemetery, Yorkville, Wisconsin.

4. **John Dawson SMITH** (1842-1920). Born: 29 Sep 1842, Boughton, Kent. Marr: Lucy Hannah BACKHUS 2 Oct 1868, Union Grove, Wisconsin, USA. Marr: Elizabeth CARTER 19 Mar 1879, Osage, Iowa. Marr: Frances Louise FRENCH 19 May 1897. Died: 24 Jun 1920, Austin, Minnesota. Buried: Oak Grove Cemetery, Mitchell, Iowa.

= Lucy Hannah BACKHUS (1847-1877), dau. of John BACKHUS (-) and Olivia Harriet LOCKWOOD (-). Born: 2 Oct 1847, Yorkville, Wisconsin. Bap: 14 Sep 1858, Yorkville United Methodist Church. Died: 6 Oct 1877, Mitchell, Iowa. Buried: Oak Grove Cemetery, Mitchell, Iowa.

5. **Clifford Henry SMITH** (1869-1939). Born: 25 Nov 1869, Union Grove, Wisconsin. Marr: Ethel Constance ECCLESTON 3 Sep 1894, Ethel's home, Austin, Minnesota. Died: 15 Jul 1939, St. Lucas Hospital, Faribault, Minnesota. Buried: Oak Ridge Cemetery, Faribault, Minnesota.

= Ethel Constance ECCLESTON (1866-1949). Born: 13 Sep 1866, Kankakee, Illinois. Died: 1 Oct 1949, St. Lucas Hospital, Faribault, Minnesota. Buried: Oak Ridge Cemetery, Faribault, Minnesota.

6. **Maurice Clifford SMITH** (1895-1972). Born: 8 Jun 1895, Carver, Minnesota. Marr: Alma Josephine Ethelyn LUNDSTOM 26 Jun 1922, Minneapolis, Minnesota. Died: 15 Mar 1972, Minneapolis, Minnesota. Buried: Sunset Memorial Park, Minneapolis, Minnesota.

= Alma Josephine Ethelyn LUNDSTOM (-).

7. **Kenneth Maurice SMITH** (1927-1978). Born: 20 Feb 1927, Minneapolis, Minnesota. Died: 17 Sep 1978, Minneapolis, Minnesota.

= F.

8. **F SMITH.**
= M JANIKOWSKI.
  9. **M JANIKOWSKI.**
  9. **M JANIKOWSKI.**
8. **Robert SMITH** (1951-1953). Born: 14 May 1951, Minneapolis, Minnesota. Died: 9 Feb 1953, Minneapolis, Minnesota.
6. **Lucy Constance SMITH** (1896-1960). Born: 22 Nov 1896, Carver, Minnesota. Marr: John Paul CHAPMAN 29 Jan 1916, Faribault, Minnesota. Died: 27 Nov 1960, Rochester, Minnesota. Buried: Grandview Gardens Cemetery, Rochester, Minnesota.
= John Paul CHAPMAN (-).
  7. **F CHAPMAN.**
  = M H. NIETULA.
  = M L SWIFT.
    8. **F SWIFT** (-).
    = M HICKS (-).
      9. **F HICKS.**
      = M JONES (-).
        10. **M JONES.**
        10. **F JONES.**
      9. **M HICKS.**
      = F HARRELL (-).
        10. **M HICKS.**
        = F NIETULA (-).
  7. **M CHAPMAN.**
  7. **F CHAPMAN.**
  7. **F CHAPMAN.**
  7. **F CHAPMAN.**
  7. **M CHAPMAN.**
  7. **M CHAPMAN.**
  7. **F CHAPMAN.**
6. **Allegra Winifred SMITH** (1901-1982). Born: 4 Dec 1901, Woodlake, Minnesota. Died: 25 Feb 1982. Buried: Columbus,

Indiana.
= Joseph Luell COOK.

   7. **M COOK.**
   = [unnamed person].
      8. **COOK.**
      = [unnamed person].

   7. **F COOK.**
   7. **M COOK.**
   = F.
      8. **M COOK.**
      8. **F COOK.**
      8. **M COOK.**

  6. **Dorene Hazel SMITH.**
  = Melville HOOVER.

5. **Howard Allison SMITH** (1871-1960). Born: 8 Oct 1871, Union Grove, Wisconsin, USA. Marr: Lenore HEWITT 24 Nov 1904. Died: 1960.
= Lenore HEWITT (-).

5. **Arthur Ellison SMITH** (1873-1965). Born: 26 Oct 1873, Union Grove, Wisconsin, USA. Marr: Mabel DICKINSON 4 Nov 1903. Died: 1965.
= Mabel DICKINSON (-).

5. **Stella May SMITH** (1876-1878). Born: 30 Nov 1876, Iowa. Died: 11 Jan 1878, Mitchell, Iowa. Buried: Oak Grove Cemetery, Mitchell, Iowa.
= Elizabeth CARTER (1853-1889). Born: 10 Jul 1853. Died: 28 Feb 1889, Mitchell, Iowa. Buried: Oak Grove Cemetery, Mitchell, Iowa.
= Frances Louise FRENCH (1859-1932). dau. of John FRENCH (-) and Mary (-). Born: 18 Mar 1859, Onieda County, New York. Died: 30 Mar 1932, Austin, Minnesota. Buried: Oakwood Cemetery, Austin, Minnesota.

5. **Mary Aileen SMITH** (1901-). Born: 7 Sep 1901, Austin, Minnesota.
= Clarence LARSON (-).

4. **Mary Anne SMITH** (1844-1904). Born: 2 Jul 1844, Boughton, Kent. Marr: John WILKINSON 13 Sep 1866. Died: 26 Jan 1904. At home, Milford. Buried: 30 Jan 1904, Milford Cemetery, Wisconsin.
= John WILKINSON (-1887). Died: 1887.

5. **Luella Eliza WILKINSON** (1867-). Born: 4 Jul 1867. Marr: William L. G. WILKINSON 3 Sep 1888.
= William L. G. WILKINSON (-).
5. **Edith Mary WILKINSON** (1873-). Born: 5 Jul 1873. Marr: George P. WOODS 7 Dec 1899.
= George P. WOODS (-).
5. **Laurence John WILKINSON** (1877-). Born: 12 Feb 1877. Marr: Ann E. MILLER 24 Feb 1907.
= Ann E. MILLER (-).
5. WILKINSON (-c. 1902). Died: c. 1902.
= FITCH (-).
4. **Helen Elizabeth SMITH** (1845-1898). Born: 28 Dec 1845, Boughton, Kent. Marr: James H. JONES 3 Oct 1872. Died: 26 Aug 1898.
= James H. JONES (-aft1898). Died: aft Aug 1898.
5. **Walter Henry JONES** (1873-). Born: 16 Dec 1873. Marr: Esabel BURNSIDE 10 Jun 1905.
= Esabel BURNSIDE (-).
6. **Margaret Elizabeth JONES** (1906-). Born: 26 Jun 1906.
5. **Ernest Stephen JONES** (1877-). Born: 8 Jul 1877.
5. **Sarah Grace JONES** (1882-). Born: 18 Aug 1882.
4. **William Goodhugh SMITH** (1847-1922). Born: 15 Apr 1847, Boughton, Kent. Marr: Eleanor May STOCK 14 Nov 1877. Died: 1922.
= Eleanor May STOCK (-).
5. **Elmo Vincent SMITH** (1879-). Born: 16 Jan 1879. Marr: Palma HARTIS 28 Dec 1904.
= Palma HARTIS (-).
6. **William B. SMITH** (1907-). Born: 12 Dec 1907.
= Althis CLARK (-).
5. **Exine Mary SMITH** (1883-). Born: 2 Jan 1883. Marr: Clarence Everett DRAKE 10 Jun 1908, Mitchell, Iowa, USA.
= Clarence Everett DRAKE (-), son of Everett E DRAKE (-) and Emma KNOULTON (-). Born:
6. **Everett Almos DRAKE** (1909-). Born: 20 Mar 1909. Marr: Ruth E. DICKSON 25 May 1935.
= Ruth E. DICKSON (1910-2004). Born: 25 Jan 1910. Died: 4 May 2004. Buried: 10 May 2004.
7. **F DRAKE**.
= M HORTON.
8. **F HORTON**.
= M COLLINS.
9. **F COLLINS**.
8. **M HORTON**.

138

= F PAULIS.
        9. **F HORTON.**
    8. **F HORTON.**
= M MOESLEIN.
        9. **M MOESLEIN.**
    8. **M HORTON.**
7. **M DRAKE.**
= F CHENG.
    8. **M DRAKE.**
= F MCLAUGHLIN (-).
        9. **M DRAKE-MCLAUGHLIN.**
        9. **M DRAKE-MCLAUGHLIN.**

4. **Walter Thomas SMITH** (1848-1925). Born: 1 Nov 1848, Boughton, Kent. Marr: Cynthia Ann CHAPPELL 1 Jan 1874. Died: 8 Jan 1925, Hartley Hospital, Battle Creek, Iowa.
= Cynthia Ann CHAPPELL (-).
5. **Aida May SMITH** (1875-). Born: 6 Apr 1875.
5. **Alfred Burton SMITH** (1877-1953). Born: 18 Feb 1877, Battle Creek, Iowa. Marr: Flora BURKHARDT 28 May 1904. Died: 1 Oct 1953, Battle Creek, Iowa.
= Flora BURKHARDT (-).
6. **Walter B. SMITH** (1905-1908). Born: 19 Apr 1905. Died: 28 Aug 1908.
6. **Florence Dawson SMITH** (1907-). Born: 18 Dec 1907.
= SIFFERD (-).
4. **Alfred Dawson SMITH** (1850-1936). Born: 29 Jan 1850, Boughton, Kent. Marr: Ida A. CHAMBERS 12 Jan 1882, Mitchell, Iowa. Died: 23 Feb 1936, at home, 817 Nicholas Street, Fulton, Missouri. Buried: Mitchell, Iowa.
= Ida A. CHAMBERS (-1931). Died: 1 Oct 1931. Buried: Mitchell, Iowa.
5. **Harriet Olive SMITH** (-). Marr: Raymond SCHAFFER 1 Sep 1935.
= Raymond SCHAFFER (-).
4. **Lever Charles SMITH** (1851-1864). Born: 10 Oct 1851, Boughton, Kent. Died: 26 Sep 1864.
4. **Sarah Dawson SMITH** (1854-aft1916). Born: 14 Feb 1854, Boughton, Kent. Marr: William Henry HELMS 14 Mar 1884. Died: aft Jul 1916.
= William Henry HELMS (-).

5. **Lillian Annanora HELMS** (1888-). Born: Jun 1888. Marr: George Francis TAYLOR, Jnr. 31 Jul 1917.
 = George Francis TAYLOR, Jnr. (-).
  6. **Elizabeth Dawson TAYLOR**.
   = Robert GOSHORN.
    7. **Kenneth GOSHORN** (1943-1991). Born: 1943. Died: 1991, Washington DC, USA.
     = F CARRIER.
      8. **F GOSHORN**.
       = M CLARKSON.
        9. **M CLARKSON**.
        9. **M CLARKSON**.
        9. **F CLARKSON**.
        9. **M CLARKSON**.
      8. **F GOSHORN**.
       = **F. CLARKSON**
    7. **F GOSHORN**.
     = M FRUCTER.
      8. **M FRUCTER** (-1992). Died: 1992.
  6. **F TAYLOR**.
4. **Mary Jane SMITH** (1855-1902). Born: 21 Nov 1855, Boughton, Kent. Marr: Clarence Augustus OSBORNE 5 Apr 1883, Minneapolis, Minnesota, USA. Died: 1902, Bancroft, Cuming County, Nebraska, USA. Buried: Bancroft Cemetery.
 = Clarence Augustus OSBORNE (1852-1936). Born: 26 May 1852, Cattaragus, New York, USA. Marr: Edith HUDSON 25 Nov 1913, Eureka, California, USA. Died: 25 Aug 1936, Canon City, Colorado, USA.
  5. **Ella Mildred OSBORNE** (1884-1977). Born: 8 Feb 1884, Milford, Dickenson County, Iowa, USA. Marr: William Lourie JACOBS c. 1903. Died: 17 Jan 1977, Omaha, Douglas County, Nebraska, USA. Buried: 20 Jan 1977, Evergreen Cemetery, Omaha, Douglas County, Nebraska, USA.
   = William Lourie JACOBS (1879-1943). Born: 26 Apr 1879, Champion, Marquette County, Michigan, USA. Died: 19 May 1943.
    6. **Florence Lourie JACOBS** (1905-1985). Born: 6 May 1905, Bancroft, Cuming County, Nebraska, USA. Marr: Theodore E CARLSON c. 1924, Council Bluffs, Pottawattamie County, Iowa, USA. Died: 15 Mar 1985, Omaha, Douglas County, Nebraska, USA. Buried: Mar 1985, Evergreen Cemetery, Omaha, Douglas County, Nebraska, USA.
     = Theodore E CARLSON (1900-1976). Born: 2 Oct 1900, Oakland, Burt County, Nebraska, USA. Died: 31 Oct 1976, Omaha, Douglas County, Nebraska, USA.

140

7. **Richard James CARLSON** (1925-1997). Born: 9 Mar 1925, Omaha, Douglas County, Nebraska, USA. Marr: Elizabeth WISELISEN 11 Aug 1951, Blair, Washington County, Nebraska, USA. Died: 9 Dec 1997, Rogers, Arkansas, USA. Buried: Cremated and buried by his mother in Evergreen Cemetery, Omaha, Douglas County, Nebraska, USA.
= Elizabeth WISELISEN (1918-1998). Born: 8 Nov 1918. Died: 8 Aug 1998, Rogers, Arkansas, USA. Buried: cremated and buried by her husband in Evergreen Cemetery, Omaha, Douglas County, Nebraska, USA.

6. **James Lourie JACOBS** (1907-1985). Born: 4 Jan 1907, Bancroft, Cuming County, Nebraska, USA. Marr: Helen SANKO 5 May 1932. Died: 17 Jul 1985, Elkhorn, Douglas County, Nebraska, USA. Buried: Cremated and buried with spouse at a later date.
= Helen SANKO (1912-1997). Born: 18 Feb 1912, Omaha, Douglas County, Nebraska, USA. Died: 12 Jun 1997, Omaha, Douglas County, Nebraska, USA. Buried: 14 Jun 1997, Prospect Hill Cemetery, Elkhorn, Douglas County, Nebraska, USA.

    7. **F JACOBS**.
    = M GOTTSCH.
        8. **M GOTTSCH**.
        8. **M GOTTSCH**.
        8. **M GOTTSCH**.

5. **Morton Henry OSBORNE** (1885-). Born: 1 Aug 1885, Milford, Dickenson County, Iowa, USA. Buried: Montana.
= Georgia MAUN (-).

5. **Emily Lucille OSBORNE** (1890-1974). Born: 3 Jan 1890, Milford, Dickenson County, Iowa, USA. Died: Nov 1974, Detroit, Michigan, USA. Buried: Michigan, USA.
= [unnamed person] (-).

    6. **[unnamed person]** (-).
    = Robert HERTEN (-). Born: South Dakota, USA. Died: Detroit, Michigan, USA.

    6. **Roland HERTEN** (1910-1996). Born: 29 Aug 1910, Presho, Lyman County, South Dakota, USA. Died: 15 Oct 1996, Titusville, Florida, USA.

    6. **Ruth Elizabeth HERTEN**.
    = Kermit Otto LAGMAN (-).
        7. **LAGMAN** (-).
        = [unnamed person] (-).
        7. **LAGMAN** (-).
        7. **LAGMAN** (-).

6. **Beryl HERTEN** (1919-1968). Born: 14 Mar 1919. Died: 31 May 1968, Detroit, Michigan, USA.

6. **Phyllis HERTEN** (1925-c. 2002). Born: 9 Apr 1925. Died: c. 2002, Detroit, Michigan, USA.

5. **Clara Augusta OSBORNE** (1893-). Born: 10 Feb 1893, Flandreau, Moody County, South Dakota, USA.

= Floyd CORKILL (-).

    6. **Donald CORKILL.**

    6. **Margery CORKILL.**

5. **Russell S OSBORNE** (1897-1972). Born: 1 May 1897, Flandreau, Moody County, South Dakota, USA. Died: 27 Jun 1972. Greenville, Michigan, USA.

= Lucille (-1976). Died: Mar 1976.

4. **Susannah Dawson SMITH** (1859-1916). Born: 20 Feb 1859, Yorkville, Racine County, Wisconsin. Marr: Fred B. SHANCKS 30 Sep 1879, West Mitchell, Iowa. Died: 4 Jul 1916, Red Oak, Iowa. Buried: 6 Jul 1916, Mitchell, Iowa.

= Fred B. SHANCKS (-1916). Died: 4 Jul 1916, 924 Highland Avenue, Red Oak, Iowa.

    5. **Naomi Dorothy SHANCKS** (-aft1916). Died: aft Jul 1916.

    5. **Courtland W. SHANCKS** (-aft1916). Died: aft Jul 1916.

    5. **Ellsworth SHANCKS** (-).

3. **Frances SMITH** (1817-1874). Born: 22 Jun 1817. Bap: Wesleyan Chapel, Faversham, Kent. Died: 31 Oct 1874, Faversham, Kent.

= James DUNN (1816-1872). Born: 1816. Died: 1872.

    4. **Charles Smith DUNN** (-).

    = Clara GRIGGS (-).

    = Marion ELLIS (-).

    4. **Frederick John DUNN** (-).

    = Mary MERRICK (-).

        5. **Sidney DUNN** (-).

        = Ann (1901-1985). Born: 1901. Died: May 1985.

            6. **Barry DUNN.**

            = Emily (-).

    4. **Fanny Smith DUNN** (-).

    = Thomas HOARE (-).

4. **Robert Smith DUNN** (1849-1926). Born: 1849. Marr: Hannah DAY 1873, Faversham, Kent. Died: 24 Feb 1926.

= Hannah DAY (1849-1937), dau. of John DAY (1815-1893) and Frances EGGLESTON (1819-1910). Born: 10 Nov 1849, Monmouthshire. Died: 19 Mar 1937.

5. **Marion Frances Eggleston DUNN** (1874-1955). Born: 18 Oct 1874. Died: 30 Jan 1955.

5. **Winifred Mawson DUNN** (1876-1947). Born: 16 Oct 1876. Marr: William FITCHEW c. May 1919, Faversham, Kent. Died: 6 Aug 1947.
  = William FITCHEW (1854-1925), son of Edward FITCHEW (c. 1810-) and Esther FAGG (-). Born: 1854. Marr: Emily Anne HAMBLIN c. Feb 1881, Wandsworth, Middlesex. Died: Aug 1925.

4. **James Smith DUNN** (1851-1925). Born: 23 Mar 1851. Died: 1925, America.
  = [unnamed person] (-).

4. **Herbert Smith DUNN** (-).
  = Mary EDWARDS (-).

4. **Mary Anne Smith DUNN** (1858-1878). Born: 1858. Died: 1878.

4. **Smith DUNN** (-).

3. **Charles Cornelius SMITH** (1818-). Born: 25 Jul 1818. Bap: 4 Apr 1819, St. Mary of Charity, Faversham, Kent.

3. **John Hawley SMITH** (1820-1833). Born: 15 Jan 1820. Bap: St. Mary of Charity, Faversham, Kent. Died: 6 Apr 1833.

3. **Sarah Ann SMITH** (1822-). Born: 20 Mar 1822. Bap: St. Mary of Charity, Faversham, Kent. Marr: Samual SZAPIRA 20 May 1856.
  = Samual SZAPIRA (1831-). Born: 1831, Volkovysk, Poland.

3. **Mary Ann SMITH** (1824-1850). Born: 2 Feb 1824. Bap: St. Mary of Charity, Faversham, Kent. Died: 23 Sep 1850.
  = Robert DUNK (-).

4. **Charles DUNK** (-).

4. **Marian DUNK** (-).
  = SKELTON (-).

3. **Thomas Elvy SMITH** (1826-1911). Born: 15 Dec 1826. Bap: St. Mary of Charity, Faversham, Kent. Marr: Eliza Ann ELLIOTT 10 Oct 1865. Died: 1911, Charing, Kent.
  = Eliza Ann ELLIOTT (1835-1922). Born: 1835. Died: Jul 1922.

3. **Stephen SMITH** (1828-1906). Born: 11 Oct 1828, Preston, Faversham, Kent. Bap: 7 Nov 1828, St. Mary of Charity, Faversham, Kent. Marr: Sarah DAWSON 2 Jun 1852, Boughton Chapel, Kent. Marr: Emily Dawson JONES aft Sep 1902. Died: 12 Dec 1906, Winchester, Hampshire. Buried: Winchester.
  = Sarah DAWSON (1827-1902), dau. of John DAWSON (1785-1850) and Ann GOODHUGH (c. 1796-1852). Born: 17 Mar 1827, Faversham, Kent. Bap: 29 Apr 1827, Wesleyan Chapel, Faversham, Kent. Died: 7 Sep 1902. Buried: River View cemetery, Oshkosh, Wisconsin.

4. **Annie Dawson SMITH** (1853-bef1855). Born: 1853. Died: bef 1855. Buried: Boughton chapel yard, Kent.

4. **Clara Elizabeth SMITH** (1854-1858). Born: 1854, Boughton, Kent. Died: 1858, Elkhorn, Wisconsin.

4. **Ernest Stephen SMITH** (1856-1941). Born: 2 Jul 1856, Elk Grove, Illinois. Marr: Ida May VANDERPOOL 8 Oct 1879, Mitchell,

Iowa. Marr: Luelia THOMPSON 6 Dec 1910, Little Rock, Arkansas. Died: 17 Jun 1941.

= Ida May VANDERPOOL (-).

5. **Emily Dawson SMITH** (1880-). Born: 20 Oct 1880, Mitchell, Iowa. Marr: Charles Robert PAYNE c. May 1910, Winchester, Hampshire.

= John S. VEGGENER (1876-). Born: 12 Nov 1876.

= Charles Robert PAYNE (-).

5. **Florence Gertrude SMITH** (1882-). Born: 2 Feb 1882.

5. **Marjorie Lucille SMITH** (1888-1945). Born: 18 Aug 1888. Marr: Clement MACMAHON 22 Jun 1910. Died: Jun 1945.

= Clement MACMAHON (1871-1930). Born: 24 Oct 1871. Died: Feb 1930.

    6. **Ida Jane MACMAHON.**

5. **Caroline May SMITH** (1894-). Born: 20 Dec 1894. Marr: Donald B. CAMPBELL 2 Nov 1918.

= Donald B. CAMPBELL (1898-). Born: Nov 1898.

    6. **Betsy May CAMPBELL.**

    6. **Bob CAMPBELL.**

    = Luelia THOMPSON (1871-). Born: 25 May 1871.

4. **Clarence Dawson SMITH** (1859-1926). Born: 23 Jan 1859, Sharon, Wisconsin. Died: 1926.

= Georgia SANFORD (-).

5. **Doris SANFORD** (-).

= William HOSKINS (-).

4. **Arthur Charles SMITH** (1860-1907). Born: 25 Nov 1860, Sharon, Wisconsin. Marr: Martha WILBOR Oshkosh, Wisconsin. Died: 1907.

= Martha WILBOR (-).

5. **Carlton Wilbor SMITH** (1890-). Born: 1890.

= Jeanette HAWES (-).

    6. **Jane SMITH** (1916-). Born: 1916.

    = James Dockray TUVERSON.

        7. **M TUVERSON.**

        = F Hitchcock BRUCE (-).

            8. **F TUVERSON.**

            = SINCLAIR.

8. **F TUVERSON.**
= DAGOSTIN.
8. **M TUVERSON.**
8. **M TUVERSON.**
= F (-).
8. **M TUVERSON.**
7. **M TUVERSON.**
= F SKELTON.
8. **F TUVERSON.**
= M WILEY.
9. **F SISCO.**
= M SISCO.
9. **M SISCO.**
8. **M TUVERSON.**
= F ROSE.
9. **F TUVERSON.**
9. **F TUVERSON.**
7. **M TUVERSON.**
= F PERKINS (-).
6. **F SMITH.**
= M KELCH.
7. **M KELCH.**
6. **F SMITH.**
= JUNK.
6. **F SMITH** (-).
= GRAEF (-).
5. **Howard Lowell SMITH** (1892-1918). Born: 1892. Died: 1918, France.
5. **Dorothy Dawson SMITH** (1896-). Born: 1896.
= Robert H ENNIS (-).
6. **Marcia ENNIS** (1918-2007) Born: 1918. Died: Jan 2007.
= John Bradford STEVENS, son of Evarts C. STEVENS (-).

145

7. **M STEVENS.**
= F RIESS.
    8. **F STEVENS.**
    8. **M STEVENS.**
      = F SIDORAK.
7. **F STEVENS.**
= M AKIN.
    8. **M STEVENS.**
7. **M STEVENS.**
= F CALHOUN.
    8. **M STEVENS.**
    8. **F STEVENS.**
7. **F STEVENS.**
= M WILSON.
    8. **M WILSON.**
    8. **M WILSON.**
5. **Marshall Henry SMITH** (1900-). Born: 1900. Marr: Charlotte PRADT Warsaw, Wisconsin.
= Charlotte PRADT (-).
    6. **Sandra SMITH.**
    = [unnamed person].
      7. **M.**
    6. **Howard Lowell SMITH.**
    6. **Stephen Altwater SMITH.**
    = Emily Dawson JONES (c. 1868-), dau. of John JONES (c. 1820-c. 1904) and Ann Staines DAWSON (1825-1915). Born: c. Feb 1868, Winchester, Hampshire. Marr: PAYNE aft 7 Sep 1902.
3. **George SMITH** (1833-). Born: 14 Feb 1833.
= Mary HANNAM (-).

HARRIS

1. **Thomas HARRIS** (-).
= Ann (-).
2. **George HARRIS** (1824-). Born: 10 Apr 1824, Upper Hardres, Kent. Bap: Upper Hardres, Kent. Marr: Johanna COLE c. May 1863.
= Johanna COLE (-).
3. **Elizabeth HARRIS** (c. 1865-). Born: c. 1865.
2. **James HARRIS** (1825-1872). Born: 14 Oct 1825, Upper Hardres, Kent. Bap: 13 Nov 1825, SS Peter & Paul, Upper Hardres, Kent. Marr: Mary Ann
SHOOBRIDGE Jan 1865, Tenterden, Kent. Died: 30 May 1872.
= Mary Ann SHOOBRIDGE (1828-1911), dau. of Thomas Hunt SHOOBRIDGE (-) and Sarah WOOD (bap.1799). Born: 27 Apr 1828. Bap: 27 Apr
1828, Halstow, Kent. Died: 24 Mar 1911.
3. **William Thomas HARRIS** (1867-1945). Born: 13 Feb 1867. Marr: Hannah SHEFFIELD 11 Sep 1891, Thanet DRO. Died: 30 Jan 1945.
= Hannah SHEFFIELD (1865-1950), dau. of Henry SHUFFILL (c. 1823-bef1877) and Harriet Ann BOFFIN (1828-). Born: 25 Jun 1865, Little
London, Whitchurch, Buckinghamshire. Died: 27 Feb 1950, Hereford.
4. **Frances Eva HARRIS** (1893-). Born: 3 Jul 1893.
4. **Martin Thomas HARRIS** (1894-). Born: 2 Mar 1894.
= Edith Norine SING (-).
5. **Gordon Sheffield HARRIS.**
= Doris (-).
6. **M HARRIS.**
6. **M HARRIS.**
6. **F HARRIS.**
6. **F HARRIS.**
6. **F HARRIS.**
5. **Murray HARRIS.**
= Jo (-).
6. **M HARRIS.**
6. **M HARRIS.**
6. **F HARRIS.**
6. **F HARRIS.**
5. **HARRIS** (-).

5. **HARRIS** (-).
5. **HARRIS** (-).
4. **Albert James HARRIS** (1895-). Born: 3 Oct 1895.
= Kathleen FRIGHT (-).
   5. **M HARRIS.**
   = F (-).
      6. **F HARRIS.**
      = M NEWIS (-).
      6. **M HARRIS.**
      = F (-).
         7. **M HARRIS.**
   5. **Tessa HARRIS** (-c. 2020). Died: c. 2020.
   = M WILT (-).
   = M TAYLOR (-).
4. **Sydney William HARRIS** (1897-). Born: 9 Mar 1897.
= Blanche SMITH (-).
   5. **M HARRIS.**
   = F (-).
      6. **HARRIS.**
      6. **HARRIS.**
      6. **HARRIS.**
      6. **HARRIS.**
      6. **HARRIS.**
   5. **M HARRIS.**
   = F (-).
      6. **F HARRIS.**
      6. **F HARRIS.**
   5. **F HARRIS.**
   = M RUTHERFORD (-).
      6. **RUTHERFORD.**
      6. **RUTHERFORD.**

4. **Florence Catherine HARRIS** (1898-1993). Born: 24 Aug 1898. Marr: William Goodhugh DAWSON 9 Apr 1923. Died: 17 Apr 1993.
= William Goodhugh DAWSON (1883-1976), son of William Goodhugh DAWSON (1851-1909) and Mary Frances DAY (1851-1933).
Born: 17 May 1883. Died: 25 Sep 1976.

   5. **William Goodhugh DAWSON.**
   = Margaret Grace HAYWARD.

      6. **William Goodhugh DAWSON.**
      = Andrea Lynne THOMPSON.

      6. **Sarah Margaret DAWSON.**
      = Philip James GRIFFIN.

         7. **Anna Elizabeth GRIFFIN.**
         7. **Owen James GRIFFIN.**
         7. **Bethany Rachel GRIFFIN.**

   5. **Martin Harris DAWSON** (1927-2006). Born: 18 Feb 1927. Marr: Shirley GREY 2 Jul 1955. Died: 29 Nov 2006, Norfolk.
Buried: 11 Dec 2006.
= Shirley GREY (1936-2005). Born: 21 May 1936. Died: 15 Mar 2005.

      6. **M DAWSON.**
      = F HARVEY.

         7. **M DAWSON.**
         7. **F DAWSON.**
         7. **M DAWSON.**
         = F DIBLEY.

      6. **M DAWSON.**
      = F MCRAE.

         7. **M DAWSON.**
         7. **M DAWSON.**
         7. **M DAWSON.**
         7. **M DAWSON.**

      6. **M DAWSON.**
      6. **M DAWSON.**
      = F.
      = F SINCLAIRE.

7. **M DAWSON**.
= F.
  7. **F DAWSON**.
6. **F DAWSON**.
= M LINES.
  7. **M LINES**.
6. **M DAWSON**.
= F DENNIS.
  7. **M DAWSON**.
= [unnamed person].
4. **Hubert Arnold HARRIS** (1900-1902). Born: 13 Aug 1900. Died: 28 Nov 1902.
4. **Ivy Kathleen HARRIS** (1902-1996). Born: 20 Feb 1902. Marr: Fred Walton COOPER 22 Aug 1925, Herne Bay, Kent. Died: 1996.
= Fred Walton COOPER (c. 1898-1986), son of Harvey William COOPER (1867-1911) and Caroline Matilda GARRETT (1868-). Born: c. May 1898, Hitchin, Hertfordshire. Died: 4 Aug 1986.
5. **Bryan Walton COOPER** Born 5 June 1928. Marr: 5 Oct 1957, Jean LINDSAY, Whitstable. Occupation: civil and structural engineer. Died: 17 Dec 2021.
= Jean LINDSAY Born 20 Nov 1930, Colombo, Ceylon (Sri Lanka).
6. **F COOPER**.
= M ANSCOMBE (-).
  7. **M ANSCOMBE**.
  7. **F ANSCOMBE**.
6. **M COOPER**.
6. **M COOPER**.
= F MCCOY.
5. **Gillian COOPER** (1931-2022). Born: Faversham, 2Q Kent 1932. Marr: John ABERDEEN 3Q 1955, Ospringe, Faversham. Emigrated to Melbourne, Australia leaving on 4 July 1957. Died: 20 July 2022, Brighton, Victoria, Australia.
= John ABERDEEN (1928-2022). Born: 1928, Bendigo, Australia. Occupation: paediatric surgeon. Died: 10 April 2022, Brighton, Victoria, Australia.
6. **F ABERDEEN**.
6. **F ABERDEEN**.
6. **F ABERDEEN**.

6. **F ABERDEEN**.
6. **F ABERDEEN**.
6. **M ABERDEEN**.
5. **M COOPER**.
= F COCKETT (-).
6. **F COOPER**.
= M BROWN (-).
7 **M BROWN**.
7. **F BROWN**.
6. **M COOPER**.
= F (-).
6. **M COOPER**.
= F (-).
4. **Kathleen Miriam HARRIS** (1904-). Born: 2 Mar 1904. Marr: Christopher PEARCE c. Nov 1930, Blean, Kent. Died: "early 1990s".
= Christopher PEARCE (-1990). Died: 1990.
5. **F PEARCE**.
= M TERRY (-).
6. **M TERRY**.
= F (-).
7. **F TERRY**.
6. **M TERRY**.
6. **F TERRY**.
4. **Hubert Arnold HARRIS** (1906-1987). Born: 28 Nov 1906. Died: 26 Dec 1987.
= Edyth KNIGHT (-).
5. **M HARRIS**.
= F (-).
5. **M HARRIS**.
= F (-).

2. **Henry HARRIS** (1828-). Born: 30 Apr 1828, Upper Hardres, Kent. Bap: Birchington, Kent. Bap: Upper Hardres, Kent.
2. **Agnes HARRIS** (c. 1830-). Born: c. 1830. Bap: 21 Nov 1830, All Saints, Birchington, Kent.
2. **Sarah Jane HARRIS** (c. 1832-). Born: c. 1832. Bap: 20 May 1832, All Saints, Birchington, Kent.

2. **Ann HARRIS** (c. 1834-). Born: c. 1834. Bap: 19 Jan 1834, Birchington, Kent.
2. **Mary HARRIS** (c. 1835-). Born: c. 1835. Bap: 21 Nov 1835, Birchington, Kent.

SHUFFILL (SHEFFIELD)

1. **John SHUFFILL** (1775-). Born: 1775.
= Ann COOK (1779-), dau. of Stephen COOK (c. 1755-) and Mary RICKARD (c. 1755-). Born: 1779.
   2. **Thomas SHUFFILL *** (1798-). Born: 1798.
   = Rebecca CHENEY * (1798-1826), dau. of Henry CHENEY (-). Born: 1798. Died: 1826, Whitchurch, Buckinghamshire.
      3. **Henry SHUFFILL** (c. 1823-bef 1877). Born: c. 1823, Whitchurch, Buckinghamshire. Marr: Harriet Ann BOFFIN c. Aug 1847, Banbury, Oxfordshire. Died: bef 1877.
      = Harriet Ann BOFFIN (1828- 1900), dau. of Jonathan CLIFTON (1080 -) and Ann BAUGHIN (c. 1810-1835). Born: 1828, Bloxham, Oxfordshire. Buried Bloxham 4 Sept 1835.
         4. **Caleb SHEFFIELD** (c. 1848-). Born: c. 1848. Bap: 1848. Marr: Aug 1879.
         = (.F.)
            5. **Caroline SHEFFIELD** (-).
            5. **Fred SHEFFIELD** (-).
            5. **Mark SHEFFIELD** (-).
            5. **Ruth SHEFFIELD** (-).
         4. **Harry SHEFFIELD** (1850-).
         4. **James SHEFFIELD** (1852-).
         = Emma (-).
            5. **Ann SHEFFIELD** (-).
            = Hugh DOW (-).
               6. **Peter DOW** (-).
               6. **Dorothy DOW** (-).
            5. **Arthur SHEFFIELD** (-).
            5. **Jessie SHEFFIELD** (-).
            = Ernest (-).
            5. **Gertie SHEFFIELD** (-).
            = Albert GODWIN (-).
               6. **Joan** (-).

```
            7.  Hilary ( - ).
              = Philip DAVIDSON ( - ).
          6.  [unnamed person] ( - ).
      4.  Joshua SHEFFIELD (1855-1855). Born: 1855. Died 1855.
      4.  Caroline SHEFFIELD (1856- ). Born: 1856. Bap: c. 1863.
      4.  Elizabeth SHEFFIELD (1860-1860/1). Born 1860.
      4.  Elizabeth SHEFFIELD (1861- ). Born: 1861. Bap: c. 1861.
        = Jo. BROWN ( - ).
            5.  Ted BROWN ( - ).
            5.  Ivy BROWN ( - ).
              = WARD ( - ).
            5.  Dorrie BROWN ( -1957). Died: 1957.
            5.  Koko BROWN ( - ).
      4.  Caroline SHEFFIELD (1862-1862/3). Born: 1862. Bap: c. 1862.
      4.  Caroline SHEFFIELD (1863- ). Born: 1863.
      4.  Hannah SHEFFIELD (1865-1950). Born: 25 Jun 1865, Little London, Whitchurch, Buckinghamshire. Marr: William Thomas
        HARRIS 11 Sep 1891, Thanet District Registry Office. Died: 27 Feb 1950, Hereford.
        = William Thomas HARRIS (1867-1945), son of James HARRIS (1825-1872) and Mary Ann SHOOBRIDGE (1828-1911). Born: 13 Feb
        1867. Died: 30 Jan 1945.
```

SEE HARRIS TREE FOR DESCENDANTS OF HANNAH SHEFFIELD AND WILLIAM HARRIS

```
      4.  Jane SHEFFIELD (1870- ). Born: 1870. Bap: c. 1873.
      4.  Rebecca SHEFFIELD (1870- ). Born: 1870. Bap: c. 1871.
        = John GREENAWAY ( - ).
            5.  Henry GREENAWAY ( - ).
            5.  Minnie GREENAWAY ( - ).
      4.  Minnie SHEFFIELD (1872- ). Born: 1872, Whitchurch, Buckinghamshire.
    3.  Elizabeth SHUFFILL (1821- ). Born: 1821, Whitchurch, Buckinghamshire.
    3.  Diana SHUFFILL (1823 - ).
```

COOPER

1. **William COOPER** (-) Marr: Nancy WALTON 25 Jun 1790, St Philip's, Birmingham.
= Nancy WALTON (1763 -) Dau of Benjamin WALTON (-) and Ann MEESON (-). Born: 1763, Walsall, Staffordshire.
  2. **Nancy COOPER** (c.1791 -) Bap: 30 Jun 1791, St Martin's, Birmingham.
  2. **Mary COOPER** (c.1793 -) Bap: 4 Jun 1793, St Martin's, Birmingham. Died: bfr 1799.
  2. **William COOPER** (c.1794 -) Bap: 8 Mar 1794, St Martin's, Birmingham.
  2. **Benjamin Walton COOPER** (c.1797 -) Bap: 8 Mar 1797, St Martin's, Birmingham. Marr: Elizabeth WILLIS 2 Dec 1818, St Martin's Birmingham
  = Elizabeth WILLIS (c.1790 -) Dau of Samuel WILLIS (1747 -) and Jane Ward (-). Bap: 16 Jul 1790, St Phillip's Birmingham.
    3. **William COOPER** (c.1821 -) Born abt 1821, Birmingham. Occupation slater and plasterer.
    = Elizabeth ROWLAND (c.1822 -) Dau of John ROLAND and Mary ?WRIGHT. Bap: 20 Oct 1822, Cefn Mawr, Denbighshire.
      4. **William COOPER** (1844 -) Born: 1Q 1844, Wrexham. Occupation slater and plasterer.
      = Sarah RABBITTS (c.1822 -) Born: abt 1822. Marr: 1Q 1846 Wrexham.
      4. **Joseph COOPER** (1846 -) Born: 3Q 1846, Wrexham. Occupation clerk then innkeeper.
      = Hannah ?ROBERTS (-) Prob marr: 2Q 1873, Wrexham.
      4. **Elizabeth COOPER** (1848 -) Born: 4Q 1848. Wrexham.
      4. **Richard COOPER** (1850 -) Born: 4Q 1850. Wrexham.
      4. **John COOPER** (1853 -) Born: 4Q 1853, Wrexham. Occupation merchant's clerk.
      4. **Mary COOPER** (c.1855 -) Born: 1Q 1855, Wrexham.
      4. **Charles Walton COOPER** (1859 -) Born: 2Q 1859, Wrexham.
      4. **Benjamin COOPER** (1861 -) Born: 2Q 1861, Wrexham. Prob died: 1Q 1863, Wrexham.
    3. **Benjamin Walter COOPER** Born: Aug 1828, Wrexham. Royal Artillery. Marr: Emma Harvey Died:4Q 1878, Gravesend.
    = Emma Amelia HARVEY (1827 – 1908) dau of James HARVEY (-) and Elizabeth HILLS (1787 – 1858). Born: 1827, Shoreham-on-Sea, Sussex. Bap: 2 Sept 1827, Brightlingsea, Essex. Marr: 19 May 1854, St George Fort, Ardersier (Nr Inverness). Died: 2Q 1908, Northampton.
      4. **Amy (?Amelia) COOPER** (1856 – 1921) Born (possibly illegitimate): 24 July 1856 Fort George, Inverness. Marr: (1) George LOOMES* (? – 1881) Southwark. Marr: (2) John George CHEER (1861 – 1926). Died: 24 December 1921, Cleethorpes. Bur: Cleethorpes cemetery.
      = (1) George LOOMES* (1854 – 1881) Born: 4Q 1854 Leicester. Died 4Q 1881, Southwark.
      = (2) John George CHEER (1861 – 1926) Born Reading. Buried Cleethorpes

5. **Reginald George CHEER** (1888 – 1924) Born: 1Q 1888 Cleethorpes. Died 1Q 1924. Bur: Cleethorpes cemetery Cleethorpes

5. **Lauretta Isabel CHEER** (1891 – 1979) Born: 10 September 1891 Cleethorpes. Marr. Cyril WYNN 1920

= Cyril WYNN (1896 – 1985) Born: 30 March 1896, Grimsby. Marr: 1Q 1920 Grimsby. Occupation fish buyer. Died 4Q 1895

5. **Benjamin Harvey CHEER** (1895 -). Born 1Q 1895 Retford, Nottinghamshire.

4. **Benjamin Walter COOPER** (also appears as Walter Benjamin Cooper) (- 1924) Born: abt 1857/58, Cork, Ireland. Partnership in hardware shop, Faversham. Marr: Jane Harriett WOOD, 15 Jul 1888, Faversham. Died: 24 Mar 1924, Faversham.

= Jane Harriet WOOD (1850 -) Dau of James Marsh WOOD (1815 - 1889) and Harriet Carr (1820 - 1873). Born: 3Q 1850. Died 1897.

4. **Flora Anne COOPER** (- 1920) Born abt 1859/60 Cork, Ireland, died Northants 1Q 1920

= Frederick (Frank) Alfred Downing (abt 1856-1938) Born Finedon, Northants abt 1856, married 3Q 1890 Faversham, occupation: decorator died Northants 3Q 1938

4. **Harvey William COOPER** (1867 – 1911) Born: Tilbury Fort, Essex,1 or 4 March 1867. Occupation plumber. Marr Caroline Matilda Garrett 24 Dec 1888, St Mary's, Reading. Died 4Q 1911, Hitchin, Hertfordshire.

= Caroline Matilda GARRETT (1868 - 1949) dau Francis GARRETT (1843-1887) and Rosina MORTON (1845 – 1908). Born 1868. Southwick. Prob died 1949, Reading.

5. **Emma Amelia COOPER** (1889 -) Born: 6 Mar 1889, Reading.

5. **Francis Harvey COOPER** (1891 -) Born: 1Q 1891, Reading.

5. **Flora Rosa COOPER** (1893 -) Born: 2Q 1893, Reading.

5. **John William COOPER** (1895-1917) Born: 3Q 1895, Reading. Killed in action 31 Jul 1917 near Ypres.

5. **Frederick Walton COOPER** (1898 – 1986) Born: 31 Mar 1898, Hitchin. Occupation: hardware shop proprietor. Died: 4 Aug 1986, Faversham..

= Ivy Kathleen HARRIS (1902 – 1996) Born: 28 Feb 1902, Birchington. Marr: 22 Aug 1925, Herne Bay Methodist Church. Died 28 Dec 1996, Faversham..

6. **Bryan Walton COOPER** (1928 - 2021). Born: 5 June 1928, Faversham. Marr: 5 Oct 1957, Jean LINDSAY, Whitstable. Occupation: civil and structural engineer. Died: 17 Dec 2021, Tunbridge Wells.

= Jean LINDSAY (1930 -) Born 20 Nov 1930, Colombo, Ceylon (Sri Lanka).

7. **F COOPER.**

= M ANSCOMBE (-).

8. **M ANSCOMBE.**

8. **F ANSCOMBE.**

7. **M COOPER.**

= F REES

155

7. **M COOPER.**
   = F MCCOY.

6. **Gillian COOPER** (1931-2022). Born: Faversham, 2Q Kent 1932. Marr: John ABERDEEN 3Q 1955, Ospringe, Faversham.. Emigrated to Melbourne, Australia 4 July 1957. Died: 20 July 2022, Brighton, Victoria, Australia,
   = John ABERDEEN (1928-2022). Born: 1928, Bendigo, Australia. Occupation: paediatric surgeon. Died: 10 April 2022, Brighton, Victoria, Australia.
   7. **F ABERDEEN.**
   7. **F ABERDEEN.**
   7. **F ABERDEEN.**
   7. **F ABERDEEN.**
   7. **F ABERDEEN.**
   7. **M ABERDEEN.**

6. **M COOPER.**
   = F COCKETT (-).
   7. **F COOPER.**
   = M BROWN (-).
      8 **M BROWN.**
      8. **F BROWN.**
   7. **M COOPER.**
   = F (-.)
   7. **M COOPER.**
   = F (-.)

5. **Eric COOPER** Born 4Q 1909 Hitchin

2. **Mary COOPER** (1799 -) Bap: 14 Oct 1799, St Martin's Birmingham. Prob. died 19 Jun 1807.
2. **Samuel COOPER** (1802 -) Bap: 1 June 1802, St Martin's Birmingham.

FAMII

THREE PEAKS
and
MALHAM

Howard Beck

Scarthin Books, Cromford, Derbyshire 1991.

FAMILY WALKS
IN THREE PEAKS AND MALHAM

Family Walks Series
General Editor: Norman Taylor

––––––––––

THE COUNTRY CODE

Enjoy the countryside and respect its life and work
Guard against all risk of fire
Fasten all gates
Keep your dogs under close control
Keep to public paths across farmland
Use gates and stiles to cross fences, hedges and walls
Leave livestock, crops and machinery alone
Take your litter home
Help to keep all water clean
Protect wildlife, plants and trees
Take special care on country roads
Make no unnecessary noise

––––––––––

Published 1991

Phototypesetting, printing by Higham Press Ltd., Shirland, Derbyshire

ISBN 0 907758 42 8

TROW GILL   Route 3

Preface

Whichever way one views the Yorkshire Dales it is walking country par excellence, the very epitome of England's green and pleasant land. It matters little whether the visitor seeks historical links with the landscape or prefers striding along the wind-swept 'tops' to a more sedate amble along the meandering, tree fringed rivers of the verdant valleys; it's all here, an infinity of contrasts simply awaiting to seduce the unprepared and guarantee that interest never wanes.

The region covered by this guide is centred upon that famous Three Peaks trilogy, which in itself needs little introduction. Some of the walks may be well known to those familiar with the area, others less so, but all are endowed with that classic ingredient which is synonymous with the Dales, beauty, variety, capricious weather and warm and welcoming Dalesfolk.

~~~~~~~~

About the author

Howard Beck works as a freelance photographer and writer of guides and books. His work has featured in many local and national publications, such as The Lady, Field, The Illustrated London News, Country Walking, Yorkshire Life and Dalesman. Family Walks in West Yorkshire is a companion volume in this series.

Other books by the author include:
GAPING GILL, 150 Years of Exploration (Hale).
BRONTE COUNTRY [joint photographer] (Trodd Pub.).
FAMILY WALKS AROUND SKIPTON (Dalesman).
Books in preparation:
WORDSWORTH'S LAKE DISTRICT.
IN SEARCH OF YORKSHIRE'S ROOTS.
CAVES OF THE CLOUD FORESTS.

~~~~~~~~

CONTENTS

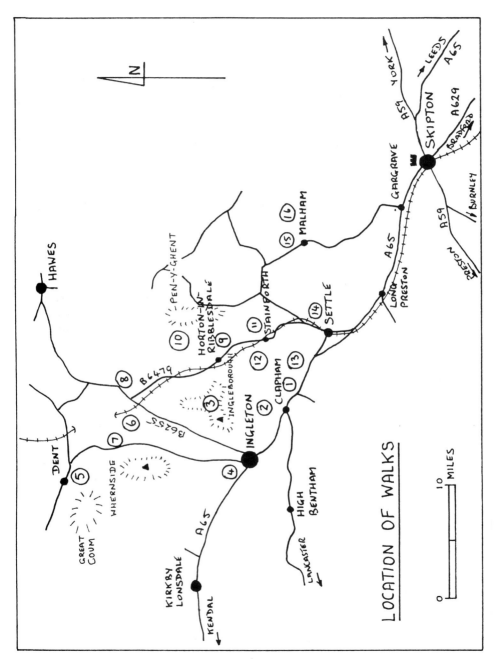

LOCATION OF WALKS

0 — 10 MILES

Introduction

The terrain described in this book is dominated by the geology of the Carboniferous Period, strata laid down in warm seas up to 350 million years ago. It unfolds like a living drama where the main characters are the limestone gorges, soaring cliffs, caves, potholes and frowning gritstone edges.

Like balconies cut into this natural theatre, tributary gills of the main valleys are draped in lush, broad-leaf woodlands. Within these verdant bowers, the boles of ash, rowan and oak stand in silent audience while a medley of the finest waterfalls play a tune by the composer Mother Earth. The area is alive with a rich flora and fauna and riddled with the country's greatest profusion of potholes and caverns.

This volume of walks is designed principally but not exclusively for the family group with children, and aims as with other books in this series, to stimulate and excite the younger generation into appreciating the finer points of the countryside. All the routes are circular walks, where possible avoiding steep gradients and too much road walking. I have planned each outing to include features which will retain the interest of children, for instance lakes, waterfalls, woods, legends, strange stones and caves.

Choosing a walk

Unless children in the party are seasoned ramblers it is perhaps advisable to select easier routes initially, moving on to more sustained expeditions at a later date. In the appendix at the end of the book an attempt has been made to grade the walks in terms of difficulty. The reader may find this of value in choosing suitable walks that avoid placing too great a demand on younger children too soon in their walking life. The aim is to nurture interest rather than put the child off walking for life!

Allowing sufficient time

Many of the walks will form the best part of a day's outing, at a child's pace, allowing time off for play, exploration and rest stops, whilst for one or two a half day will suffice. It is infinitely better to over-estimate rather than under-estimate the time required; there is nothing worse than having to route march the last stages of the journey. As a rough guideline, allow a pace of around one mile per hour for a very young child, graduating to two miles an hour for a more experienced ten-year old.

What to wear

The British weather being what it is demands that walkers go prepared for the worst. Robust, but comfortable fell shoes or walking boots are more desirable than wellingtons, even though the latter have their place in English folk heritage! They do tend to chafe on long walks. Waterproof outer garments are an essential rather than a luxury, while underneath several layers of thin woollies are far better than one thick jumper. They tend to be warmer when the conditions are cold and in hotter weather (we do get it warm now and again) allow greater flexibility. Don't forget a woolly hat and gloves. A strong rucksack is essential for carrying spare clothing, food, drink, maps and so on.

Finding the way

Most of the walking described is along well defined and marked public footpaths, bridleways and green lanes, with the occasional stretch of road where this is unavoidable. Though each of the route descriptions and maps should be sufficiently detailed for navigation it is recommended that the relevant Ordnance Survey sheet is taken along as well. Should the reader find a path obstructed then the line of least resistance around it should be sought and the problem reported either to the Ramblers Association or to the relevant District Council.

Refreshments

Most of the pubs along these walks allow children on the premises if accompanied by an adult. Many cater for young children and may include play areas or special rooms. Bar meals and lunches are usually available but a good alternative, and one which will go down well with the younger walker, is to take along a picnic. Places on route where this is ideal are mentioned, as are the locations of cafes and tea shops.

Public transport

Although these days most families possess a car or other means of transport, I have included relevant details on bus operators, trains, etc in the appendices.

THWAITE LANE NEAR AUSTWICK

Symbols used on the route maps

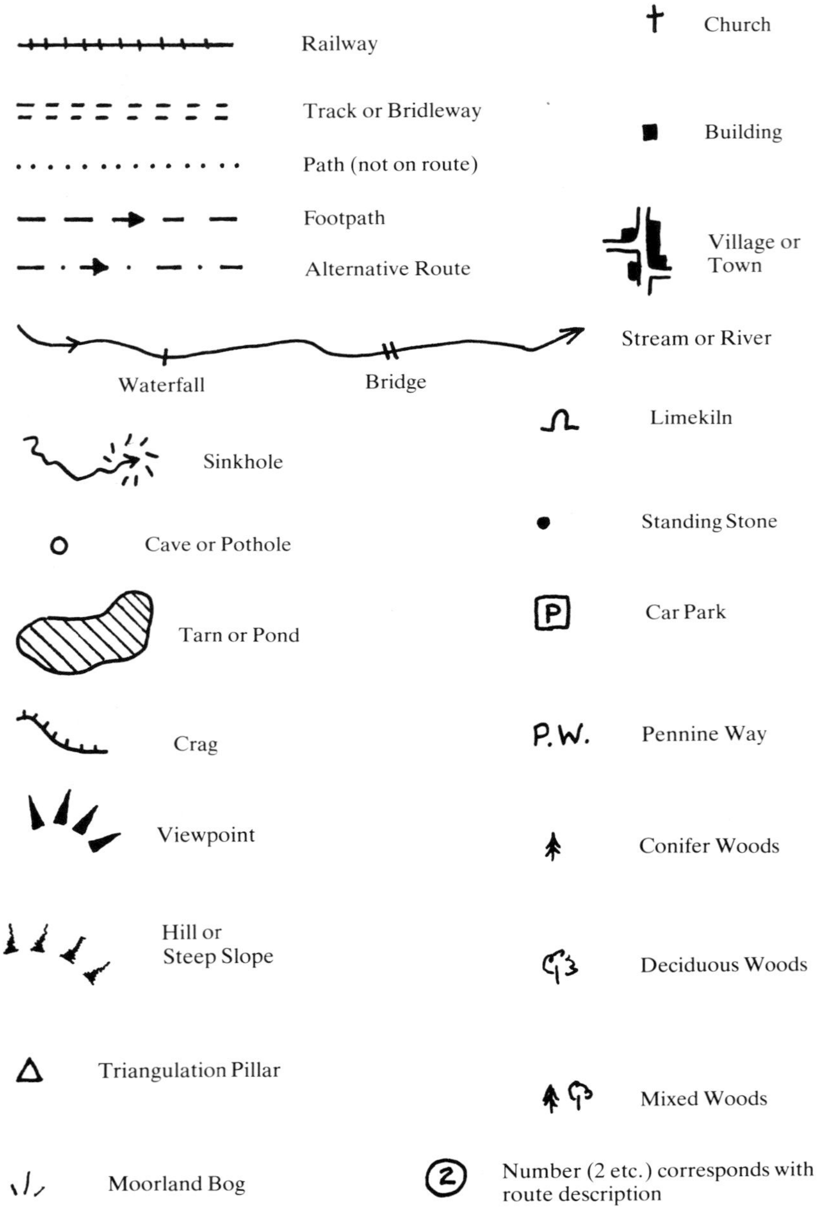

┼┼┼┼┼┼┼┼┼	Railway
= = = = = = =	Track or Bridleway
· · · · · · · · · · · ·	Path (not on route)
— — ➤ — —	Footpath
— · ➤ · — · —	Alternative Route

Waterfall   Bridge   Stream or River

Sinkhole

○   Cave or Pothole

Tarn or Pond

Crag

Viewpoint

Hill or
Steep Slope

△   Triangulation Pillar

Moorland Bog

†   Church

■   Building

Village or
Town

Limekiln

●   Standing Stone

P   Car Park

P.W.   Pennine Way

🌲   Conifer Woods

Deciduous Woods

Mixed Woods

②   Number (2 etc.) corresponds with
route description

8

Route 1

Austwick and Norber Erratics

Outline   Austwick ~ Norber Brow (standing stones) ~ Thwaite Lane (green track) ~ Clapham ~ Visitor Centre ~ Austwick.

Summary   This pleasant walk, mostly along easy field paths and green lanes, links Austwick with the neighbouring village of Clapham. Both villages possess fine examples of vernacular architecture so typical of the Yorkshire Dales. At Norber Brow the scarp edge enjoys expansive panoramas, but it is the erratic boulders that catch the eye. There are plenty of places here and on route for play and adventure.

Attractions   Clapham is without doubt one of the prettiest of Dales villages, its focal point being the beck which divides the village and is spanned by several bridges. The stream is a favourite haunt of dippers and is a delight with young children for duck feeding or stick dipping.

The Dales National Park Visitor Centre (parking nearby) provides a welcome escape should the weather prove inclement. It has many permanent displays as well as audio-visual productions featuring various aspects of the region.

One of the lesser known claims to fame at Clapham is the fact that the parents of Michael Faraday, the Father of Electricity, lived here. Oddly enough the railway station was one of the last in the country to have electric lighting installed on the platform!

The walk starts north of Austwick. After a short climb the scarp edge is reached where the alignment of the Craven Fault has created Norber Brow. This overlooks the village and offers some choice views across the River Wenning to the Bowland Fells and Pendle Hill, deep in the heart of Lancashire's witch country.

The many huge boulders of Silurian slate here perched like sentinel trolls on the scarp edge, balance precariously upon the underlying limestone. This vision will no doubt stimulate a vivid imagination of giants at play. These erratics were of course deposited by retreating glaciers at the end of the last Ice Age.

The green track of Thwaite Lane, was formerly part of an 11th century road plied by Cistercian monks travelling from Fountains Abbey to their estates in the Lake District. Today it forms an important walkers' link between the two villages.   *continued on page 12*

9

Route 1

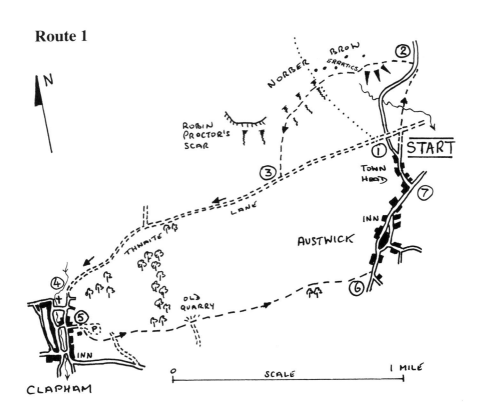

N

NORBER BROW
ERRATICS

ROBIN PROCTOR'S SCAR

START

TOWN HEAD

LANE

THWAITE

AUSTWICK

INN

OLD QUARRY

CLAPHAM

INN

0   SCALE   1 MILE

NORBER ERRATIC

Huxson Beck

Route 1

Austwick and Norber Erratics

4 miles
(shorter variation 2½ miles

START   *Parking for one or two cars can be found at the cross roads on the Austwick to Crummack lane a quarter mile north of the village. O.S. Outdoor Leisure Sheet 2. (G.R. SD769692).*

ROUTE

1. *From the cross-road walk east along the bridleway for 100 yards to pick up a footpath turning left (uphill). The path crosses a small stream and, still climbing, eventually meets the lane to Crummack once again.*
2. *Across this a path leads off along the edge of Norber Brow. Away from this the Norber erratics will be seen. The continuing path is a little unclear in places. However, by heading for Robin Proctor's Scar and more or less keeping to the scarp edge the path is found descending slightly west of south to enter Thwaite Lane.*
3. *Turn right and follow this track for almost a mile, passing through a tunnel to enter Clapham village by the church.*
4. *Walking down either side of the beck reaches the National Park Visitor Centre.*
5. *Walk to the left of the centre and follow a path between the car park and toilet block. After an iron gate trace a field path to an old wall quarry. From here the well defined path continues for ¾ mile, entering Austwick at its south-western extremity.*
6. *Turn left and walk up the main street past the Gamecock Inn to a left turn 100 yards beyond the school.*
7. *Walking uphill, bear right at the fork to reach a bridleway cutting across the path. Turn left to return to the starting point.*

SHORTER VARIATION

For those wishing only to see the erratics at Norber, the route to Clapham may be omitted.

As for 1 to 3 above to Thwaite Lane then:

i *Turn left and, in a little over half a mile, return to start.*

ACCESS BY BUS

Pennine service from Skipton to Austwick.

Thwaite Lane eventually dives through a curious tunnel emerging in Clapham by the village church. The tunnel was built by the Farrer family beneath the grounds of Ingleborough Hall to afford some privacy from people using the right of way. Behind the church Clapham Beck thunders over a waterfall, before racing off through the centre of the village.

Refreshments The New Inn, Clapham. Meals and bar snacks. Spindle Tree Cafe, Clapham. Gamecock Inn, Austwick (lawn with children's slide).

INGLEBOROUGH CAVE

Route 2   3 miles

Clapdale and Ingleborough Cave

Outline   Clapham ~ Nature Trail ~ Victorian Grotto ~ Show Cave ~ Clapdale Castle ~ Clapham.

Summary   For sheer variety this walk has it all and is guaranteed to retain the interest of adults and children alike. The walk takes the reader through fairytale woodlands, by lakes and beckside, along open dale and by mysterious caves.

Attractions   The route through the Ingleborough grounds passes initially alongside a lake created in the early 19th century by the Farrer family. It is set amongst mature broad leaf woodlands that are the subject of the Reginald Farrer Nature Trail (leaflets from the Visitor Centre). This was set up in memory of the famous local botanist. A nominal fee is payable for entry through what are private grounds.

Water fowl abound on the lake, whilst the sharp eye will spot many exotic plant species brought back from places as remote as Burma and the Himalayas. The woods are alive with flowers, birdlife and squirrels which will delight the children. An added bonus in late August are the many wild strawberries growing alongside the trail.

Part way through the grounds a grotto created for Victorian ladies provides the walker with shelter if caught out by the rain. Some quarter of a mile beyond this the woods are left behind for the open reaches of Clapdale. A clear running brook forms an ideal place for picnics or simply to rest and let the children paddle.

The stream can be traced as far as Beck Head where the water emerges from a low cave mouth. Beside this is Ingleborough Cave where guided parties are treated to a glimpse into the subterranean world for which the region is famed. The amazing array of calcite stalactites and stalagmites make this one of the finest caves open to the public.

The return to the starting point involves retracing your steps for a short distance to pass Clapdale Castle. This is really a fortified farmstead which featured in the Wars of the Roses, when it was held by the House of Lancaster. Local tradition has it that the building is haunted and that knights of the Clapham family are interred in an upright posture beneath the floor. Whether there is any truth in this has never been proved, yet it is a nice story to fire the imagination.

Refreshments   Kiosk at the cave. The New Inn (Beer garden and children's room), and Spindletree Cafe in the village.

13

Route 2

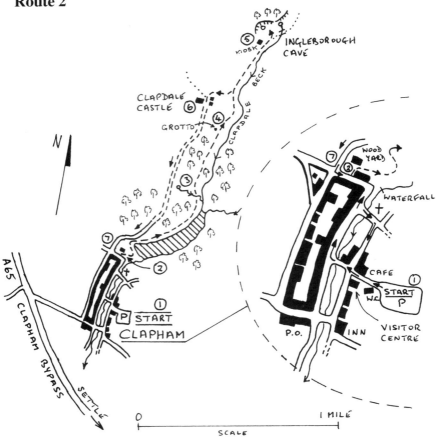

Route 2

Clapdale and Ingleborough Cave   3 miles

START   *The Central car park in Clapham, located just off the B6480. O.S. Outdoor Leisure Sheet 2. (G.R. SD745692).*

ROUTE

1. *Turn right out of the car park and immediately left over the footbridge. Turn right again and walk to the head of the village, bearing left to the entrance to the woodyard (signposted Ingleborough Cave).*

2. *Turn right through the gate, and after paying at the cottage, bear right through a gate and trace the path uphill and around to the left through an arch of trees to follow it alongside a lake.*

3. *Shortly after leaving the lake behind a normally dry stream bed is crossed and the path continues through mature woodlands with the stream flowing in a ravine down to the right. A Victorian grotto is passed on the left, and soon afterwards the woods end at a gate.*

4. *Clapdale is now more open with the beck babbling nearby. The path continues to the Show Cave and Beck Head after a further ¼ mile.*

5. *Retracing your steps take a stony track heading uphill on the right, through a gate, to reach Clapdale Castle.*

6. *Keeping left of the farmhouse pass a second gate and follow a stony track downhill through pastures eventually entering Clapham by the woodyard.*

7. *Turn left then right and walk down to the footbridge where a left turn returns to the start.*

ACCESS BY BUS
Pennine buses and Mountain Goat Bus between Skipton and Ingleton call at Clapham.

TROW GILL

16

Route 3   7 miles
Rigodunum Hill Fort

Outline   Clapham ~ Clapdale ~ Trow Gill ~ Gaping Gill Hole (famous pothole) ~ Ingleborough Hill (Rigodunum Hill Fort) ~ Newby Cote ~ Newby ~ Laithbutts Lane (path) ~ Clapham.

Summary   This walk starts as for the previous route, but by way of contrast, heads for the most famous of that Three Peaks trilogy. The walker attaining the summit of Ingleborough will be amply rewarded for his efforts. It forms a fitting climax to a walk which will give the children in the party a real sense of achievement. In the past people believed the summit was a mile high! Children can play 'King of the Castle' in style.

Attractions   Leaving Clapham by the woodyard Ingleborough grounds are traced into Clapdale as with the previous route. From the entrance to Ingleborough Cave a narrowing valley flanked with cliffs is a picture of beauty in late summer and autumn when the red berries of rowan add a splash of colour to contrast with the grey limestone.

The valley has that mysterious feel about it that has a child wondering what waits around each corner. Black holes and crevices beckon enticingly. Soon the valley opens dramatically into Trow Gill, a rock walled ravine rising steeply to a narrowing cleft. At the top of this on the left is the Devil's Kitchen, a wide but low cave extending a few yards back into the rock.

The continuing dry valley climbs steadily as far as a stile by a rocky pothole. At this point the walker gains his first glimpse of his goal. From Bar Pot the obvious trail heads off through a patch of clints then bears around to the right along a peaty stretch which is notoriously boggy after prolonged rain.

Gaping Gill appears suddenly at the walker's feet. At 340ft. it is the deepest natural shaft in Britain, an awesome place which demands respect, for the rocks can be slippy. Fell Beck plunges over twice the height of Niagara Falls! At Whitsuntide week and August Bank Holiday local potholing clubs lower visitors by winch to explore a chamber vast enough to accommodate a cathedral. It is an experience never forgotten.

Ingleborough is now within striking distance though still 1¼ miles away. At 2372ft. above sea level it falls well short of being a mile high and is overshadowed by its neighbour across Chapel-le-Dale by 46ft. However the view from the summit plateau is unparalleled, extending to Morecambe Bay and the peaks of the Lake District.

continued on page 20

17

Route 3

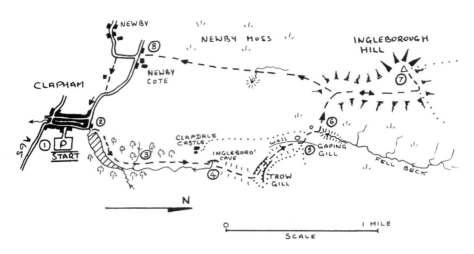

BECK HEAD CAVE

Route 3
Rigodunum Hill Fort

7 miles

START   *The Main car park in Clapham (G.R. SD745692) just off the B6480. O.S. Outdoor Leisure Sheet No. 2.*

ROUTE

1. *Turn right out of the car park and walk up the lane to the church. Follow the lane left in front of this, then right, and left again to reach the entrance to the woodyard.*

2. *Turn right into this, and after paying to enter Ingleborough grounds, aim for a gate over to the right of the cottage and trace the pathway uphill and around to the left.*

3. *Walk alongside the lake and after this ends cross Cat Hole Beck (normally dry) and continue through the woods, eventually to reach a gate. Continue ahead to reach the entrance of Ingleborough Cave.*

4. *From the kiosk walk over the bridge at Beck Head and pass through a gate to follow a dry valley gently ascending to reach a second gate. Follow the path around to the left and climb up through the gorge of Trow Gill. After a further ½ mile following a wall a step stile is met at Bar Pot corner.*

5. *Crossing this follow an easy path through an area of clints and around to the right with Ingleborough visible dead ahead. Aim for a fence to reach the shaft of Gaping Gill Hole.*

6. *The path now climbs to the north-west with increasing gradient toward the summit of Little Ingleborough. At the cairn turn right (north) and follow the ridge with level going for a while prior to the final pull up to the top. Head across the plateau to the west to reach the trig point and wind shelter.*

7. *Retrace your steps to find the path back down and follow this back to the cairn on Little Ingleborough, but here bear half right and descend a path which crosses Newby Moss to enter Newby Cote adjacent to a disused quarry.*

8. *Walk down to the cross-roads and carry on straight ahead towards Newby. Just where the lane starts to bend right walk up the banking on the left to find an obscure pathway (Laithbutts Lane) heading east. After ⅓ mile this rejoins the old road. Turn right and shortly enter Clapham by the woodyard.*

19

It is here that the Brigantian leader Venutius built his hill top stronghold and in the 1st century A.D. led the resistance against the Romans. The plateau is ringed with the tumbled remains of the perimeter wall and dotted with several cairns, an O.S. trig point, the remains of a lookout tower and a substantial wind shelter. A competition could perhaps be held amongst the younger members of the group to see who can spot the most hut circles. All told the foundation of 13 of them may be picked out amongst the hardy grasses.

The descent back into the valley passes through Newby Cote and Newby before entering Laithbutts Lane. Like Alice in Wonderland the walker leaves behind the sealed lane and all of a sudden an ancient pathway leads off. This is part of the monks' road from Fountains Abbey. Less frequented than most paths it is usually overgrown with nettles and briars (**shorts not recommended**), however the aspiring young botanist will no doubt enjoy identifying the wild blooms that colour its hedgerows in spring and summer.

Refreshments   New Inn, beer garden and childrens' room. Spindle Tree cafe. Both in Clapham.

ACCESS BY BUS
The Pennine bus from Skipton to Ingleton and Mountain Goat service
  call at Clapham.

THORNTON FORCE

20

Route 4   4½ miles
Ingleton Glens Waterfalls Trail

Outline   Ingleton Town ~ Swilla Glen ~ Pecca Falls ~ Thornton Force ~ Raven Ray ~ Scar End ~ Rival Falls ~ Beezley Falls ~ Baxenghyll Gorge ~ Snow Falls ~ Cat Leap Force ~ Ingleton.

Summary   Although a much commercialised walk this route has been included for there are few of comparable distance that can boast so much idyllic scenery. The entire route is way marked on well laid paths. Where there are gradients steps have been provided. **Extra special care should be taken** with children as the edges of vertical drops are not protected.

Attractions   The profusion of cascades, rapids and waterfalls invite superlatives. In combination with limestone gorges and natural woodlands rich with a varied flora and fauna, this trail is a delight for all the family. The scenery is superb and though a refreshment hut exists, it is recommended that a picnic be taken along so a whole day may be spent in order to enjoy to the fullest such magnificent surroundings.

If you prefer quiet and solitude this is not the walk for you. The outstanding natural beauty of the Ingleton Glens, and its wealth of geological features, has ensured that it is as popular today as when first opened to the public 115 years ago. Though busy there are ample compensations.

Thornton Force is the highest of the waterfalls at 40ft. One of the classic geological non-conformities is to be seen here where the Carboniferous Limestone sits upon the Ordovician Slates. It is possible to walk behind the waterfall, in normal water conditions that is, and within a single hand width span 20 million years in the earth's history! The trail offers some fine views of Ingleborough Hill and Chapel-le-Dale.

Though Ingleton has striven to live up to its popular appellation of Beauty Spot of the North I'm not all that convinced it has succeeded in marrying this ideal with its tarnished industrial heritage. In the past there has been lime burning, cotton spinning, quarrying and coal mining. It achieved a brief heyday when the railway came this way in 1849, but all that survives of the now disused line is the sweeping viaduct which carried the railway over the river Greta.

Refreshments   The Craven Heifer and Wheatsheaf pubs in Ingleton. A cafe by the ticket office at the start of the walk. Refreshments kiosk near the head of Pecca Falls.

Route 4

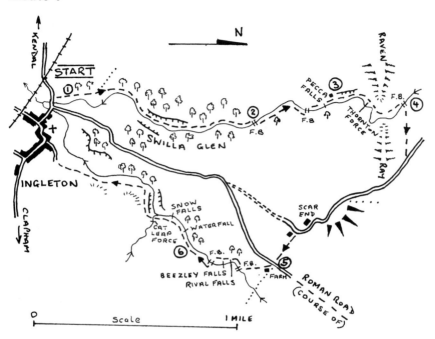

HARTS TONGUE FERN

22

Route 4

Ingleton Glens Waterfalls Trail   4½ miles

START   *The car park at (G.R. SD693733), reached by a road descending from Ingleton main street down towards the viaduct. The town is just off the A65. O.S. Outdoor Leisure Sheet 2.*

ROUTE

1. *From the ticket hut by the cafe a good path follows the meandering banks of the River Twiss into the rocky confines of Swilla Glen. The valley narrows and the path eventually reaches Manor Bridge.*

2. *Cross to the far bank and follow the pathway left, in ¼ mile crossing again at the next bridge. A good view upstream is obtained here. The way to Pecca Falls is by climbing some concrete steps along an especially picturesque stretch of the glens. The path bursts all of a sudden into the open at a refreshments hut.*

3. *Continue to Thornton Force. Here the path winds left up the hillside and continues upstream passing through a large bank of glacial drift, known as the Raven Ray. This originally dammed up the river, forming a lake in nearby Kingsdale. Around a couple more bends yet another foot bridge is met.*

4. *Crossing the beck the path climbs to a green lane. Turn right and walk as far as a farm. Pick up a path bearing left, past Twistleton Hall and descend to the road.*

5. *Follow a sign for Beezley Falls across the road and descend the track to the farm. Ignore the path going straight on. Bear right by the farm and descend to the River Doe. Ignoring the first footbridge, continue downstream, passing the magnificent Rival Falls and Beezley Falls. Cross the second bridge, and for the next stretch the stream has cut a deep slot at Baxenghyll Gorge.*

6. *Below the canyon is Snow Falls where the path then becomes less steep, passing Cat Leap Force on the tributary of Skirwith Beck. The way on then passes some disused quarries before becoming a bridleway entering Ingleton. A right turn at the T junction, down past the church towards the viaduct and the car park at the start is soon regained.*

ACCESS BY BUS

Pennine Motors or Mountain Goat bus services between Skipton and Ingleton.

MAIN STREET, DENT

The Dentdale Vampire

Outline   Mill Bridge ~ Deepdale Beck ~ Dent ~ Flinter Gill ~ Occupation Road ~ Scow ~ Mill Bridge.

Variation   Mill Bridge ~ Deepdale Beck ~ Dent ~ River Dee ~ Tommy Bridge ~ Mill Bridge.

Summary   An excellent walk at any time of the year, though for option 2 dry weather is necessary to cross a ford on the Dee. The route follows field paths, riverside meadows, packhorse trails and green lanes, which apart from the steep haul up Flintergill provide mostly easy walking.

Attractions   Dent town is in my opinion set in one of the prettiest of all the Dales, presided over by a handful of the finest fells in the region. It still retains much of its olde worlde charm by virtue of its narrow cobbled streets and hotch-potch of quaint stone cottages.

The eminent Cambridge Professor of geology Adam Sedgwick was born here in 1795, and to commemorate the fact there is a drinking fountain in the town centre incorporated into an inscribed boulder of Shap granite.

Dent is an interesting place to explore and has often been described as the Clovelly of the North. Should the weather prove less than a match for Devon there is a craft centre as well as art and photography galleries in which to browse. The church too is worth a look. The story of the Dentdale Vampire will be sure to excite the children.

One George Hodgson was believed, because of his uncommonly good health, to have dealings with the Devil. After his death in 1715 many villagers claimed to have seen him wandering on moonlit nights. Several mysterious deaths and the fact that he had prominent canine teeth merely served to strengthen their suspicions.

He was exhumed and reburied, they say, with a stake through his heart. The grave may be seen near the church porch and indeed has a square hole where it is said an iron stake was driven through the stone into the corpse!

The valley of the Dee and its many tributaries offers some excellent walking, idyllic in spring and summer when riverbanks, meadows and woods are a riot of colour from the variety of wild blooms.

Refreshments   The Sun and the George and Dragon pubs. The Stone Close Cafe (tea rooms) all in Dent town. Afternoon teas available at Scow Cottage.

Route 5

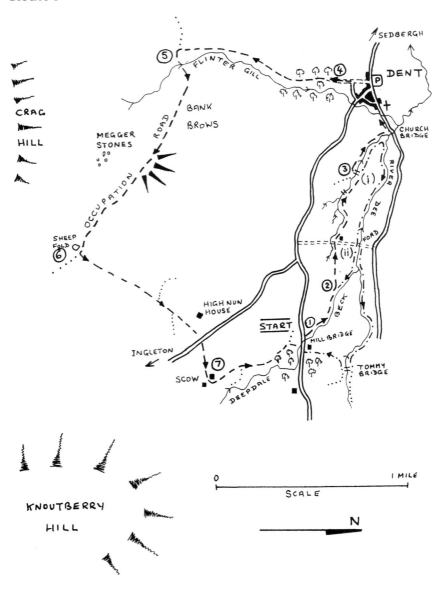

SEDBERGH

DENT

CRAG
HILL

FLINTER GILL

BANK
BROWS

MEGGER
STONES

ROAD

OCCUPATION

CHURCH
BRIDGE

RIVER DEE

FORD

SHEEP
FOLD

BECK

HIGH NUN
HOUSE

START

MILL BRIDGE

INGLETON

TOMMY
BRIDGE

SCOW

DEEPDALE

KNOUTBERRY
HILL

0   1 MILE
SCALE

N

26

Route 5

The Dentdale Vampire

6 miles
(Shorter Variation 2½ miles)

START   *At Mill Bridge one mile south-east of Dent there is room for a couple of cars to pull off the road at G.R. SD720861. O.S. Outdoor Leisure Sheet 2.*

ROUTE

1. *From Mill Bridge follow a path (signposted Church Bridge), soon reaching a ladder stile. From here the path traces the course of Deepdale Beck, crossing several more stiles.*

2. *After ½ mile the path divides. Turn left (more stiles). The path crosses a bridleway at Double Croft, passing to the left of the farm to reach a gap stile in a wall. Immediately through this turn left along a sunken track before following a small stream. Ignore the first wooden bridge to reach a ford and stepping stone. Keeping to the right bank, pass through a gap stile straight ahead and turn left over a concrete bridge.*

3. *Follow the stream now as far as Church Bridge and turn left up the hill past the church into Dent. Almost opposite the car park turn left up a short road to the village green. At the far side of this a narrow wooded lane twists uphill.*

4. *When the tarmac lane ends an old packhorse trail climbs steeply up Flinter Gill, eventually joining the Occupation Road. Ahead rise the slopes of Crag Hill and Great Coum.*

5. *Turn left following the green lane to a sheep fold where another green lane is met.*

6. *Turn left (downhill) as far as the Dent to Ingleton road. Cross this and take the field path to Scow.*

7. *After Scow the path bears left (north) and ½ mile later turns right to return to the parking spot by Mill Bridge.*

SHORTER VARIATION

i *After visiting Dent return to 3 and cross the footbridge. Turn left following a field path along the bank of the River Dee to reach a ford.*

ii *If the river is not dry continue up Deepdale Beck to return to the start, otherwise cross to the far side and turn right, following the river as far as Tommy Bridge. Cross again and follow a field path back to Mill Bridge.*

ACCESS BY TRAIN

Trains to Dent station. Taxi service into town. Tel. Dent (058 75) 203.

LIMESTONE PAVEMENT NEAR INGLEBOROUGH

Route 6

2 miles

Winterscales and Craven Way

Outline   Station Inn ~ Ribblehead Viaduct ~ Ivescar ~ Kirby Gate ~ Winterscales ~ Craven Way ~ Roger Kirk Rocks ~ Station Inn.

Summary   A pleasant level walk of short duration within sight of the Settle Carlisle Railway and the famous Three Peaks. It is ideal for the spare couple of hours on a dry afternoon.

Attractions   This walk starts and finishes at a pub, definitely an attraction some would say! It takes in the spectacular Ribblehead Viaduct on the recently reprieved Settle Carlisle Railway, just the ticket for train spotting if the walk coincides with the times when steam specials are passing through.

What an impressive sight it is to see a loco under full steam crossing this great monument to Victorian engineering. The structure is 160 feet high and curves 1300 feet across the moor. Some of the blocks from which it was built weigh as much as 8 tons. Story has it that the pillars upholding this amazing structure were supported on bales of fleece. In fact they extend 30 feet down into the peat to reach a firm footing on bedrock.

The route crosses Batty Moss, passing beneath the 24 arch span. After crossing Winterscales Beck the walk passes through Ivescar and, via the ancient Kirby Gate, the neighbouring settlement of Winterscales, two Dales farmsteads reflecting Viking settlement over 1000 years ago.

The Settle Carlisle Railway is crossed again close to Blea Moor Tunnel to follow the Craven Way. This is an old packhorse trail once linking Settle with Dent.

Rock outcrops at Roger Kirk Rocks provide exciting scrambling for the budding rock climber in the party. From these limestone scars Batty Green is crossed on the return to the car. It was here that the shanty towns sprang up to house the labour gangs who built the viaduct and nearby tunnel. These settlements were given colourful names like Jericho, Salt Lake City, Belgravia and Sebastopol.

Refreshments   The Station Inn, Ribblehead.

Route 6

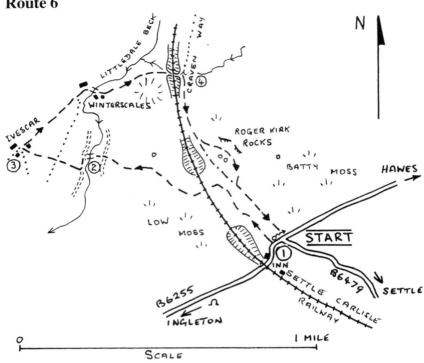

N

LITTLEDALE BECK

CRAVEN WAY

④

WINTERSCALES

IVESCAR

③

②

ROGER KIRK ROCKS

BATTY MOSS

HAWES

○○

LOW MOSS

START

①

INN

B6479

SETTLE CARLISLE RAILWAY

SETTLE

B6255

INGLETON

0   1 MILE

SCALE

INGLEBOROUGH

Howard Beck

Route 6

Winterscales and Craven Way   **2 miles**

START   *Parking on common land by the road junction at Ribblehead. G.R. SD765792. O.S. Outdoor Leisure Sheet 2.*

ROUTE

1. *Between the pub and a low cave mouth (from which a strong stream emerges in wet weather) a track leads north-west across Batty Green. Follow this bridleway beneath the viaduct, passing Gunnerfleet Caves on the right, to a bridge over Winterscales Beck.*

2. *Turn left after the bridge, then right along a path leading to Ivescar.*

3. *Turn right along a bridleway (Kirby Gate) and at Winterscales take the bridge and follow the track under the railway to join the Craven Way.*

4. *Turn right alongside the railway for ½ mile, where a path veers left around by the limestone outcrop of Roger Kirk Rocks. From here a path strikes directly across Batty Moss to the road junction. Turn right to regain the starting point and refreshments if required.*

ACCESS BY TRAIN

Trains to Ribblehead station.

COMMON SUNDEW

Leaves red, flowers white.
June-Aug.

RIBBLEHEAD VIADUCT

Route 7   7 miles
Whernside via Little Dale

Outline   Ribblehead ~ Little Dales ~ Whernside ~ Broadrake ~ Ivescar ~ Ribblehead Viaduct ~ Ribblehead.

Summary   This walk starts as for the previous route but by contrast is a real expedition, taking the walker into the heart of Three Peaks country. Its aim is to gain the summit of the highest of those three famous hills. A day out to blow the cobwebs away, offering choice views of the Howgill Fells and peaks of the Lake District.

Attractions   For some reason Whernside never seems as popular as its neighbours, Ingleborough and Pen-y-ghent, certainly the ascent from Chapel-le-Dale is not as easy as from Kingsdale Head. As compensation however, it presents a superb vantage point from which to view the majestic sweep of Dentdale, the Howgills, Wild Boar Fell and high country as far away as the Lake District.

After walking alongside the railway from Ribblehead the walker is drawn into Little Dale, a secretive nook sequestered between the dreary wastes of Blea Moor and the long slopes extending via Greensett to the summit of Yorkshire's highest peak.

It was in this tiny valley during the last century, that some 34,000 cubic yards of rock was quarried to build the nearby viaduct.

The Craven Way crosses the rail line just before Blea Moor Tunnel curiously enough by way of an aqueduct, the walker sharing this with the waters of Force Gill. Upstream a short distance is a quite spectacular waterfall worthy of the diversion necessary to reach it and an ideal spot for a picnic.

Continuing via Grain Head and Knoutberry Hill the ridge leading to the summit of Whernside is gained. From this the Settle-Carlisle railway appears like a child's toy train set laid out in the valley way below. On the right Chapel-le-Dale draws the eye south-west into the Lune Valley. Beyond may be seen the shimmering of Morecambe Bay.

Refreshments   The Station Inn, Ribblehead.

Route 7

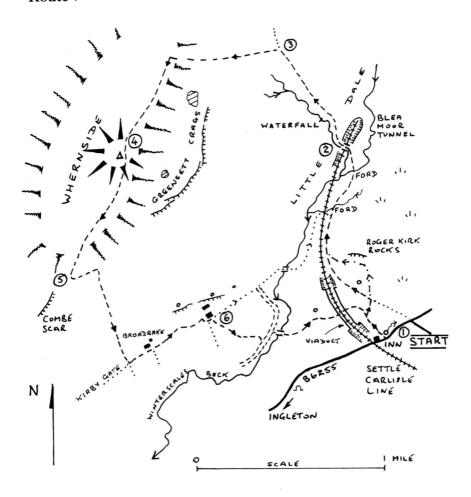

WHERNSIDE

GREENGETT CRAGS

WATERFALL

LITTLE

Dale

BLEA
MOOR
TUNNEL

③

④

②

⑤

COMBE
SCAR

BROADRAKE

KIRBY GATE

WINTERSCALES

BECK

FORD

FORD

ROGER KIRK
ROCKS

⑥

VIADUCT

INN

① START

B6255

INGLETON

SETTLE
CARLISLE
LINE

N

| 0 | SCALE | 1 MILE |

34

Route 7

Whernside via Little Dale   7 miles

START   *Parking at Ribblehead G.R. SD765792. O.S. Outdoor Leisure Sheet 2.*

ROUTE

1. *Take the dirt track north by the cave entrance. Ignore the bridleway passing under the viaduct, but instead trace the footpath alongside the railway. This fords two streams then crosses the railway line at an aqueduct bridge.*
2. *Walk up by the side of Force Gill and, as the path bears to the north-west, Force Gill Waterfall may be heard over to the left. It is a short and worthwhile diversion to view the cascade. Climbing back to the path, ascend this to a fence at Grain Head.*
3. *Leaving the Craven Way turn left and, climbing almost in a straight line, gain the ridge after one mile. Turn left and follow the edge south along the boundary wall with views of Greensett Tarns. After a mile the O.S. trig point is reached.*
4. *Continuing south the path descends at Skelside and again at High Pike, and where the ridge levels out toward Combe Scar, the path leaves the ridge.*
5. *The route now doubles back and begins a steep descent to the Kirby Gate. Turn left through Broadrake to Ivescar.*
6. *Turn right here and walk down to a farm track. Turn left, then right, crossing Winterscales Beck. Continue across Low Moss, passing beneath Ribblehead Viaduct to reach the starting point.*

ACCESS BY TRAIN
Trains to Ribblehead station.

PEN-Y-GHENT IN WINTER

Route 8   4½ miles
Gearstones and Devil's Causeway

Outline   Gearstones ~ Thorns Gill ~ Packhorse Bridge ~ Drumlins ~
Nether Lodge ~ Ling Gill Bridge ~ Pennine Way ~ Devil's Causeway
(Roman Road) ~ Gearstones.

Summary   A delightful walk taking in miniature limestone gorges, the
glacial landscape of drumlins, old bridges and trails varying from old
pannier trails to Roman military roads. The walk offers locations for
picnics, play and exploration.

Attractions   The walk starts at Gearstones which until 1911 was a
drover's hostelry. Weekly corn markets were held here until late into the
last century.

   The area around Ribblehead is notable for the profusion of
drumlins. These are low hills of boulder clay left behind by retreating
glaciers of the last Ice Age, and weathered into their present rounded
form over the intervening thousands of years.

   Due south of Gearstones is Thorns Gill, hereabouts forming a
narrow canyon where streams play cat and mouse in secretive caverns.
The gorge is spanned at its narrowest point by a 17th century packhorse
bridge. This carried the Craven Way, a packhorse road between Settle
and Dent.

   Wending its way around several drumlins this walk continues to Ling
Gill, a designated nature reserve whose species are fortunately protected
by the precipitous nature of the wooded ravine.

   At the head of Ling Gill the Pennine Way long distance path climbs
up from Horton to cross the beck by a delightful little arched bridge. The
shallow stream and low turf banks make this an ideal picnic spot for a
halfway halt. The Pennine Way is followed for the next stage of this walk,
to Cam End.

   Here the Devil's Causeway is met. This is really a Roman road built
around the time when Julius Agricola was Governor of Britain. It linked
the fort at Virosidum (Bainbridge) in Wensleydale with another fort at
Calacum (Overburrow) in the Lune Valley.

Refreshments   The Station Inn at Ribblehead is the nearest.

Route 8

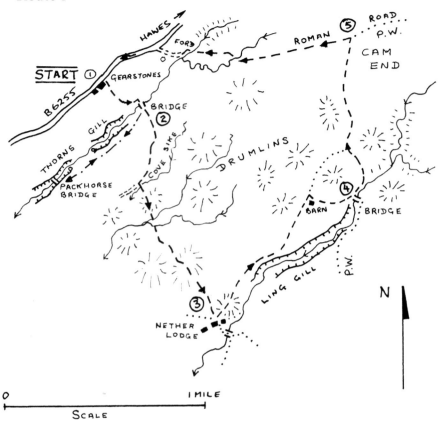

Route 8

Gearstones and Devil's Causeway   4½ miles

START   *The roadside at Gearstones on the B6255. G.R. SD780800. O.S. Outdoor Leisure Sheet 2.*

ROUTE

1. *Take a path down the left side of Gearstones which heads for Thorns Gill. This is crossed at a bridge. (A short way down the gill from this point is a quaint little packhorse bridge.)*
2. *A pleasant track winds around to a group of deserted farm buildings at Thorns. Pick up a path left after the last barn and, walking along the wall, pass through a gate left by a barn, the way now threading its way south-east between drumlins to Nether Lodge.*
3. *Turn left on a path which climbs over Swinesett Hill and traces a wall as far as a barn. Turn right here down the wall side to meet the Pennine Way at Ling Gill Bridge.*
4. *Turn left alongside the beck for a few yards then climb for 1 mile to a fingerpost at Cam End. (The Pennine Way turns right here along the Devil's Causeway.)*
5. *Turn downhill to cross a ford over Gayle Beck to the B6255. Turn left along the road to reach Gearstones after ¼ mile.*

ACCESS BY TRAIN

Train services to Ribblehead station.

ASPEN

39

STAINFORTH FOSS

Route 9   2 miles

Horton-in-Ribblesdale

Outline   Horton ~ River Ribble ~ Ford ~ Horton Beck ~ Church ~ Squirrel Cottage ~ Horton.

Summary   An easy amble for a short half day which takes in riverbank and beckside landscapes and includes an exciting river crossing (wellies advisable) if the water is low enough. If it isn't then walkers must be prepared to retrace their steps. Do not attempt to cross the ford if the river is high.

Attractions   To my mind Horton is not the most picturesque of Dales villages since it tends to be overshadowed by the nearby quarry, although operations here have been scaled down somewhat since its kilns were shut down.

It is however, a convenient starting point for expeditions on to two of the Three Peaks, as well as serving as base for other low level excursions.

The village is extremely linear, straddling the B6479 for ¾ mile with a public house at either end. The oldest part of the village is undoubtedly St. Oswald's church which dates from the reign of Henry I (1100-1135). This is located opposite the Golden Lion pub where with the church as foreground photographers may obtain an excellent viewpoint of Pen-y-ghent. A few yards east of the church, just before the bridge over Horton Beck, is a curious little cottage with a postbox built into it.

It is not without good reason that Ribblesdale is nicknamed drizzledale by many of the potholers that frequent the area. Should the weather take a turn for the worse a refuge can always be sought in either of its two hostelries or the nearby Pen-y-ghent Cafe.

Refreshments   The Crown (children welcome, beer garden and swings) and Golden Lion (childrens' room and playground) pubs. Pen-y-ghent Cafe.

Route 9

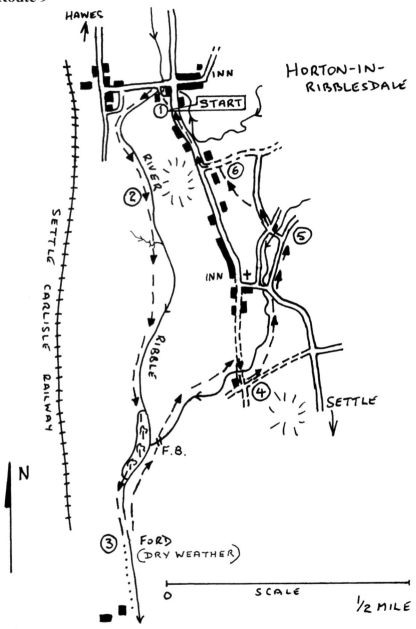

HAWES

INN

HORTON-IN-
RIBBLESDALE

START

RIVER

②

⑥

SETTLE CARLISLE RAILWAY

RIBBLE

⑤

INN

+

SETTLE

④

F.B.

N

③   FORD
(DRY WEATHER)

0   SCALE   ½ MILE

42

Route 9

Horton-in-Ribblesdale

2 miles

START   *The main car park at the north end of the village at G.R. SD807726. O.S. Outdoor Leisure Sheet 2. Horton is 6 miles from Settle along the B6479.*

ROUTE

1. *From the car park walk in front of the toilet block across the footbridge and turn left through a gap stile (signposted Helwith Bridge) into a riverside meadow. Follow the river to where it bends south. At the fence bear left heading for a ladder stile. Cross this and turn left along the Ribble Way. The path, initially along a pipeline, follows the river, soon tracing a clear path to the water treatment plant.*

2. *The obvious way follows a short stretch of wall to a footbridge over a small stream. Once over this turn left, still following the riverbank. Pass through a stand of trees and 200 yards later reach a ford.*

3. *Water level permitting cross the river and turn left to reach and cross a footbridge over Horton Beck. Bear right and continue for about ½ mile to a farm track. Turn right past the barn to a junction then turn left.*

4. *A few yards up here go through a stile on the left, following a path by the beck. At the road cross another stile and walk left along the lay-by to the bridge. Take the leafy lane up the right side of the beck to reach a footbridge just before the school.*

5. *Turn left over this, then immediately right. Where the lane divides bear left up a stony track (signposted Pennine Way). After 50 yards turn left through a gap stile and climb the hill, around the wall corner, and drop to a stile in the bottom left corner.*

6. *Turn left down the track past Squirrel Cottage, then right into the village to return to the car park.*

ACCESS BY TRAIN
Train services to Horton station.

THE NORMAN CHURCH, HORTON

Route 10 5½ miles

Pen-y-ghent — Hill of Winds

Outline Horton ~ Horton Scar Lane ~ Hunt Pot ~ Pen-y-ghent ~ Pennine Way ~ Gavel Rigg ~ Brackenbottom ~ Horton.

Summary This, the lowest of the famous Three Peaks, has a strong Celtic component in its name, 'pen' meaning hill. The name is believed to mean 'hill of winds', a title which it can certainly justify at times. It is an interesting walk through limestone country embodying all of the classic features associated with caves, dry valleys, sinkholes, limestone pavements.

Attractions The well known crouching lion appearance of Pen-y-ghent dominates the eastern aspect of Ribblesdale and Horton, from where most people begin the ascent.

A lane forming part of the Pennine Way departs from the village by Squirrel Cottage. Any children in the party will probably be quick to spot the unusual stone which gives the dwelling its name.

The lane climbs gradually for 1½ miles but nowhere does the gradient become tiresome. On the contrary, wild flowers vie for attention, while fissures by the wayside tantalise with the sounds of falling water drifting up from some mysterious cavity. To the right Pen-y-ghent is seen to advantage, the foreground rising from the valley below being dotted with low scars and boulders of limestone, like the bleached bones of long dead dinosaurs.

At a shooting hut where the way turns right a path continues straight forward. This leads to the huge quarrylike feature know as Hull Pot. This is well worth the diversion, especially after very heavy rain when an impressive waterfall thunders almost 50 feet into the bottom.

The path leading to the summit angles its way through the Yoredale strata where with luck you might catch sight of ravens. These rocky heights also offer refuge to the rare purple saxifrage, a native perennial, flowering in springtime.

Refreshments The Golden Lion (playground behind and childrens' room) and The Crown (beer garden and swings). Pen-y-ghent Cafe.

Route 10

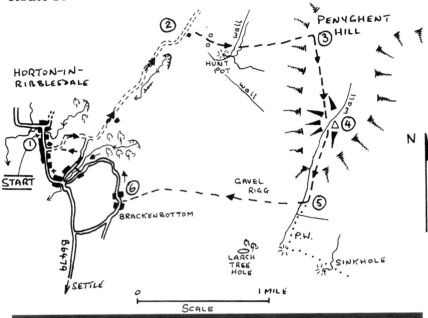

WINDPOWER

Route 10

Pen-y-ghent — Hill of Winds   5½ miles

START   *Main car park in Horton at G.R. SD807726 on the B6479. O.S.*
Outdoor Leisure Sheet 2.

ROUTE

1. *Turn right from the car park and walk up the road turning left up the
   stony lane (Pennine Way) after 250 yards. Walk up this for 1½ miles as
   far as a shooting hut.*

2. *Turn right up the slope and then head for a ladder stile ahead. After
   crossing this the route ascends towards a wall, beyond which a stream is
   crossed in a deep channel. This sinks into the deep fissure of Hunt Pot
   200 yards downstream. The path has been the focus of attempts to
   reduce erosion and climbs to reach the scarp edge.*

3. *Turn right contouring to eventually reach the fell wall on the summit.
   The trig point is at the far side of this, beyond a ladder stile.*

4. *From the summit walk down the left side of the wall, after a quarter mile
   descending some rocky steps to a stile, then trace the wall for ½ mile.*

5. *Leave the Pennine Way by turning right through a gap in the fell wall
   and striking across Gavel Rigg on a raised wooden pathway erected by
   the National Park to combat erosion. This eventually descends into
   Brackenbottom.*

6. *Turn right and walk down the lane to the footbridge over the normally
   dry Horton Beck. Turn right, then fork left up a stony farm track. After
   50 yards go through a gap stile left and walk over the hill to a stile in
   bottom left corner. Cross this and turn left to enter the village.*

ACCESS BY TRAIN
Train services to Horton station.

STEPPING STONES IN STAINFORTH

Stainforth & Catrigg Force

Outline   Stainforth ~ Lower and Upper Winskill ~ Catrigg Force ~ Goat Scar Lane ~ Stepping Stones ~ Stainforth.

Summary   An attractive but less frequented route overshadowed by more popular walks. Despite this the walk gives wide vistas across the Wenning to the distant Fells of Bowland. It presents no special difficulties although the path on the first section is a little indistinct. If a longer walk is required both this and walk 12 could be combined.

Attractions   Stainforth is a pre-conquest settlement where the presence of a ford suggests that an important highway existed here long before the Normans entered the dale.

The village sports a fine set of hippings (stepping stones) over the stream which runs through its centre. Although the nearby Foss with its deep natural swimming pool, waterfall and graceful packhorse bridge are obvious attractions, the highlight of this short walk is Catrigg Force.

Although located only ¾ miles east of the village it is not an especially well known waterfall, being 'hidden' in a small wooded dell where Stainforth Beck has delved a narrow gorge from the surrounding fellsides.

It is an impressive feature for all that, though it is difficult to obtain a good viewpoint from which to see the 60 feet cascade. The only recommended path gives access to the brink of the chasm where the beck takes its impetuous leap into space. It would be less than prudent to attempt to find a way to its foot.

There is plenty of car parking space complete with picnic area on the outskirts of the village. The way to reach Catrigg Force climbs out of Stainforth through a line of wooded scars where natural steps were believed to have been hewn by a local giant called Winskill. The route passes through two isolated farmstead of this name before meeting Goat Scar Lane from which a path descends to the waterfall.

Refreshments   Craven Heifer pub and a cafe across the road.

Route 11

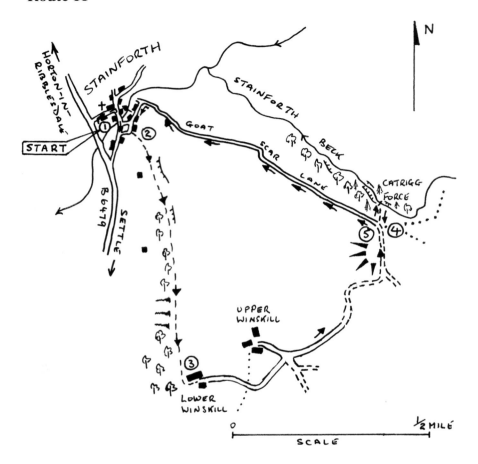

Route 11

Stainforth & Catrigg Force

2 miles

START   *The car park G.R. SD821673 O.S. Outdoor Leisure Sheet 2. Stainforth is located on the B6479 2½ miles north of Settle.*

ROUTE

1. *Turn right out of the car park and follow the road through the village, around to the right, over the bridge to the pub.*

2. *Opposite this a narrow lane quickly leads to the edge of the village (signposted Winskill). Pass through a gate and trace a vague path towards the wooded crags. At the edge of the woods a natural rocky stairway climbs diagonally to gain the open pastures where field paths are indicated by the presence of ladder stiles. Shortly a lane is met at Lower Winskill Farm.*

3. *Walk left up the lane proceeding straight forward at a junction. The lane levels out but soon becomes indistinct. However, ladder stiles again point the way, so follow the path which eventually descends to Stainforth Beck.*

4. *Head for the bottom corner of the field and cross the right hand of two stiles. This leads on to a path ending on the edge of the waterfall.*

5. *Return to the stile and from here enter Goat Scar Lane. This leads right into Stainforth where it bends sharp left. Almost immediately a right turn crosses the beck at the stepping stones. Turn left, then first right to regain the start.*

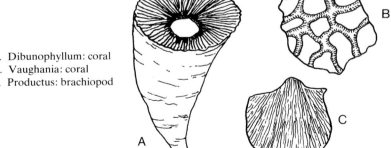

a. Dibunophyllum: coral
b. Vaughania: coral
c. Productus: brachiopod

THIRSTY WORK, WALKING

Route 12   7 miles

Knight Stainforth to Feizor

Outline   Stainforth ~ Packhorse Bridge ~ Knight Stainforth ~ Feizor ~ Tumuli ~ Stackhouse ~ River Ribble ~ The Foss ~ Stainforth.

Summary   This is definitely a full day's expedition, linking Stainforth with the sleepy hamlet of Feizor along an old packhorse trail. The only refreshments available are at the start and finish, therefore a packed lunch or picnic would go down well.

Attractions   There is a superb packhorse bridge spanning the Ribble just outside Stainforth. It is now in the care of the National Trust. Just downstream from this is The Foss, a popular swimming hole and picnic halt.

After crossing the river the way takes the walker through the neighbouring Knight Stainforth whose hall is reputed to be haunted. By the roadside is an old well though now heavily silted.

The route west across the fells to Feizor takes a stony lane to the left of the well. The lane quickly becomes a pathway threading its sinuous way among crags and limestone pavements (clints) before descending into Feizor.

This quaint little collection of dwellings is tucked away from busy roads, a haven of peacefulness. At the top of the village is a small green complete with old water pump, while to the right of this are some of the oldest cottages. One of these bears a fine example of Witch's Seat.

In the 17th century the belief in the dark arts was rife, the night skies were thought to be thronged with commuting witches. To appease them some people incorporated slabs of slate into chimney stacks so they protruded thus providing a warm resting spot for the dark travellers.

To the north-west out of Feizor is Oxenber Wood where in autumn hazel thickets provide food for free in the form of succulent filberts.

The return route to Stainforth crosses another area of exposed fell country beneath frowning limestone scars. There is a hole called Dead Man's Cave here, though I have never managed to find it. The path passes two Bronze Age burial mounds before entering Stackhouse to reach a pleasant riverside pathway. This is followed upstream to The Foss and its graceful bridge.

Refreshments   The Craven Heifer and nearby cafe in Stainforth. There is a picnic site located beside the car park, but a far better place would be beside the Foss, or just before dropping down into Feizor.

Route 12

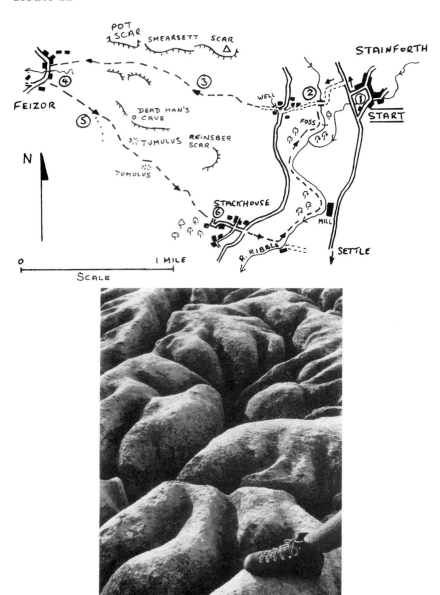

CLINTS ON MALHAM LINGS   Route 16

54

Route 12

Knight Stainforth to Feizor
7 miles

START   *The car park on the outskirts of Stainforth located on the B6479 2½ miles north of Settle. G.R. SD821673. O.S. Outdoor Leisure Sheet 2.*

ROUTE

1. *From the car park turn right up the main valley road and take the first left, tracing this stony track downhill to cross the narrow packhorse bridge.*

2. *Continue west along the green lane into Knight Stainforth. Immediately across the road is a well. Walk up the track on its left and out along a path ascending to the open fell where, below Smearsett Scar, the gradient eases.*

3. *Below Pot Scar the crags close in as the path begins its descent into Feizor, just coming into view with the Bowland Fells forming a backdrop. Soon a lane develops and this enters the settlement. Turn left and, within 100 yards, turn left up a bridleway.*

4. *This climbs gradually alongside a wall for almost ½ mile, where the bridleway bears right.*

5. *Continue straight ahead along a level path passing two burial mounds. The path passes close to one of these before beginning the descent into Stackhouse.*

6. *The path dives into a leafy lane through Stackhouse, soon to emerge at a T-junction with a tarmac lane. Walk straight forward down a lane leading to the river. Just before the locks, a riverside path takes off left. After 1½ miles, Stainforth Foss is reached, and just upstream is the packhorse bridge and lane leading back into the village.*

AUSTWICK

Route 13

5 miles
(Shorter Variation 3 miles)

Austwick and Wharfe

Outline   Austwick ~ Austwick Bridge ~ Wood Lane (bridleway) ~ The
Fleet ~ Wharfe ~ Midge House ~ White Stone Lane (bridleway) ~
Norber Sike ~ Town Head ~ Austwick.

Shorter Alternative   Austwick ~ Austwick Bridge ~ Wood Lane ~ The
Fleet ~ Wharfe ~ Dam House Bridge ~ Thwaite Lane ~ Town Head ~
Austwick.

Summary   The trim village of Austwick is the start for two options for
circular walks along mostly bridleways and green tracks. It combines
excellent easy strolling with some interesting village architecture.

Attractions   The -wick component of this place-name gives us a clue to
its Saxon origins. At the time of the Norman Conquest the Domesday
Survey records that the Saxon thane Thorfinnr held Ousteuuic, where
along with neighbouring manors some 48 carucates of taxable land was
under the plough.

Austwick is a peaceful community with a village green and market
cross reflecting days of yore when regular marts were held here. One of
the more interesting buildings is Austwick Hall located just off the
Crummock road at Town Head. Dating from the 12th century the
structure incorporates the remains of a fortified pele tower with walls as
much as 6 feet thick. Winston Churchill once stayed here; now however it
is converted to a residential home.

The nearby hamlet of Wharfe is a real backwater, a fact no doubt
enhanced by the fact that no sealed road leads into its midst. Again
steeped in history, this tiny cluster of stone-built dwellings sits on what
was once an important monastic highway linking Fountains Abbey with
Borrowdale in the Lake District.

Wharfe Manor is reputed to have been built by monks in the 13th
century. The ornate door lintel, dated 1715 reflects an 18th century
addition to the structure. This has an interesting terraced chimney and
mullioned windows, as well as some interesting internal features. On the
outskirts of Wharfe is peculiar Midge House, named thus on account of
its size.

The route to Wharfe from Austwick follows bridleways and field
paths, returning either by a leafy trail and the quaint Dam House Bridge
or via Midge House. The ford where White Stone Lane crosses Austwick
Beck offers a fine viewpoint and lunch halt.

Route 13

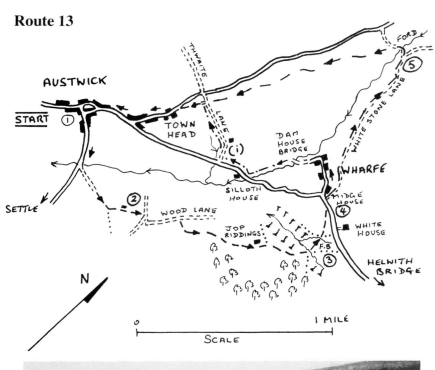

VICTORIA CAVE   Route 14

58

Route 13

Austwick and Wharfe

5 miles

(Alternative 3 miles)

START   *The centre of Austwick village G.R. SD767685, located just off the A65 north of Settle. O.S. Outdoor Leisure Sheet 2.*

ROUTE

1. *From the road junction in the village centre walk left of the market cross down the road to Austwick Bridge. Just past this, turn left following a bridleway around a bend to a parting of the ways.*

2. *Turn right and immediately left along Wood Lane and, after 250 yards, pick up a track climbing up to the right. Bear left at the fork, passing below a small copse and following a wall past Jop Riddings to where the route dips into Wharfe Gill Sike.*

3. *As the track climbs the bank, a path takes off left, over a stile and a footbridge, to join the lane west of White House.*

4. *Turn left then first right along a dirt road (The Fleet) leading into Wharfe. Just as this is reached a bridleway takes off uphill on the right. Passing the curious Midge House and skirting Wharfe, continue up the hill to a left branch. Follow this across a ford.*

5. *Just after this follow a footpath left, downhill, across Thwaite Lane to enter Austwick at Town Head. Continue down into the village, turning right at the foot of the hill to return to the centre.*

SHORTER ROUTE: Continue as below.

4. *Instead of turning right up bridleway continue through Wharfe past the old hall to a parting of the ways after 300 yards. Turn right and crossing Dam House Bridge the way is then left through a gate. Follow a beckside trail overhung with ash trees and hemmed in by elder, bramble and haws to reach the road by Silloth House.*

 i *Turn right, then take the first right up Thwaite Lane. After ½ mile turn left down a field path returning to Austwick via Town Head.*

ACCESS BY BUS

Pennine buses run a service to Clapham and Ingleton which calls at Austwick.

Refreshments   The Gamecock Inn, Austwick. Children welcome but not in main bar. Lawn area with children's slide.

THE NAKED MAN, SETTLE

Settle — Attermire & Victoria Caves

Outline   Settle ~ Constitution Hill ~ Warrendale Knotts ~ Attermire
Scar ~ Victoria Cave ~ Clay Pits Plantation ~ Settle.

Summary   Though this walk begins with a steep pull out of Settle the
rapid gain of altitude allows for expensive panoramas. But for a short
stretch on the approach to Victoria Cave, the whole walk is usually dry
underfoot. The route passes through some dramatic limestone scenery
where the children will find plenty to dissipate their energies.

Attractions   Settle stands at the meeting place of several ancient market
roads and remains today a popular venue.

One of the town's main claims to fame is being the birthplace of the
Rev. Benjamin Waugh (1839-1908), founder of the R.S.P.C.C. He was
born in a cottage which once occupied the site of the T.S.B. bank, a
plaque on the wall commemorating the fact.

Don't be in too much of a hurry to dash off walking, for the town is
well worth spending time exploring. There are a number of buildings of
note, The Folly for instance, representing a fine example of 17th century
architecture, until recently housing an antique business.

The famous Shambles presides over the old market place. This row
of shops and dwellings dates from c.1680 when they were used by
butchers. Nearby is the Town Hall, a site where the tollbooth and lockup
once stood.

At the opposite side of the street the reader will find a cafe offering a
choice of refreshments at the end of the walk. Before entering however,
look above the entrance at the unusual sign dated 1663. This appears to
depict a man without any clothes. Before becoming a cafe this was once
the Naked Man Inn.

Towering above the eastern side of Settle is Castlebergh Rock,
which seems to overhang the town in a somehow threatening manner.
This high buttress of limestone offers a bird's eye view of the town, the
neighbouring Giggleswick and the Ribble Valley for those with the
energy to negotiate the steep trail to the top.

A 'sprint' up the town's own crag might form an ideal means of
stretching the legs prior to tackling something further afield. Settle forms
a convenient base for some excellent walking. The area north-east of
town is dominated by some classic features of limestone landscape, the
Warrendale Knotts in particular being weathered into rugged scars and
long scree slopes.

continued on page 64

Route 14

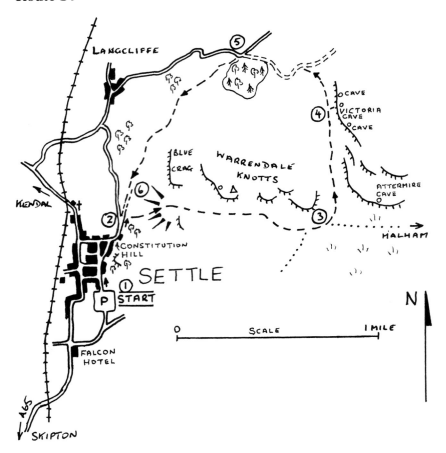

Route 14

Settle — Attermire & Victoria Caves   4 miles

START   *The main car park at Greenfoot G.R. SD820634 located just off the A65. O.S. Pathfinder Series Maps, sheet SD86/96.*

ROUTE

1. *From the car park walk north into town, passing The Folly, the Talbot Hotel and taking off uphill along a narrow lane on the right just by the T.S.B. bank. At the top of the hill the lane bends right, then left, and levels briefly.*

2. *Leave the tarmac lane, bearing right up a stony track to a gate. Shortly, a path takes off to the right (uphill) and climbs steeply over a pass below Blue Crag. The path levels off and descends to a gap stile, continuing below Warrendale Knotts to a parting of the ways.*

3. *Turn left, climbing between Warrendale Knotts and Attermire Scar and following a well defined path to a wall corner. Walk along the wall side for 300 yards, to where a path climbs the slope to reach Victoria Cave.*

4. *From the cave the path continues north along the foot of Langcliffe Scar, eventually to meet an indistinct track. There are fine views from here across to Ingleborough Hill. Cross a ladder stile and make a beeline for the right hand bottom corner of a small wood seen below. The moor road out of Langcliffe is met here.*

5. *Take off along a bridleway on the left almost immediately, following this below the plantation and across the field below Blue Scar.*

6. *Below the latter the outward bound route is met and a return to the car made down Constitution Hill.*

ACCESS BY PUBLIC TRANSPORT

Pennine or Mountain Goat bus services. Trains to Settle railway station.

After climbing out of town via Constitution Hill a field path crosses over a divide and descends to a wide basin below Attermire Scars. The name is believed to be derived from Otters Mere, suggesting that a tarn once existed here.

Fissures and cave entrances stare like blank eye sockets from the white cliffs overlooking the trail which if pursued eventually crosses Pikedaw before dropping into Malham. High in the cliff face can be seen the vertical fissure entrance of Attermire cave.

Many of these caves are important archaeological sites both Attermire and Victoria Caves also yielding artifacts dating from Romano-Celtic times.

Victoria Cave was originally discovered by a walker's dog which chased a rabbit into a small hole. Subsequent excavation revealed a large cavern containing the remains of hyena, brown bear, elk and wolf from an interglacial period around 120,000 years ago.

Its huge entrance is an obvious attraction to young people, however it is not recommended that walkers attempt to explore beyond the daylight chamber. The latter is often very muddy.

Refreshments The Royal Oak (children welcome). The Talbot Hotel (beer garden). Settle Down Cafe. Naked Man cafe.

MALHAM COVE

Route 15

Malham and The Cove

Outline   Malham Car Park ~ Malham Beck ~ Celtic Fields ~ The Cove ~ Moons Bridge ~ Malham Car Park.

Summary   An ideal starter walk for families with young children not yet accustomed to strolling further than the corner sweet shop! Excellent under foot with plenty to retain the wandering attention of youngsters.

Attractions   Malham is a settlement of considerable pedigree, going back to the times before the Norman Conquest as Malgun, a manor in the ownership of Bjornulfr. From the Domesday Book we learn that the manor afterwards passed into the hands of William de Percy.

In the 13th century the surrounding moors and indeed the village were divided between the estates of Fountains Abbey and Bolton Priory, many local place-names reflect this fact. The beck running through the village formed the boundary between these lands and today is a delight with young children for stick dipping, duck feeding and paddling.

The stream is spanned by a number of structures most interesting being Moons Bridge, an ancient clapper bridge upstream of Beck Hall. Just a few yards down the road from here is the Cove Centre, providing a welcome retreat should the weather turn sour.

The Craven Fault, a geological weakness in the strata passes just north of Malham. As a result the area is endowed with classic limestone features that find their way into geology and geography textbooks throughout the country. Malham Cove is very popular in summer, especially with rock climbers. This can sometimes detract from a visit, yet the walker can only marvel at the climber's gymnastic manoeuvres whilst swinging from the huge overhanging face.

It was at Malham Cove, where the river Aire has its source, that Charles Kingsley was inspired to write that perennial children's favourite The Water Babies.

Refreshments   Beck Hall (riverside tea gardens). The Cove Centre coffee shop. The Buck Inn has a hikers' bar.

Route 15

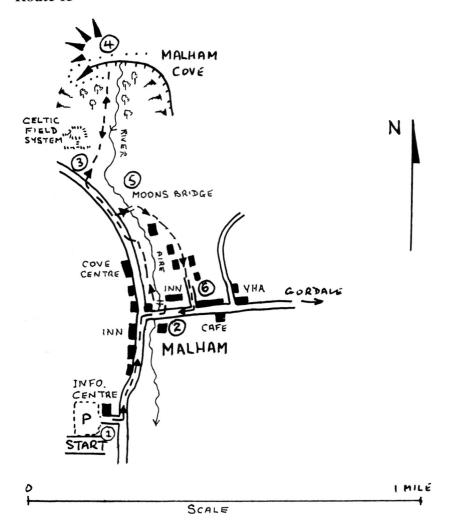

MALHAM COVE

④

CELTIC FIELD SYSTEM

③

RIVER

⑤

MOONS BRIDGE

N

COVE CENTRE

AIRE

INN

⑥

VHA

GORDALE

INN

②

CAFE

MALHAM

INFO. CENTRE

P

①

START

0

1 MILE

SCALE

Route 15

Malham and The Cove
1½ miles

START   *The Main car park adjacent to the Yorkshire Dales National Park Information Centre. G.R. SD900628. O.S. Pathfinder Series Sheet SD86/96. Malham is 5 miles north of Gargrave.*

ROUTE

1. *Leaving the car park, turn left into the village and right over the hump back bridge.*

2. *Turn left towards the Listers Arms pub, alongside Malham Beck to a footbridge. Pass through a gap stile in the wall, and walk alongside the beck through the trees. The path enters the lane, which is then followed uphill to a gate on the right. The Cove comes into view at this point.*

3. *Follow a descending path across pastures ahead. (To the left of the path is the outline of a field enclosure system dating from the Iron Age. These are best seen in evening light from the top of the Cove.) The path wends its way through sparse tree cover to the base of the huge cliff.*

4. *A few yards back from the cliff, a pathway winds its way up the left flank of the valley to twin ladder stiles, beyond which the path crosses limestone pavements to the head of the Cove. Return back down the valley to the road. Turn left down this, then pick up an overgrown path left for Moons Bridge.*

5. *Cross this and in a few yards turn right along a path ascending into a narrow lane. This leads back into Malham at the village green.*

6. *Turn right, cross the bridge, then left to return to the starting point.*

ACCESS BY BUS
Pennine bus services from Skipton to Malham.

GORDALE SCAR

Janet's Foss & Gordale

Outline   Malham ~ Pennine Way ~ Gordale Beck ~ Janet's Foss and Cave ~ Gordale Scar ~ Malham Lings ~ Tarn Sinks ~ Watlowes Valley ~ Malham Cove ~ Moons Bridge ~ Malham.

Summary   An excellent walk with plenty to captivate the attention of youngsters with waterfalls, legends, mysterious caves. Easy walking throughout on well defined paths alongside streams and across classic limestone scenery.

Attractions   Malham is nearly always busy and so the best time for this walk is perhaps in late autumn when things will be easing off.

Although one of the traditional 'honeypots' of The Dales I have included this route simply because it is a classic with so much going for it. It begins by following beckside meadows and pathways leading to the sylvan nook of Janet's Foss. Here a waterfall has been formed where mineral rich tufa deposits have built a cascade.

There is a cave nearby which according to local mythology, was the abode of the local fairy Jenet. In spring the wooded dell is dotted with the bright 'eyes' of sorrel and anemone and suffused with the ethereal blue haze of wild hyacinth. In summer ramsons or wild garlic takes over with its sickly aroma.

Upstream from Janet's Foss the narrowing Gordale canyon suddenly confronts the rambler, when around a corner a spectacular waterfall plummets through an eyehole. The name is derived from the old Norse geir, meaning an angular place and the anglicized version of dalr for valley. Beside the path leading into Gordale may be seen traces of foundations where the Canons of Bolton Priory held their manorial court.

Above Gordale a clear path through limestone clints provides distant views of Pendle Hill and passes close to Seaty Hill, site of a Bronze Age burial. Mastiles Lane leads to Tarn Sinks where a dry valley turns south, ending on the brink, literally, of the famous Malham Cove (extreme caution required).

A stepped pathway wends its way to the foot of the cliff to where the river Aire bubbles up crystal clear from some flooded cave. Recently cave divers have explored this underwater system for over ½ mile.

Refreshments   Cove Centre (coffee shop) or Beck Hall (beck-side tea shop). The Buck Inn (hiker's bar).

Route 16

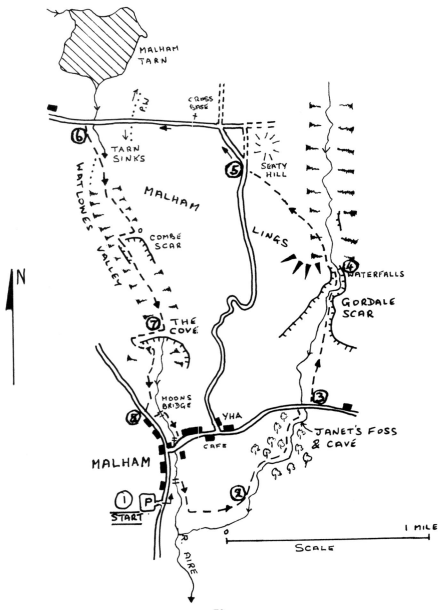

Route 16
Janet's Foss & Gordale

6½ miles

START *The starting point is as for the previous route, being the main car park on the outskirts of the village. G.R. SD900628. O.S. Pathfinder Series Sheet SD85/95.*

ROUTE

1. *Turn left out of the car park and quickly reach a path on the right. This crosses a footbridge over the beck. Turn right and follow the Pennine Way almost to Gordale Beck. Near a barn turn left.*

2. *Keeping to the left bank trace the path upstream for almost a mile, through the trees to Janet's Foss. Take the path up to the left of the cascade and enter the lane at a stile. Turn right, over the bridge to pick up a stile on the left.*

3. *Turn left and walk along a well made pathway leading into the mouth of Gordale Scar. Around a bend you reach a double waterfall.*

4. *Climb the tufa slope on large bucket steps carved from the deposits and emerge at the top of the waterfall. The path climbs half left to reach a ladder stile. Follow the path across Malham Lings through fields of limestone pavement to meet the moor road from Malham.*

5. *Turn right then bear left to the T junction. Turn left and after ½ mile cross the outlet from Malham Tarn. Turn left through a gate just beyond this.*

6. *A clear path follows the stream to a sink, beyond which a deepening dry valley is followed to Combe Scar. The way turns sharp right, then left over a stile to reach the continuing valley. This is traced to the head of The Cove.*

7. *Bear right across a limestone pavement to reach twin ladder stiles. Follow the path left downhill to reach the foot of the cliff. A path now leads down the valley, and enters the road at the gate.*

8. *Turn left and walk down the hill. Just after the village is entered look for an overgrown path on the left leading to Moons Bridge. Turn left and cross the clapper bridge and follow a muddy path up and to the right, following this to the village green. Bear right, over the bridge, then left to return to the car park.*

ACCESS BY BUS
Pennine buses run a service from Skipton.

LAITHBUTTS LANE   Route 3

Appendices

ROUTES IN ORDER OF DIFFICULTY

The walks are arranged into four categories according to distance, and within each category they are listed in order of difficulty. This is assessed on the basis of how strenuous the walks are relative to other routes in the same category.

Easy Walks *(up to 3 miles)*

Route 15 — *Malham and The Cove — 1½ miles*
Route 6 — *Winterscales and Craven Way — 2 miles*
Route 9 — *Horton in Ribblesdale — 2 miles*
Route 2 — *Clapdale and Ingleborough Cave — 3 miles*
Route 5 — *The Dentdale Vampire (Variation) — 2½ miles*
Route 13 — *Austwick and Wharfe (Variation) — 3 miles*
Route 1 — *Austwick and Norber Erratics (Variation) — 2½ miles*

More strenuous walks (up to 5 miles)

Route 1 — *Austwick and Norber Erratics — 4 miles*
Route 4 — *Ingleton Glens Waterfalls Trail — 4½ miles*
Route 14 — *Settle — Attermire and Victoria Caves — 4 miles*
Route 8 — *Gearstones and Devil's Causeway — 4½ miles*
Route 11 — *Stainforth and Catrigg Foce — 2 miles*

Easy longer walks *(5 miles or more)*

Route 12 — *Knight Stainforth to Feizor — 7 miles*
Route 16 — *Janet's Foss and Gordale — 6½ miles*
Route 13 — *Austwick and Wharfe — 5 miles*

Strenuous walks (5 miles or more)

Route 10 — *Pen-y-Ghent — Hill of Winds — 5½ miles*
Route 7 — *Whernside via Little Dale — 7 miles*
Route 5 — *The Dentdale Vampire — 6 miles*
Route 3 — *Rigodunum Hill Fort — 7 miles*

BUS AND RAIL INFORMATION

Pennine Buses .... Tel. (0756) 749215
Mountain Goat Buses .... Tel. (096 62) 5161
Tel. (076 87) 73962

British Rail enquiries. Tel. Leeds (0532) 448133
Skipton (0756) 792543
Carlisle (0228) 44711

NATURE RESERVES/TRAILS

Reginald Farrer Nature Trail. Route through Ingleborough Grounds from Clapham. Exotic plant species from Burma, Tibet, China and Japan. Wildlife and lake. Leaflets from the National Park Information Centre in Clapham.

Globe Flower Reserve located (SD873667) in a walled enclosure ½ mile east of Capon Hall on Malham Moor.

Ingleton Glens Waterfall Trail at Ingleton just off the A65. Trail follows the course of the rivers Twiss and Doe taking in 9 waterfalls, gorges and glens. Noted for its geology, abundant birdlife, plants and ferns.

Colt Park Nature Reserve just off the B6479 near Ribblehead. Abundant plants of the limestone pavements. Permit holders only, available from Nature Conservancy Council. Tel. (0904) 412429.

Malham Tarn Reserve 2½ miles north of Malham. Permits only. Famous for its wetland habitats, plants and wildlife, including deer.

Ling Gill Nature Reserve located (SD800785) 4 miles north from Horton-in-Ribblesdale. Noted for several tree species including wych elm, aspen, bird cherry and a rich ground flora, such as globe flower, melancholy thistle and mosses. There are no official rights of way at Ling Gill but a permit is not required. For further details contact the Nature Conservancy Council. Tel. (0904) 412429.

WET WEATHER ALTERNATIVES

Museums and Historic Buildings

Museum of North Craven life, Settle. Exhibits featuring landscape, settlement, farming and other aspects of the region.

Craven Museum, Skipton. Exhibits on archeology, prehistory and settlement of the Craven region. Tel. (0756) 794079.

Skipton Castle. Impressive building dating back to the twelfth century, with many interesting medieval and later features. Tel. (0756) 792442.

St. Oswald's Church, Horton-in-Ribblesdale. A fine building dating from the reign of Henry I. It has a 15th century tower. The south doorway, arcades and font are Norman.

St. Andrew's Church, Dent. Founded in Norman times, the present structure is 15th century with surviving Norman pillars. The chancel floor is made from beautiful Dent marble. Outside is the tomb of the so-called Dent Vampire.

Show Caves

White Scar Caves, underground lakes and waterfalls amid a unique landscape of stalactites and stalagmites.

Ingleborough Cave. Perhaps the finest cave open to the public. Good paths and electric lighting display ¾ mile of living cave passage. Stalactites and Stalagmites in bewildering variety.

National Park Visitor Centres

Clapham. Tel. (04685) 419.
Malham. Tel. (07293) 363.
Sedbergh. Tel. (05396) 20125.

Steam Railway

The Yorkshire Dales Steam Railway, Embsay Station near Skipton. Tel. (0756) 794727.

Craft Centres and Galleries

Malham Cove Centre, outdoor wear, buttery and craft units. Tel. (07293) 432.
Ingleton potteries, The Tanyard, Ingleton. Tel. (05242) 41363.
Dent Crafts Centre, Helmside, Dent. Tel. (05875) 400.
Low Bentham Pottery, Oysterber Farm. Tel. (05242) 61567.
Curlew Crafts and Gallery, Main Street, Ingleton. Paintings, prints and photographs by local artists. Tel. (05242) 41608.

Swimming Pools

Ingleton Pool. Tel. (05242) 41147.
Settle Pool. Tel. (07292) 3626.

OTHER PLACES OF INTEREST

Hoffman lime kiln, ¾ mile south of Stainforth (SD823663). The largest of its type in the country.

Ribblehead Viaduct on the Settle to Carlisle line is a listed monument, testifying to the Victorian engineering skills.

Settle Folly, a superb example of 17th century house.

Ebbing and Flowing Well located (SD803654) at the bottom of Buckhaw Brow on the old A65 out of Giggleswick. Ancient well exhibiting strange fluctuating water flow.

Rigodunum Celtic Hill Fort. Located on the summit plateau of Ingleborough at an altitude of 2373 feet. Fortification dating from 1st century A.D. include the tumbled remains of perimeter wall and foundations of around 13 hutments.

TOURIST INFORMATION

Ingleton (summer only). Tel. (05242) 62252.
Pen-y-Ghent Cafe. Horton-in-Ribblesdale. Tel. (07296) 333.
Settle. Tel. (07292) 3617.
Skipton. Tel. (0756) 792809.

OTHER USEFUL INFORMATION

Viewpoints

High Moss (SD724825) at the head of Kingsdale on the Ingleton to Dent road. Sweeping views of Deepdale and Dentdale.

Denthead (SD779842) Magnificent views of the Settle Carlisle Railway and Dentdale.

Cam End (SD801804) on the Pennine Way. Superb views of the Three Peaks.

Buckhaw Brow (SD798659) located on the A65 2 miles north-west of Settle. Views of Bowland, Settle and Pendle Hill.

Ebor Gate (SD853620) on the Settle to Kirkby Malham moor road. Extensive panoramas south towards Airedale and Bronte Country.

Weets Cross (SD926631), ¾ miles east of Gordale Bridge. Views south towards Skipton, Ilkley Moor and Airedale hills.

Seaty Hill (SD907653), located 200 yards south of Street gate on Mastiles Lane. Excellent views of Malham Tarn, Great Close Scar and, given a low sun angle, the Roman marching camp on Mastiles Lane.

Councils and Other Bodies

Craven District Council, Granville Street, Skipton, BD23 1PS. Tel. (0756) 2304.

Nature Conservancy Council, Archbold House, Archbold Terrace, Newcastle-upon-Tyne, NE2 1EG. Tel. (091) 2816316.

Yorkshire Wildlife Trust, 10 Toft Green, York, North Yorkshire, YO1 1JT. Tel. (0904) 59570.

The Yorkshire Dales National Park, Colvend, Hebden Road, Grassington. Tel. (0756) 752748.

The Ramblers Association, 1-5 Wandsworth Road, London, SW8 2XX. Tel. (071) 5826878.

Forestry Commission, 1a Grosvenor Terrace, York, YO3 7BD.

Footpath Difficulties. Tel. (0756) 793344.

Fell Rescue. Dial 999 or Settle Police. Tel. 2542 and ask for fell rescue service.

Market Days

Bentham	Wednesday
Ingleton	Friday
Settle	Tuesday
Skipton	Mon., Wed., Frid., Sat.
Sedbergh	Wednesday

Youth Hostels

Youth Hostel Association. Tel. Skipton (0756) 752400.
Taitlands, Stainforth.
Dee Side, Denthead, Dentdale.
Ingleton.
Malham.

STEAM SPECIAL AT HORTON-IN-RIBBLESDALE

PERSONAL SAFETY ON THE HILLS

It cannot be stressed enough that ramblers should go prepared for all eventualities. Pennine weather can change suddenly and be a complete contrast between the valleys and high fellsides. If crossing exposed moorland or high ground always:

Wear appropriate footwear and carry suitable waterproofs.

Carry map and compass and have the knowledge of how to use them.

Carry a torch, whistle and spare food.

Never walk alone and always leave details for your route.

Take extra caution with children near deep water.

Never enter caves or approach the brink of shafts. Any interest in caving should be developed through one of the recognised caving clubs for the area.

In the event of an emergency never leave an injured person alone. If injuries allow it, move to a sheltered position safe from additional hazards, water, loose boulders or cliff edge. If unconscious leave in a position where vomiting is unlikely to cause choking.

Cover the injured party with spare clothing, or better still, place in an exposure bag. Remember the universally recognized distress signal is six long blasts on a whistle or flashes with a lamp, repeated at one minute intervals.

To summon help dial 999 or Settle police and ask for Fell Rescue.

FAMILY WALKS SERIES

Family Walks in the Lake District. Barry McKay. ISBN 0 907758 40 1.

Family Walks in West Yorkshire. Howard Beck. ISBN 0 907758 43 6.

Family Walks in Three Peaks and Malham. Howard Beck. ISBN 0 907758 42 8.

Family Walks in South Yorkshire. Norman Taylor. ISBN 0 907758 25 8.

Family Walks in Cheshire. Chris Buckland. ISBN 0 907758 29 0.

Family Walks in the Staffordshire Peak and Potters. Les Lumsdon. ISBN 0 907758 34 7.

Family Walks in the White Peak. Norman Taylor. ISBN 0 907758 09 6.

Family Walks in the Dark Peak. Norman Taylor. ISBN 0 907758 16 9.

Family Walks in Snowdonia. Laurence Main. ISBN 0 907758 32 0.

Family Walks in Mid Wales. Laurence Main. ISBN 0 907758 27 4.

Family Walks in South Shropshire. Marian Newton. ISBN 0 907758 30 4.

Family Walks in the Teme Valley. Camilla Harrison. ISBN 0 907758 45 2.

Family Walks in Hereford and Worcester. Gordon Ottewell. ISBN 0 907758 20 7.

Family Walks in the Wye Valley. Heather and Jon Hurley. ISBN 0 907758 26 6.

Family Walks in the Cotswolds. Gordon Ottewell. ISBN 0 907758 15 0.

Family Walks in South Gloucestershire. Gordon Ottewell. ISBN 0 907758 33 9.

Family Walks in Oxfordshire. Laurence Main. ISBN 0 907758 38 X.

Family Walks around Bristol, Bath and the Mendips. Nigel Vile. ISBN 0 907758 19 3.

Family Walks in Wiltshire. Nigel Vile. ISBN 0 907758 21 5.

Family Walks in Berkshire and North Hampshire. Kathy Sharp. ISBN 0 907758 37 1.

Family Walks on Exmoor and the Quantocks John Caswell. ISBN 0 907758 46 0.

Family Walks in Mendip, Avalon and Sedgemoor. Nigel Vile. ISBN 0 907758 41 X.

Family Walks in North West Kent. Clive Cutter. ISBN 0 907758 36 3.

Ready Spring 1992

Family Walks in the Weald of Kent and Sussex
Family Walks in North Yorkshire
Family Walks around Luton and Dunstable
Family Walks in Northumbria
Family Walks in Nottinghamshire
Family Walks on the Isle of Wight
Family Walks in Clwyd
Family Walks in Dorset
Family Walks in Rossendale, Pendle and Bowland

Other titles under consideration

The Publishers, D. J. Mitchell and E. G. Power welcome suggestions for further titles in this Series; and will be pleased to consider other manuscripts of Derbyshire and regional interest from new or established authors.
